Beatlemania in America

Beatlemania in America

Fan Culture from Below

ANDREW HUNT

BLOOMSBURY ACADEMIC
LONDON · NEW YORK · OXFORD · NEW DELHI · SYDNEY

BLOOMSBURY ACADEMIC
Bloomsbury Publishing Plc
50 Bedford Square, London, WC1B 3DP, UK
1385 Broadway, New York, NY 10018, USA
29 Earlsfort Terrace, Dublin 2, Ireland

BLOOMSBURY, BLOOMSBURY ACADEMIC and the Diana logo are trademarks of
Bloomsbury Publishing Plc

First published in Great Britain 2023

Copyright © Andrew Hunt, 2023

Andrew Hunt has asserted his right under the Copyright, Designs and Patents Act, 1988, to be identified as Author of this work.

Cover design: Akihiro Nakayama
Cover image © Trinity Mirror/Mirrorpix/Alamy Stock Photo

For legal purposes the Acknowledgments on pp. x–xi constitute an extension of this copyright page.

All rights reserved. No part of this publication may be reproduced or transmitted in any form or by any means, electronic or mechanical, including photocopying, recording, or any information storage or retrieval system, without prior permission in writing from the publishers.

Bloomsbury Publishing Plc does not have any control over, or responsibility for, any third-party websites referred to or in this book. All internet addresses given in this book were correct at the time of going to press. The author and publisher regret any inconvenience caused if addresses have changed or sites have ceased to exist, but can accept no responsibility for any such changes.

A catalogue record for this book is available from the British Library.

A catalog record for this book is available from the Library of Congress.

ISBN: HB: 978-1-3502-9157-7
PB: 978-1-3502-9156-0
ePDF: 978-1-3502-9158-4
eBook: 978-1-3502-9159-1

Typeset by Newgen KnowledgeWorks Pvt. Ltd., Chennai, India
Printed and bound in Great Britain

To find out more about our authors and books visit www.bloomsbury.com and sign up for our newsletters.

For Bob Goldberg.
Scholar, mentor, friend.

Contents

List of Figures viii
Acknowledgments x

Introduction 1

1 Early Stirrings 9

2 Hysterical Girls and Long-Haired Boys 33

3 The Beatles for Sale 59

4 The Beatles and Black America 79

5 Beatlemania's Discontents 101

6 The Spirit of '66 119

7 In Such a Groove 143

Epilogue 167

Notes 175
Index 217

Figures

0.1 Beatles fans arrive early at the Arena to welcome their idols at their evening concert, Milwaukee, Wisconsin, September 4, 1964 6

1.1 Ringo Starr of the Beatles in New York City, dancing at the Peppermint Lounge, Tuesday, February 11, 1964 11

2.1 A group of Beatles fans—accompanied by an amused adult chaperone—reacts enthusiastically to the Beatles playing at the Boston Garden in Boston, Massachusetts, September 12, 1964 40

2.2 American fan magazines such as *All About the Beatles*, published at the height of the Beatlemania craze in 1964, were widely circulated among fans and often contained articles encouraging young men and women to style their hair like the band members 44

2.3 Officer Robert Yocum informs Beatles fans Chelie Mylott and Melody Yapscott that they'll have to move from their spot in front of the Hollywood Bowl, August 23, 1964 47

3.1 These memorabilia items appeared in a 2014 CBS program called *50 Years: The Beatles*, a live interactive multimedia event to mark the 50th anniversary of the Beatles' February 9, 1964, debut on the *Ed Sullivan Show* 72

3.2 Carol Valentine, ten, of the Bronx, inspects Beatles dolls that were being introduced during a Toy Fair, March 9, 1964 76

4.1 Twenty-one-year-old American pop singer Mary Wells (1943–1992) rehearses with members of Sounds Incorporated at the Prince Of Wales Theatre, London, in preparation for a five-week UK tour with the Beatles, October 8, 1964 82

4.2 Fans gathered outside the Delmonico Hotel in New York City to cheer for the Beatles during the band's North American tour, ahead of their concert in Forest Hills, August 28, 1964 97

5.1 Beatles fan club members, Helena Rand, Linda Schooley, Danielle Anderson, and Lee McGurr at the Hilton Hotel in San Francisco, looking forward to the Beatles' arrival, August 14, 1964 105

5.2 Young Beatles fans picket with "Ringo for President" sign on July 13, 1964, at the Republican National Convention, held at the Cow Palace in Daly City, California 115

FIGURES

6.1 Teenagers gather at a "Beatles Burning," staged by WAYX-AM in Georgia, where records, books, and wigs are burned in a bonfire in response to John Lennon's comment that the Beatles are more popular than Jesus Christ 122

6.2 St. Louis—August 21: Scores of young female fans scream in sheer delight as the Beatles play at Busch Stadium, August 21, 1966, in St. Louis, Missouri 134

6.3 Beatles fans at Shea Stadium display their enthusiasm for the band, August 15, 1965 137

7.1 Newlyweds John Lennon and Yoko Ono in their bed in the presidential suite of the Hilton Hotel, Amsterdam, March 25, 1969. The couple was staging a "bed-in for peace" and intended to stay in bed for seven days "as a protest against war and violence in the world," specifically the Vietnam War 159

Acknowledgments

I found the researching and writing of this book to be immensely rewarding, in part because of the help that I received from a lot of amazing people along the way. I would like to start by thanking the wonderful folks at Bloomsbury Publishing, who were supportive of this project at every step along the way. Thank you to Abigail Lane, Maddie Holder, Paige Harris, Megan Harris, and the other helpful staff at Bloomsbury. Thank you, too, to the meticulous eye of Bloomsbury's extraordinary copy editor. I appreciate the deep care that went into the editing of this book. And I am grateful to the readers that provided superb feedback and tips on how to revise the proposal and manuscript. Their commentary resulted in striking improvements to the finished product.

Here at the University of Waterloo, I'd like to thank my colleagues in the Department of History for their friendship and support, especially Sue Roy, Dan Gorman, Ian Milligan, Geoff Hayes, Talena Atfield, and Kate Bruce-Lockhart. Thank you, also, to Robyn Wilkinson and Susan King, for your constant support. A special thank you goes to my good friends Patrick Harrigan, Jeffrey Shallit, and John Sbardellati. For nourishing my spiritual side, I am immensely grateful to Rabbi Moshe Goldman and the many wise lessons he has passed along to me while I was writing this book. Thank you, Rabbi Goldman, for always inspiring me.

Back in Utah, thank you to Kay and Jodie Hunt, Linda Hunt, and my history comrade, Spencer Hunt, and your beautiful family. Even though we live far apart, we are close together in spirit, and all of you have a special place in my heart. Closer to home, here in Canada, thank you to Maddox and Charlie, Aidan and Zaria, and Ruth and Tony, for bringing so much happiness to my life. I love each one of you. My heart, of course, belongs to Luisa D'Amato. Thank you, my beloved Lieba, for taking this journey with me. Thank you for the magical dinners, and the long soul-restoring walks, and every cherished moment we've spent together.

Lastly, I would like to acknowledge my lifelong debt to Professor Robert Alan Goldberg, or Bob as he always preferred to be called. From the moment I first set foot in his US History survey course, in that enormous, packed auditorium at the University of Utah back in 1986, and saw him work his magic, I was hooked. Bob brought history to life in a way that no other professor was able to come close to matching. I learned from him about how deeply enriching it is to study the past, and to bring it to life in the classroom and on paper for others to discover. Bob, you are the reason why I am a historian. I know I will never be able to fully repay my debt to you. But I can start by dedicating this book to you, with my deepest gratitude. Thank you for all you've done for me, Bob.

Introduction

For approximately three years, between January 1964 and the fall of 1966, Beatlemania—large-scale public expressions of enthusiasm for the British rock band the Beatles—emerged as the biggest, most influential example of fandom in the history of the United States. This countrywide fan community, which was like no other before it, and unmatched in size and breadth in the decades that followed it, touched countless facets of American life in its heyday. Beatlemania spread rapidly, offering its followers an immersive experience. At its height, one could surround oneself with all things Beatles. It became a way of life for multitudes of young people from a wide range of backgrounds, forging memories that would last lifetimes.

Various elements made Beatlemania equal parts memorable and indelible. It added color and humor to American society, a reflection of the foursome that inspired it. It contained dramatic and funny and exhilarating moments. It placed the four Beatles—George Harrison, Paul McCartney, John Lennon, and Ringo Starr—at the center of American pop music, making them the biggest stars in the country. It triggered one of the most vital developments in the ever-expanding genre of rock and roll: the so-called British Invasion, the renaissance of English rock music, which burst through the previously impenetrable Fort Knox-like walls of American pop culture. British rock acts such as the Rolling Stones, the Dave Clark Five, Dusty Springfield, the Animals, Gerry and the Pacemakers, the Kinks, Herman's Hermits, Marianne Faithfull, the Yardbirds, the Who, the Hollies, Lulu, and too many other groups and singers to list, delivered sizable doses of rock music with a distinctly English flavor. Their debt to the trailblazing Beatles for this unprecedented access to American society could never be repaid.

Beyond its instantaneous impact on popular culture, Beatlemania shone a spotlight on complex issues such as race and gender, conformity and authenticity, generational divides and consumerism, religion and technology. It coincided with resistance struggles of the 1960s, namely the Civil Rights and Anti-Vietnam War Movements, and it overlapped with the early stages of second-wave feminism. Unlike those protest campaigns, Beatlemania was not an overtly political movement. However, it contained some vaguely political subtexts and undercurrents. It often involved a startling level of commitment from adolescents, motivating them to participate in fan clubs and attend public events such as concerts. Boys grew their hair long to imitate the Beatles, putting them at odds with the dominant values at the time, while young women unhesitatingly screamed and exhibited more emotion in public than their mothers and grandmothers. Beatlemania motivated and mobilized young people, some of whom would go on to participate in acts of resistance against the Vietnam War, or institutionalized racism or sexism.

Beatlemania gave rise to dynamic fan communities in every state. Beatlemaniacs—the people at the center of it all—evolved along with the band they loved. Some of them lost interest in the Beatles when they thought the Liverpool foursome had strayed too deeply into "far out" territory. But others stayed steadfastly loyal to the Fab Four. Beatle people grew more assertive when it came to giving voice to what they wanted, a characteristic often nurtured in the post-Second World War baby boom generation. These young Beatle people—male and female alike—felt, often for the first time in their lives, like they had found, and belonged to, something larger, grander, more epic, than their day-to-day lives had been prior to Beatlemania. A remarkable number of them attributed these changes in their lives to embracing Beatles fandom.

Beatlemania in America explores American Beatlemania during its zenith, and the influence it had on US society. While fans heavily populate this narrative, they are not the only people who inhabit it. More broadly, this history of Beatlemania in America is told from a wide scope. Myriad points of view are found in these pages, including the standpoints of fans, detractors, experts, religious figures, political activists (on the right and left), parents, prominent African Americans, media and show business personalities, and the police who provided security at concerts and other Beatles events. The aim of *Beatlemania in America* is to tell a larger story than that of fans, or the Beatles themselves. It is about a phenomenon of great importance, a fan leviathan that assumed a life of its own for a few years, and its impact on America during one of the most eventful decades of the country's history, the 1960s.

The body of Beatles literature has gotten to be vast, and it keeps growing. Books about the four individuals who comprise the group, and about the band collectively, number in the thousands by now. Certain chroniclers stand out as exceptional: Philip Norman, Mark Lewisohn, Bob Spitz, Hunter Davies, and

Kenneth Womack.[1] These authors have written meaningful additions to the expanding library on the Beatles, and they—along with a number of others—have helped to set the bar high for future contributors.

Even with all these essential histories, the Beatles need no introduction. To this day, they are one of the few rock bands—maybe even the only one—whose members' names are almost universally known without having to look them up. Their first names are even uttered in a familiar order: John, Paul, George, and Ringo. Astonishingly, because so much has been written about the Beatles, their daily, almost hourly, movements from the time McCartney met Lennon at the garden fete of St. Peter's Church, Woolton, Liverpool, on July 6, 1957, until the official announcement of the Beatles' breakup on April 10, 1970, have been painstakingly documented.

The Beatles' music and lives have also been contextualized against the turbulent tapestry of the 1960s, with the rise of protest movements and the counterculture forming a vivid backdrop behind their striking evolution. These books include Jon Wiener's *Come Together: John Lennon in His Time* (1990), Ian MacDonald's *Revolution in the Head: The Beatles' Records and the Sixties* (1994), Steven D. Stark's *Meet the Beatles: A Cultural History of the Band That Shook Youth, Gender, and the World* (2005), Jonathan Gould's *Can't Buy Me Love: The Beatles, Britain, and America* (2007), John F. Lyons's *Joy and Fear: The Beatles, Chicago and the 1960s* (2021), Christine Feldman-Barrett's *A Women's History of the Beatles* (2021), and Kenneth L. Campbell's *The Beatles and the 1960s Reception, Revolution, and Social Change* (2021).[2] In addition, a handful of books have focused on Beatles' fan communities.[3] The literature on fandom history is largely an early twenty-first century innovation, with many of these books being written by the fans themselves. *Beatlemania in America* is unique because it is the first in-depth history of Beatlemania written from an array of perspectives, including those of Beatlemaniacs, Beatlephobes, and ordinary Americans, from all walks of life, who had, in one way or another, experienced this remarkable phenomenon.

This is not another book about the Beatles per se. *Beatlemania in America* places the group in the background, drawing instead on a variety of sources, including oral histories, Beatles fan magazines and fan club newsletters, press coverage from all parts of the United States, personal memoirs, and an array of other materials, to present a richer, fuller portrait of Beatlemania. It will also demonstrate that far from being universally accepted by Americans in the mid-1960s, the arrival of The Beatles on American soil touched off debates—sometimes quite contentious—in the United States about a host of weighty issues, on everything from masculinity to race relations to religion to fears of youth running amok.

Beatlemania in America is not merely a book about controversies sparked by the arrival of the Beatles in the United States. It is a cultural history that includes the voices of fans, critics, parents, teachers, experts, politicians, disc jockeys, record store employees, self-described "Beatle haters," and others. More than any generation before or since, the impassioned Beatlemaniacs of the 1960s gave collective voice to their preferences on a large scale in the streets of America. They celebrated their idols in bold ways, never witnessed in the history of American youth.

Dismissed by disparaging adults as "screaming fans," young first-generation Beatles lovers departed in fundamental ways from those who took part in previous fan manias by creating cohesive communities that deepened their identification with the band, and they fortified their bonds with each other. They discovered networks of kindred spirits, cultivated friendships, and populated a fan culture that was unprecedented in its enormity, animated by a fervor that some observers at the time likened to a religion. *Beatlemania in America* rests on the assumption that this fan culture matters, and understanding its growth and evolution is key to comprehending the full significance of The Beatles' impact on the United States, and the rapid, dizzying changes of America's most eventful of eras, the 1960s.

The passage of time since Beatlemania's halcyon years obscures the excitement that young people across the country felt when the Beatles arrived in the United States in that bitter cold February of 1964. Beatlemania seemed so fresh and new and thrilling in those days. It had been less than three months since the tragic assassination of President John F. Kennedy on November 22, 1963, and people were traumatized by his horrifying killing in a motorcade in Dallas, Texas. A dark pall had fallen over the land, and the Beatles gave adolescent Americans a reason to be hopeful and excited once more. Days after the Beatles made their electrifying *Ed Sullivan Show* debut on February 9, 1964, a journalist in Elmira, New York, interviewed a man who perceptively connected the excitement that so many youths felt about the arrival of the English rock and roll band to the recent death of the American president:

> The country is just beginning to emerge from the shock of President Kennedy's assassination. It was disturbing to everyone, but I think it was particularly shocking to the teenage group of citizens; so many of them identified themselves with the young president. Something had to give. Along comes this crazy, far-out group of kids with their wild hair styles and youthful enthusiasm and the kids have something to counterbalance the long stretch of somber days. The pendulum had to swing.[4]

The Beatles' whirlwind visit to the United States in February 1964 revealed the pent-up energy possessed by American teenagers that was finally being unleashed by Beatlemania. When the Beatles flew to Miami aboard a National Airlines DC-8 after their *Ed Sullivan Show* appearance, the scene that greeted them at Miami International Airport was one of pandemonium. A crowd of adolescents broke through police lines, resulting in—according to one account—"smashed doors, smashed windows, smashed furniture, a smashed auto roof and one badly cut teenager."[5] Police watched as wild-eyed teens kicked over ashtray stands at the airport restaurant, and used chairs to break widows and shatter a heavy plate glass door. The city's incensed airport director, Alan Stewart, blamed the chaos on local disc jockeys and journalists. "This wouldn't have happened," he insisted, "if those radio stations and news media hadn't stirred the kids up."[6]

But as always is the case with history, all one has to do is turn the prism slightly to find a different perspective. The day the Beatles' airplane touched down in Miami, sixteen-year-old Becky Pierce, a student at Coral Gables High School, was at the airport, assigned by the *Miami News* to cover their arrival from the unique standpoint of a teenager. She witnessed thousands of young fans flooding into the terminal, desperate to catch a glimpse of this new rock and roll sensation. Standing on an observation deck, she looked down at a sea of heads churning below, surging toward the tarmac doors. The Beatles were not Pierce's favorite group. "I'm an Andy Williams fan myself," she confessed. Yet there she stood, alongside adult reporters, staring in awe at the spectacle unfolding all around her. The sights and sounds she beheld that day overwhelmed her. "Then it happened. A mophead was seen, and then another. Everybody started shrieking and I felt a tingle inside, we were all so happy because we had waited for so long." The Beatles appeared briefly before the screaming crowd, waving and smiling, before sliding into automobiles that whisked them away. Pierce overheard a flight attendant who flew on the DC-8 with the band remark that "the Beatles were all very courteous and impressed her as being nice English gentlemen." Before leaving, Pierce encountered "older people" who "kept shaking their heads and muttering what is the younger generation coming to." Becky Pierce had a response for them in the following day's paper: "The younger generation was coming to see a singing group that is real sharp."[7]

The mayhem that took place at the Miami International Airport, and the cultural divide it illuminated, was but a foreshadowing of events to come. Beatlemania generated levels of excitement on a scale never seen before in the history of American fandom, not even during Elvis Presley's early years. But this was not always a positive or admirable thing. Infamous were the screams and shrieks and cries of tens of thousands of concertgoers who drowned on Beatles' songs during their 1964, 1965, and 1966 North American tours. The Beatles would later claim that they could not hear themselves playing above the steady, deafening din. And then there were the objects thrown on stage by people in the audience, which came raining down on the Beatles while they performed hits such as "I Want to Hold Your Hand," "She Loves You," and "Can't Buy Me Love." When the Beatles played a live concert at the Milwaukee Arena, Wisconsin, on September 4, 1964, a dazed reporter described the frenzied response of the concertgoers: "They clapped, waved, laughed, cried, shouted, groaned, kicked, held their ears, jumped up, sat down, wailed, and stomped. They threw jelly beans, chocolate, hair pins, hair rollers, paper and flash bulbs" (see Figure 0.1).[8]

Not all fans who came out to greet the Beatles were so unruly. But polite youths who idolized the Fab Four, those gentler souls who were orderly and respectful of property and authority, rarely made the news. Sheryl Claussen Jones, age sixteen, was among the 30,000 fans packed into the Met Stadium in Bloomington, Minnesota, to see the Beatles concert on August 21, 1965. She remembered one zealous fan climbed over a security barrier guarding the field. "Instantly security was on her as they dragged her screaming,

FIGURE 0.1 *Beatles fans arrive early at the Arena to welcome their idols at their evening concert, Milwaukee, Wisconsin, September 4, 1964.*
Source: *Photo by Underwood Archives via Getty Images.*

frantic body back and literally threw her back over the fence. Other than that, everyone, albeit delirious with delight, was very well-behaved."[9]

Beatlemania had its foes, some in positions of power and influence. At different points, clergy, politicians, celebrities, and a variety of experts warned the American public about it. They regarded Beatlemania—and the group that inspired it—with contempt or suspicion. A handful of right-wing extremists even insisted that the Beatles and their adoring followers posed an existential threat to the United States. Yet the Beatles faced far more formidable challenges than those coming from the far right in America. Alas, at times, the Beatles' worst enemies were overzealous fans, the ones who screamed too loudly and too long, who hurled dangerous projectiles, and who threatened to overwhelm security and come washing down over the Beatles like a tidal wave. The Beatles later made no secret of the fact that screaming audiences were one of the reasons they decided to cease touring in the fall of 1966 to spend their time making music in EMI Studios, which effectively ended Beatlemania.

By 1967, the gusty waves of Beatlemania had largely dissipated in the United States. With the Beatles no longer touring, fans' expressions of love for the band had moved from the public realm to the quieter settings of homes, dormitories, bars, record stores, and other places where smaller groups of people gathered to listen to music together. Three years later, when the four men in the Beatles went their separate ways, Beatlemania had been reduced to a largely overlooked footnote, seen at the time as an interesting but ultimately meaningless groundswell of fan enthusiasm that was a product of its times and existed no longer.

But remnants of it lingered long after its demise. Beatlemania in its American form offers a window into a time in history before the turbulence of the late 1960s—the upheavals, violence, division, assassinations, and cultural revolution—arrived in full force. It is a snapshot, frozen in amber, that has much to teach us about a nation in perpetual conflict with itself, lurching forward through gale-force winds, toward what many hoped would be something better on the other side of the storm.

1

Early Stirrings

Nightfall came early on Sunday, and bitter cold prevailed in many parts of the nation on February 9, 1964, when Americans—some 73.7 million of them—gathered around televisions that evening to see the *Ed Sullivan Show* on their local CBS affiliate. Earlier that day, newspapers across the United States had featured stories—often with photos—announcing that a big new British sensation, The Beatles, would be the guest stars on tonight's episode of the beloved variety television program. The bushy-haired foursome had landed aboard Pan Am flight 101 at New York's John F. Kennedy Airport two days earlier, greeted by thousands of screaming adolescents. Inundated with over 50,000 requests for tickets, CBS television's Studio 50 in New York City filled up to capacity with 728 people that night, most newly minted teenage fans of the band. "This craze is phenomenal, a powerful thing—you can feel it in the air," remarked a photographer, present at the performance.[1]

That night, tens of millions of curious adults and excited youths alike got comfortable as a familiar orchestral fanfare spilled out of TV speakers at the top of the hour. Onscreen, elegant curtains rose from the stage, the words the *Ed Sullivan Show* appeared, and the long-faced, dark-eyed host emerged to applause. Stiff suit, high-shouldered, black hair slicked back helmet-tight, Sullivan calmed the audience with outstretched arms.

> Now, yesterday and today our theatre's been jammed with newspapermen and hundreds of photographers from all over the nation, and these veterans agree with me, that the city never has witnessed the excitement stirred by these youngsters from Liverpool, who call themselves the Beatles. Now, tonight, you're gonna twice be entertained by them, right now and again in the second half of our show. Ladies and gentlemen, the Beatles![2]

The arrival of the Beatles in the United States in February 1964 proved to be an event of profound importance, one that transcended all other pop culture milestones in the nation's history. Its impact was felt far and wide, from the nation's largest metropolises and mid-sized cities to small towns and rural areas. It stirred a level of enthusiasm among youth not seen since the rise of Elvis Presley in the previous decade. Communities of adoring fans coalesced overnight. And while they bore certain similarities to earlier fan enclaves that emerged around the likes of Rudolph Valentino, Frank Sinatra, and the King himself, the sheer size and scope of Beatlemania, from the time of its inception in America, lacked any sort of precedent. And the experience of being part of it became etched in the memories of adolescents across the nation who witnessed—and in some instance, directly participated in—this nationwide community of Beatles fans.

"This Country Will Never Be the Same Again"

The night the Beatles debuted on the *Ed Sullivan Show*, future author and editor Amanda Vaill, a self-described "bookish, rather nerdy adolescent," was attending the Madeira School, a private prep school in McLean, Virginia, near Washington, DC She gathered with classmates around a "small television set" in the school's library, enchanted from the start of "All My Loving'." The Beatles played with energy and charisma, performing in the center of an immense circle, surrounded by giant curved arrows on all sides pointing inward at them. "My pastel-clad peers and I looked at the screen as the TV cameras panned over the auditorium," Vaill recalled, "normally full of people who looked like our parents, and what we saw was ourselves reflected back at us: teenaged girls and young women, dressed in proper little wool jumpers or tidy tailored suits with circle pins on the collar, all gasping and clutching their faces in paroxysms of innocent desire, primal but somehow not prurient."[3] Reactions varied among the millions of younger viewers to The Beatles' appearance on the *Ed Sullivan Show* (see Figure 1.1). Some screamed or openly wept or squealed with delight, while others watched in silence, stunned by what they were witnessing, or—in some cases—wondering what all the hubbub was about. "I was twelve years old that Sunday night," recalled Carolyn Tanner, of Macon, Georgia. "I remember getting so angry at the cameraman who kept showing the screaming girls in the audience. I didn't care anything about them. I wanted to see The Beatles!"[4] Thirteen-year-old Gay Stilley, daughter of Associated Press reporter Francis Stilley, wrote an op-ed piece days before the *Ed Sullivan Show* aired. Her purpose in writing it, she explained, was to

FIGURE 1.1 *Ringo Starr of the Beatles in New York City, dancing at the Peppermint Lounge, Tuesday, February 11, 1964. The Beatles arrived in America on Friday, February 7, 1964, to make their first live US television appearance, on the* Ed Sullivan Show *two days later, to perform for an audience of 73 million viewers, about two-fifths of the total American population. Starr and his band mates were here still basking in the glory of their historic performance two days earlier.*
Source: *Photo by Don Smith/Mirrorpix via Getty Images.*

help adults make sense of the overwhelming popularity of The Beatles with America's youngsters. Hundreds of newspapers across the country ran her short, yet insightful, column. "To the average adult," Stilley wrote, "it would sound like nothing more than a conglomeration of noises, screams, howls and other unclassified sounds. To the ecstatic teenager lying in front of her hi-fi, it's sheer heaven."[5]

Despite Gay Stilley's best efforts to explain The Beatles' meteoric rise to fame in America, few parents understood why their children had fallen so fast, and so hard, for these strange looking musicians from England. Sure, the four lads exhibited gusto on the television screen, but wasn't there already plenty of that to be found in the United States? Fuelling doubts among adults was the widely dismissive response of the American press to The Beatles' arrival in the country. With few exceptions, journalists and critics alike dismissed the band as talentless and faddish newcomers who would soon vanish from the already overcrowded pop culture landscape. Headlines told the story: "The Beatles: Boston Votes Bushy Britons One-Way Ticket to Cuba"[6]; "Barnyard

Braying Better'n Beatles"[7]; "Please Take Beatles Back, John Bull"[8]; "TV Brings Americans Shaggy Dogs' Tale"[9]; "The Ridiculous British Beatles"[10]; and "Critic Doesn't Think She'll Ever Become a Beatle Nut."[11]

Long-time *New York Daily News* cultural critic Ben Gross—known for his hyperbolic verdicts—sounded the alarm when he declared: "Take to the fallout shelters ... or better still, board a plane for Antarctica! The Beatles, as if you didn't already know, made their American live TV debut on the *Ed Sullivan Show* last night. This country will never be the same again."[12] Cynthia Lowry, a former Second World War correspondent, who now covered television for the Associated Press, fixated on the band's hair and fashion style. "They sing close harmony, stomp their feet and play electric guitars, but so do a lot of crew-cut American boys in slacks and sweaters, and the Americans cause no riots. Beatle clothes look about two sizes too small, and I've seen sheep dogs with more attractive hairdos."[13] Even more grimly, *Newsweek* magazine—finding no redeeming qualities in the Beatles performance that night—concluded: "Visually they are a nightmare: tight, dandified Edwardian-Beatnik suits and great pudding bowls of hair. Musically they are a near disaster, guitars and drums slamming out a merciless beat that does away with secondary rhythms, harmony, and melody. Their lyrics (punctuated by nutty shouts of 'yeah, yeah, yeah') are a catastrophe, a preposterous farrago of Valentine-card romantic sentiments."[14]

To reinforce such negative coverage, the press amplified the ho-hum reactions of dissenting youths who felt no love for The Beatles. A disappointed youngster from Weymouth, Massachusetts, declared: "I don't think they have anything to offer. What they played on the *Ed Sullivan Show* wasn't music. All the great composers must be rolling in their graves right now."[15] The Monday morning after The Beatles appeared on the *Ed Sullivan Show*, a group of seventh and eighth graders at St. Mary's Grade School in Bismarck, North Dakota, formed the Anti-Beatles Club, which had a female president. The club's officers issued a news release to the press, quoted extensively in a front-page story in Bismarck's local newspaper: "They're ruining the whole tone of music, and playing teenagers as suckers ... The Beatles would not be a hit if they didn't where [sic] those flinky high-heeled shoes and hairdos."[16]

Inevitably, the pervasive cynicism of journalists who covered the band's US debut rubbed off on parents who harbored doubts about the band. Especially perplexing to many adults was the suddenness of the craze. A mere month earlier, most screaming youngsters hadn't even heard of the band. "My dad didn't want anything to do with it," remembered Penny Wagner, a Beatlemaniac raised near Milwaukee, Wisconsin. Her father, it turns out, was out of town on the night of the broadcast, and her more liberal mother allowed her to see it. His absence proved advantageous, because Wagner—like millions of other young fans—slipped into a hysterical state, of which her father would've strongly disapproved. "That was it. I couldn't stop myself. I started screaming and carrying on, and my mother didn't know what to do ... [M]y grandmother thought something was wrong with me."[17] Liz Gatzman, a teenager from Fresno, California, often made fun of Ed Sullivan's distinctive mannerisms, to the annoyance of her father, especially when the host promised viewers "a really great shew." But when The Beatles appeared on his popular variety program, Gatzman's attitude about Sullivan abruptly changed. "I was singing and dancing with the Beatles, having a great time, but after one too many shakes of their bangs and 'We Love You, Yeah, Yeah, Yeahs,' my dad popped up out of his recliner, puffed up, and stomped out of the living room saying, 'Oh, good Lord.' "[18] In Furlong township, north of Philadelphia, the father of a young Beatles fan, Michelle Isacoff Rothstein, kept saying, "Oy vey!" while his daughter sat riveted in front of the television, hanging on to every note played by The Beatles. "Dad, they're so cute," Michelle insisted. Her father replied: "Look at that hair, it's so long."[19] Adolescent Beatlemaniac Elizabeth Abbe watched the *Ed Sullivan Show* on the family's television in Connecticut. To the dismay of her father and mother, she cheered on her new favorite band. "Our parents hated The Beatles. They complained about the Beatles' long hair, collarless suit jackets, and their music ... Our parents couldn't understand the attraction of The Beatles, so naturally they couldn't understand us."[20]

While a generational divide undeniably influenced viewers' reactions to the Beatles' *Ed Sullivan Show* appearance, not all adults succumbed to hostility, just as not every young person embraced the band. Many parents—men and women in their thirties, forties, and fifties—who gathered with their kids around televisions on February 9, 1964, were pleasantly surprised—some, even favorably impressed—by what they heard and saw. They detected genuine talent in the rising stars. Bert Shipp, a respected cameraman and news correspondent who spent more than forty years at television station WFAA in Dallas, Texas, developed a deep and abiding respect for the Beatles. He was in his mid-1930s when he watched them on the *Ed Sullivan Show*, and subsequently saw them in concert at the Memorial Auditorium in Dallas on September 18, 1964. "The Beatles were good for the country. Their songs were popular; they were such a spirited group. A healthy atmosphere followed them wherever they went," Shipp recalled.[21] Across the nation, fair-minded grown-ups found reasons to be impressed with The Beatles, even if the group's music did not resonate with them. Bob Precht, producer of the *Ed Sullivan Show*, and husband of Sullivan's only daughter, Elizabeth, furnished a thoughtful verdict, shared by millions of mature observers: "With all their success, you never met four youngsters as unspoiled, level-headed—nice kids. They're very quick-witted, too."[22] A mother of three teenage Beatles fans in Orlando, Florida, expressed relief that her children were staying home and listening to the British foursome, rather than joining rambunctious

Spring-break partiers in Daytona Beach for the long Easter weekend. "I'll admit that there are times when I could scream listening to these records over and over again, but ... I'll take knowing where my children are, and what they're doing—listening to good, clean Beatles records at home," she said.[23]

In the span of an hour, the *Ed Sullivan Show* broadcast that aired February 9, 1964, had stamped itself indelibly into the American public's collective memory, and secured a venerable place in the history of modern popular culture. It became an instant milestone. In the ensuing decades, millions of viewers would be able to recall the most minute details of that memorable night. The episode also marked the starting point of Beatlemania writ large in the United States. Overnight, the band's fan base grew to nationwide in scope, fueling an insatiable demand for all things Beatles. Beatles records, Beatles wigs, Beatles dolls and bobbleheads, and other types of Beatles merchandise instantly flooded the marketplace. "The Beatles wigs cost $2.98 and represent a cool $15 million ... for this one item alone," marveled the *Indianapolis Star* by early March.[24] Beatles songs crackled on millions of transistor radios. Teen periodicals such as *16* and *Dig* that featured the Beatles on the cover sold briskly at newsstands. Kids bought glossy one-off Beatles magazines containing profiles and photos of the band faster than they could be printed. Predictably, the press responded to The Beatles' newfound success with sarcastic jabs. "We Wanta Hold Your Purse," said a headline in the *Spokane Chronicle*.[25]

Recurring jabs at the Beatles failed to slow their momentum. On the contrary, such put-downs only strengthened the fans' love for the band. Wherever John, Paul, George, and Ringo went, publicity followed, much of it scornful in tone. Yet each Beatle managed to shrug off criticisms in the press. "It came mostly from the more serious people," Paul McCartney noted dismissively.[26] Ultimately, the band's whirlwind visit to the United States in February 1964—consisting of three appearances on the *Ed Sullivan Show*, sold-out concerts at Washington Coliseum in Washington, DC, and New York City's Carnegie Hall, an upbeat meeting with boxer Cassius Clay at Miami's Fifth Street gym, and a flurry of interviews and public appearances—amounted to an epic US debut. Each day brought photo ops and radio, television, and newspaper coverage. Promotion-wise, the trip exceeded The Beatles' highest expectations.[27] They returned home on February 22 to crowds of around 12,000 fans cheering them on at the airport.[28]

A Trip to Benton

Four months before the *Ed Sullivan Show* broadcast, on September 16, 1963, twenty-year-old George Harrison arrived in the United States with his older brother, Peter, to visit their sister, Louise Caldwell.[29] Louise lived in Benton, a small town in southern Illinois (population approximately 7,000), with her Scottish-born engineer husband, Gordon, who worked for a mining company based there. The couple lived in a five-bedroom bungalow at 113 McCann Street. In those last days of summer, George savored his time in the United States, where he could still go places without encountering screaming crowds. Back in Great Britain, The Beatles had soared to the top of the record charts with their number one hit "She Loves You." By contrast, in the United States, the band still wasn't famous, and had no following. "It really was the calm before the storm. No one here had heard of him, and it was a nice, calm and quiet time," Louise later recalled.[30]

George savored the two weeks he spent with Gordon and Louise, their two children, and their dog. He went to a drive-in theater in his sister's Dodge Dart to see a movie. He filled up on American junk food. He played with his nephew's electric train set. Camping trips introduced George to the serene beauty of the countryside. Back in Benton, he jammed on stage with a local band, the Four Vests, at a hall belonging to the Veterans of Foreign Wars. He shopped for records in a local furniture store, and he purchased a red Rickenbacker 425 and paid to have it refinished black to match his band mate John Lennon's guitar. Thanks to the relentless boosterism of his older sister, George took part in an interview at radio station WFRX in West Frankfort.[31] Disc jockey Marcia Schafer was among the earliest American DJs to play Beatles' records on the air.[32] "It really didn't dawn on me that this group would ... become as big as Elvis, or bigger than Elvis," Schafer later told an interviewer. "I played their records because it was a unique situation and the music was different."[33]

George Harrison journeyed to the United States at a time of transition. In September 1963, he had no way of anticipating the coming of the Beatlemania juggernaut to America. Its eventual blossoming owed as much to historical circumstances as to the talents of the band's four members. Americans—young and old alike—sensed change in the air. Looking back with the benefit of 20/20 hindsight, historians have identified the year 1964 as a turning point, roughly marking the end of the so-called "Long Fifties"—a period extending from the 1940s to the early 1960s—and the start of what is often referred to as "the Sixties"—an age of countercultural experimentation, youthful rebellion, greater openness, polarization, war in Vietnam, and turmoil in America's streets. In the aftermath of the hard-fought Birmingham, Alabama, desegregation campaign in 1963, the Civil Rights Movement had peaked at high tide the following year. Buttressed by Martin Luther King Jr. receiving the Nobel Peace Prize in Oslo, Norway, several movement organizations unleashed the effective Mississippi Summer Project (or Freedom Summer) voter drive, which established Freedom Schools, and registered the local Black population to vote. Meantime, the assassination of President John F. Kennedy in a Dallas motorcade on November 22, 1963, remained a raw wound in the nation's psyche at the start of 1964. Although a committed Cold Warrior in the foreign policy arena, and cautious when it came to Civil Rights, Kennedy enjoyed a remarkable level of popularity among Americans from all walks of life, and he effectively tapped into a youthful zeitgeist. Emphasizing optimism in his rhetoric, Kennedy spoke of "new frontiers" and the nation's ability to overcome the challenges it faced. His quoted poets and philosophers in his speeches. He prioritized inviting artists, literary figures, and musicians to the White House. Elegant, and with an air of sophistication, the president and first lady embodied, in the eyes of millions of Americans, a nation bright with promise. The horrific ringing of gunfire that ended Kennedy's life in Dallas on November 22, 1963, established President Lyndon Johnson as the custodian of the martyred Kennedy's legacy. For the time being, Johnson's brand of sweeping federal liberalism dominated politics in Washington, D.C., in the form of his War on Poverty and Great Society programs. When The Beatles performed on the *Ed Sullivan Show*, it was evident that a sea change of some sort was already underway.[34]

Culturally, too, the country had reached a crossroads by the time George and Peter Harrison visited their sister's family in Illinois. It had only been a decade since rock and roll had burst onto the national scene with a seismic impact that caught Americans off guard. The new music borrowed heavily from earlier traditions of blues, country, jazz, and rhythm and blues. What began on the fringes of radio dials and in the corners of record shops in the mid-1950s had, by the early years of the next decade, blossomed into the dominant genre of popular music in the United States. Its early stars—Elvis Presley, Chuck Berry, Buddy Holly, Fats Domino, Jerry Lee Lewis, Little Richard, Carl Perkins, and the Everly Brothers—graduated to household names. Their hits filled the airwaves, sales of their singles overtook those of old-school crooners such as Nat King Cole and Frank Sinatra, and their faces dominated teen magazines. But rock and roll hit a rough patch in 1959. The crash of the Beechcraft Bonanza 35 in Clear Lake, Iowa, on February 3 of that year, killing young rockers Buddy Holly, J.P. "the Big Bopper" Richardson and Ritchie Valens, and pilot Roger Peterson, shocked legions of rock and roll fans at home and abroad. By this time, Elvis Presley had been drafted into the Army, Little Richard had enrolled in Oakwood College in Huntsville, Alabama, to study to become a Seventh Day Adventist preacher, and sex scandals threatened to wipe out the careers of Chuck Berry and Jerry Lee Lewis. In the fall of 1959, the heavily publicized Payola scandal—an investigation of age-old pay-for-play practices in the radio industry that zeroed in particularly tightly on rock and roll disc jockeys—generated front-page newspaper headlines and newsreel footage in movie theaters from coast to coast. The press widely proclaimed rock and roll to be "dead," or at least slipping into extinction.[35] *Time* noted in December 1959:

Newly sobered by the Payola scandal, the nation's top jocks were acknowledging what everybody has suspected for some time—that their teenage audience has begun to walk out on them ... Of the top ten pop hits last week, three were out-and-out rock 'n' roll. In Manhattan, Sam Goody's famed record shops reported a 40% drop in rock 'n' roll sales compared to a year ago. What happened to the kids? "It seems," says a Chicago jock, "like they just got tired."[36]

But rock and roll was made of tougher stuff. Rather than dying out, it changed with the times. The executives who dominated America's pop music industry during the Payola scandal—an empire symbolized by the autocratic Brill Building, a Manhattan office complex housing a number of important music businesses—paid little attention to new music scenes flourishing beyond their reach. Such vibrant locales as Greenwich Village, with its thriving folk music community, Detroit, home to the new Tamla label (also known as Motown), and Southern California, epicenter of the emerging surf rock craze, among other notable places, served as gathering spots for daring and experimental musicians. Rock and roll not only survived the misfortunes of 1959, it flourished. On the other side of the Atlantic, rock and roll found fertile ground in Great Britain, home to multiple thriving communities of musicians in cities such as London (Dusty Springfield, the Dave Clark Five, the Rolling Stones, the Kinks, the Yardbirds), Manchester (the Hollies, Herman's Hermits, Wayne Fontana and the Mindbenders), and the Merseyside port city of Liverpool, which gave the world Cilla Black, Gerry and the Pacemakers, the Searchers, Billy J. Kramer and the Dakotas, and The Beatles.[37]

Postwar Great Britain—which still bore the scars of the Second World War—consumed more rock and roll music than any country in the world outside of the United States. Such conditions led to a compelling synergy between youthful English rock bands, formed in the late 1950s and early 1960s, and their American counterparts across the "Big Pond." Young British men and women—in their teens and twenties—voraciously consumed American blues, R&B, jazz, country, and especially rock and roll. They furnished fan bases for the likes of Elvis Presley, Bill Haley, Little Richard, Chuck Berry, and Buddy Holly that was equal parts enthusiastic and loyal. Like American youths, they purchased singles in music stores, pored over teen magazines, and founded fan clubs. British teenagers inaugurated the age of Beatlemania on October 13, 1963, when they gathered outside the building where the Beatles performed on ITV's Sunday Night at the London Palladium for 15 million viewers. Three weeks later, the word "Beatlemania" appeared in a headline for the first time in the *Daily Mirror*, accompanied by images of cheering fans.[38] By this time, rock and roll fandom among young Brits had existed for eight years.[39] For George Harrison and his bandmates, the years of hard work they had put into perfecting their sound and stagecraft—in backyards and living rooms, at church grounds and fairs, on countless stages, in Scotland, in Liverpool's Casbah Coffee Club and the Cavern Club, in the seedy, neon-drenched venues of Hamburg—had paid off. "A Beatle who ventures out unguarded into the streets runs the very real peril of being dismembered or crushed to death by his fans," noted *Life* magazine, in the days before Beatles fandom exploded in North America.[40]

Yet the Beatles' success in Great Britain did not guarantee fame and fortune in the United States. By the time Louise was showing her brothers George and Peter Harrison the sights in southern Illinois in September 1963, only a handful of English music acts had made any headway on American charts. The list of Brits who could boast a number one hit on US radios was a study in brevity: teenager Laurie London (with his 1957 version of the African American folk spiritual "He's Got the Whole World in His Hands"), clarinetist Acker Bilk (performing the easy listening "Stranger on the Shore," 1962), and the upbeat pop group The Tornados (and their futuristic instrumental tune "Telstar," 1962). Americans who watched flickering images of Laurie London's 1958 visit to the United States on their televisions marveled at the gaunt young lad from England. "The most unlikely thing to hit the top in pop records would be a fourteen-year-old English kid with a cockney accent singing old-time American spirituals. Yet Laurie London has rock 'n' rollers on both sides of the Atlantic clapping their 'hands' with a broad 'A' while a choir sings in the background," observed an Iowa journalist.[41]

Unlike Laurie London, most talented UK musicians found the Billboard Hot 100 impenetrable. American record buyers, it seems, consumed only homegrown music. Meantime, back in England, with the rise of rock and roll, American pop had become a mainstay of the British charts, and bands from the United States drew large crowds when they toured the country. So widespread was US music in the United Kingdom that by the spring of 1961, Paddy Roberts, president of the Songwriters' Guild of Great Britain, lamented: "Much of the rock output isn't really music, and quite a bit of it is illiterate. And yet, for years, our hit parade has sounded like an echo of America's. Let's face it: The kids buy what they hear, and what they were hearing was American music."[42] Such cultural hegemony extended beyond rock and roll in England, into the genres of classical and jazz music. Conductors and musicians from the United States routinely topped the bills of London's music halls and concert venues, much to the chagrin of the country's music critics. In December 1957, a spokesperson for a prominent British impresario who wished to remain anonymous told a journalist: "The large numbers of young American artists who have been doing this since World War II have helped to establish American dominance of London's musical life."[43]

Like their fellow British entertainers, The Beatles knew all too well how hard it was to break into the American music scene. Inhospitable pop charts weren't kind to their earliest US singles, and success initially eluded them. Chicago-based Vee-Jay, a small record label founded in 1953 that specialized in blues, jazz, and R&B, released "Please Please Me" in February 1963, followed by "From Me To You" in May 1963. Both singles flopped—essentially, dead on arrival—due to minimal radio airplay.[44] Their dismal showing left the four band members, their producer, George Martin, and their manager, Brian Epstein, discouraged yet undaunted. For the time being, they remained content to focus on their rising stardom in the United Kingdom, temporarily shrugging off the leviathan that was the American market. The band's uncertain future in the United States in the summer and fall of 1963 makes George Harrison's trip to Illinois in September even more intriguing and poignant. He glimpsed the Midwest—"Middle America," as many liked to call it at the time—in the final moments before Beatlemania struck landfall in North America. Weeks later, in the fall of 1963, two nightly network news programs in the United States, on CBS and NBC, would air brief snippets of the Beatles performing onstage, and crowds of young Brits standing outside their concert venues screaming for their idols. On January 3, 1964, television host Jack Paar was the first to air extended footage of the Beatles performing "She Loves You" and "From Me to You" on his popular *Jack Paar Program*, piquing the curiosity of millions of curious viewers, especially the legions of teenagers who stayed up late to watch his show that night.

And yet, even at that point, George had no way of knowing that the next time he arrived in the United States, mobs of fans would besiege him. Had he been looking, he could have found antecedents to Beatlemania. One did not need to harken all the way back to the nineteenth century, when female fans of charismatic Hungarian composer and pianist Franz Liszt fainted in his presence, or to the 1920s, when silent screen star Rudolph Valentino sparked hysteria among millions of admirers, mostly young women, to find historical parallels. More recent examples of fandom—expressed publicly, on a large scale, like the giant expressions of adoration for The Beatles—could be found much more recently in the United States.

Laying the Foundation

In August 1964, Charles O. Finley, owner of the Kansas City Athletics baseball team, announced that he was paying The Beatles an unprecedented $150,000 to give a concert at Municipal Stadium, the Athletics' home field. The news that the exciting new British rock and roll band would be adding Kansas City to their list of North American tour stops created a major buzz in the community, and became the stuff of headlines, TV news broadcasts, and disc jockey talk.

An excited Finley told the press: "We're going to be able to seat 37,500, with some seats on the field. It will be the biggest arena they'll perform in on their tour here."[45] When Ernest Mehl, sports editor for the *Kansas City Star*, expressed astonishment over Finley's "extraordinarily generous offer," the wealthy businessman grinned at Mehl and defended his decision thusly:

> Now let me ask you a question. I suppose you were young once. Now maybe you didn't do this, but I'll bet you knew girls who swooned at the very mention of Rudolph Valentino. I've been doing some research. Youngsters not only swooned, but some even committed suicide. So here's the question: "Which is healthier, to swoon over Valentino or scream at the Beatles?" Include Rudy Vallee, Elvis Presley, and Frank Sinatra.[46]

Charles Finley's spirited defense of his decision to pay The Beatles what was then a colossal sum of money to perform only one concert introduced some valuable perspective. His comments came at a moment when Beatlemania's mesmerizing spell on young people left many adults perplexed. He was right that such mass outpourings of celebrity adoration did not suddenly start in 1964. But nor was this a very old phenomenon, either. The large-scale displays of fandom in public places of the sort increasingly common by the mid-1960s—at airports, hotels, concert venues, record stores, and radio stations—had roots twenty years earlier, in the zealous following amassed by Frank Sinatra.

The famous crooner stirred the passions of his young female followers with a series of high-profile solo performances between 1942 and 1944 at the Paramount Theater in New York City. Around this time, the press coined the name "bobby-soxers" for his fans, after the short, frilly socks worn by these screaming devotees. "By 1944, Sinatra's popularity was such that disturbances arose outside the theater when thousands of girls were unable to gain entry, provoking what came to be known as the Columbus Day Riots," writes Sinatra chronicler Karen McNally.[47] The Columbus Day Riots happened on October 12, 1944, at the Paramount Theater. Outside of the theater, between 25,000 and 30,000 Sinatra fans, mostly young women, swept through the streets of Times Square and charged at a line of 200 New York Police Department reinforcements while attempting to enter the packed venue. Inside the Paramount, according to one account, "the audience stamped, screamed, and ran up and down the aisles."[48]

The Columbus Day Riots occurred at the same time a new youth market and distinct teenage culture emerged in the United States, with its own collective identity. During the October 1944 upheavals, the label "teenager"—used to describe the population between thirteen and nineteen in the United States—was still novel, only used in the press since the mid-1920s.[49] Prior to the twentieth century, boys and girls in their teen years were considered "young adults." Conventional wisdom held that by their mid-teens, they were capable of marrying, finding full-time employment, starting families, and living independently. But such notions were on the retreat during the final quarter of the nineteenth century. Changing concepts of youth came about in part due to sweeping reform movements. Enforcing universal public education—particularly at the high school level—became a high priority in the Progressive Era, which spanned the 1890s to around 1920. These efforts continued into the Great Depression, with the outlawing of child labor brought about by President Franklin D. Roosevelt's New Deal. These sea changes coincided with the rise of a distinct youth culture by the turn of the twentieth century, fed by a new ethos of consumerism spreading across the nation.[50] The launch of *Seventeen* magazine in September 1944—the first periodical in the United States aimed exclusively at a teenage audience—proved to be a major milestone in the formation of a youth culture. The magazine's editors did not anticipate the enormous demand for their new publication. With an original print run of 400,000 for its premier issue, *Seventeen* surpassed the million mark in circulation within sixteen months of its founding.[51]

Meantime, the bobby-soxer subculture continued to thrive for the rest of the 1940s, spilling into the next decade. Bobby Betz, who wrote a nationally syndicated youth-focused column for King Features and drew cartoons for *Seventeen* magazine, observed at the height of the craze in 1947: "When I think of bobby-soxers, I think of the little groups who swoon over crooners, mob celebrities for autographs, and otherwise make themselves obnoxious."[52] On the radio, actress Louise Erickson played teenage bobby-soxer Judy Foster in the popular NBC program *A Date With Judy*, on the air from 1941 to 1950. In the Oscar-nominated Warner Bros. Looney Tunes cartoon *Swooner Crooner* (1944), directed by Frank Tashlin, a farmer (played by Porky Pig) confronts a Frank Sinatra-esque rooster whose crooning is distracting his lovesick hens from laying eggs. Porky enlists the aid of a pipe-puffing Bing Crosby-like rooster who uses his smooth singing voice to lure the hens away from the skeletal Sinatra rooster. Eventually, the talented roosters team up, and their duet so excites Porky that he starts laying eggs.[53] Three years later, the RKO comedy *The Bachelor and the Bobby-Soxer* (1947), starred Shirley Temple—by now in her late teens—as Susan Turner, a bobby-soxer who has a crush on playboy artist Richard Nugent (Cary Grant). Susan's older sister, Margaret (played by Myrna Loy), happens to be a judge, as well as Susan's legal guardian. Margaret concocts an elaborate scheme with Nugent with the goal of curtailing Susan's starry-eyed infatuation with him. Hilarity ensues, as Margaret slowly begins to fall for Richard.[54] *The Bachelor and the Bobby-Soxer* fared well at the box office, becoming the sixth highest grossing film of 1947.[55]

These and other pop culture contributions helped to mainstream bobby-soxers in the United States. But the postwar juvenile delinquency scare cast a shadow over the craze. Newspapers routinely ran stories about "underage" bobby-soxers running wild, playing hookey, drinking liquor, toking and peddling reefers, stealing, and engaging in premarital sex. In February 1952, a reporter for Long Island-based *Newsday* described a "North Shore bar ... packed to the doors with beer drinking bobby-soxers on Saturday date night."[56] Around the same time, Nashville journalist Raymond Moley warned of bobby-soxers attempting to sell "marijuana cigarettes" to "little girls." "The little girls scuttled away and told their teacher. The bobby-soxers moved on, looking for more customers," he wrote.[57] When a seventeen-year-old self-described "bobby-soxer" testified before the California State Legislature in 1954 about obtaining beer, vodka, and Benzedrine tablets from a seedy Bay Area "thrill spot" called Tommy's Place, a shocked PTA official expressed her dismay: "I have no daughters, but if this youngster were my child, I would just die of shame."[58] Elsewhere, newspaper headlines across the nation told similarly troubling tales about bobby-soxers: "Sinatra's Bobby-Soxers in Line at 4:30 A.M.; 53 Held by Police"[59]; "Object to 'Good, Clean Kids' Being Called Bobby-Soxers"[60]; "13-Year-Old Bobby-Soxer Held for Setting Churches Afire"[61]; "Bobby-Soxer Roots for Joe Stalin"[62]; "Bobby-Soxers Send Crooner to Hospital"[63]; and "Thrill-Seeking Bobby-Soxers Follow New Fad: Haunt Atlanta Jail to Look at Men."[64] Such negative publicity inevitably took a toll. By 1953, Alice Thompson, editor and publisher of *Seventeen* magazine, assured adults that the bobby-soxer phenomenon was nearing its end in America. "The girl under 20 today is—in essence—a throwback to her staunch, stern, strong ancestors who helped to pioneer this country," Thompson wrote.[65]

Around the time the bobby-soxer was taking their place alongside the flapper on the ash heap of history, mid-century America was witnessing the birth of rock and roll. In a relatively brief span of time, rock and roll had become ubiquitous in the United States. Signs of it could be found in record stores, movie theaters, and local concert venues. A growing number of radio stations now included rock and roll shows aimed mainly at young listeners. For most pundits, politicians, cultural critics, and moral guardians, rock and roll surfaced on the nation's airwaves with a suddenness and intensity they found bewildering. A handful of experts were quick to point out that rock and roll borrowed from earlier traditions of American music, such as Blues, R&B, and Country, but conventional wisdom of the mid-1950s emphasized the music's newness and the sway it held over the nation's youth. "There is no middle ground on the subject of rock 'n' roll. Either it warms your heart or it chews your nerves and, as for me, I am cold and frazzled," wrote journalist and syndicated columnist Phyllis Brattelle in 1955.[66]

Perhaps the harshest verdict on rock and' roll came from Frank Sinatra, patron saint of bobby-soxers, during his testimony before Congress in January 1958: "Rock 'n' roll smells phony and false. It is sung, played, and written for the most part by cretinous goons and by means of its almost imbecilic reiteration, and sly lewd, in plain fact, dirty lyrics ... it manages to be the martial music of every sideburned delinquent on the face of the earth."[67] Once again, the experts weighed in, often with a racist subtext coursing through their commentary. In the *New York Times*, psychiatrist Francis Braceland referred to rock and roll as "cannibalistic and tribalistic."[68] Another psychiatrist, Jules Masserman of Northwestern University, characterized rock and roll as "primitive quasi-music that can be traced back to prehistoric cultures."[69]

Like the bobby-soxers that came before them, young rock and roll enthusiasts encountered resistance from adults who blamed an array of problems—including juvenile delinquency, riots, violence, crime, sexually provocative behavior, vandalism, and drug and alcohol consumption—on the music's influence. Rock and roll polarized Americans in the 1950s, but not all grown-ups decried the new sounds. In the summer of 1956, Mitch Miller, a beloved musician, conductor, and record producer who made no secret of his disdain for rock and roll, spoke for enlightened parents when he observed: "No music can hurt kids who haven't already been hurt by their home environment. Rock 'n' roll is simply this: a safe form of rebellion against mother, father and teacher. It's a way they can take out their feelings of independence without hurting those they love."[70] Meantime, the music's admirers put up a spirited defense, collectively articulating their personal preferences in a manner that was bolder and more outspoken than their bobby-soxer predecessors. "All my friends are rock 'n' roll fans and not one of them is delinquent. They like to dance, that's all. All kids like to dance," reasoned a female teenager from Long Island, New York, in July 1956.[71] A high school student from Boston furnished a lively explanation for her attraction to the music: "It gives you a sort of feeling of freedom. It makes you relax and want to jump. Youth's gotta have freedom today, you know?"[72] Hugh White, an eighteen-year-old rock and roll fan from Nashville, put it even more succinctly: "This type of jive sends me, man!"[73]

Of all the early rock and rollers, Elvis Presley commanded the largest and most dedicated youthful fan base. Supporters established fan clubs in every state, and throngs of screaming teenagers greeted him wherever he went. "There just isn't an adjective in the dictionary that can describe him ... We want him to realize we are behind him in anything he does," explained nineteen-year-old Jeanelle Alexander, president of the Shreveport, Louisiana, branch of the Elvis Presley fan club, a "loose-knit" organization with 6,000 members. Self-proclaimed "honor roll student" Linda Deutsch, from Asbury Park, New Jersey, ran an Elvis Presley Fan Club with 10,000 members. "The fans know his background, and they know about the religious young Southern boy who struggled until he reached the top. Maybe each hopes that some day he or she can be half as great a person and credit to the Lord and country as Elvis Aaron Presley is."[74] Lest anyone claim Presley's following consisted solely of adolescents, a group of thirty "mothers and grandmothers" from El Paso, Texas, and the surrounding environs, founded a group of so-called "Presley-Grams" in 1957, many of whom also happened to be "widowed" and "faithful workers in their churches." It buttressed the group's credibility to have a Sunday School teacher as its president. These mature Presley fans released a statement to the press proclaiming: "Elvis won't drink alcoholic beverages, and he has left parties in his honor when the guests had too much. He doesn't smoke either."[75] Further north and east, Baltimore fan club president Pat Kolb held monthly Saturday night meetings of the local Elvis Presley Fan Club in her family's spacious house, which drew members from all parts of the city. Kolb loved showing off her Christmas card inscribed with a message from Elvis (wishing her a "cool Yule and a frantic First"), and a "brown and white striped" shirt given to her by the singer that she wore "everywhere except to school."[76]

Such activities garnered public attention across the country. Indeed, it was difficult to ignore the legions of Elvis Presley fans. During the 1950s, there was at least one qualitative attempt to understand this thriving community of youths and their patterns of behavior. In March 1958, Eugene Gilbert, a researcher from Chicago who established his influential Gilbert Youth Research Group when he was nineteen years old in 1945, released the results of an extensive study of teenage Presley fandom. By this time, Gilbert had established a reputation among business executives as a guru of the thriving "teenage market," and the findings of his surveys carried a great deal of weight. His study of Elvis Presley fans—with its reliance on murky methodology and the clinical language of social scientists so popular in academic circles at the time—appeared in newspapers across the country. Gilbert polled "about 100 teenagers at random," asking a variety of questions about their extracurricular activities, "scholastic achievements," and thoughts about the future. The responses, he said, "produced a definite pattern."[77] Teens who spent time "idolizing" Presley were not joiners, and thus far less likely to pay dues to fan clubs than "fans of Frank Sinatra, Perry Como and Pat Boone." Instead, youths in the Presley camp were too rebellious and too apathetic to get involved with appreciation societies. One Presley admirer allegedly told Gilbert: "Who's got time for school clubs? I'd rather sit around with my pals."[78] This pervasive aimlessness, Gilbert claimed, resulted in a lack of ambition among the young men and women he surveyed. For instance, Elvis lovers typically received lower grades in school—averaging in the C range—than those less partial to him. Moreover, "Presley fans were shockingly unconcerned about the future," Gilbert observed.[79] In broad brushstrokes, Gilbert dismissed Presley's "rabid" fan base as "infantile" and "insecure" youngsters who maintained unhealthy obsessions with the rock and roll star. Gilbert concluded that Presley's diehard fans listened to his music as a means of fitting in with their fellow Elvis-adoring peers. Presley's appeal, the researcher concluded, was based on his status as "unacceptable to the adult world," and "to the unadjusted teenager, he seems to mock its cultural taboos."[80]

The findings of Eugene Gilbert's survey, which dismissed Presley's fans as childlike and lacking goals, meshed well with nationwide crusades by politicians, prominent religious figures, and defenders of more traditional forms of cultural expression to delegitimize rock and roll. Since its inception a few years earlier, the music had fostered divisions that ran deep in American society. And the press in the late 1950s eagerly printed critiques of it, especially those made by dismissive adolescents. Youthful denunciations of rock and roll were soon commonplace. "Rock 'n' roll music isn't the best type of music. It seems to bring out the worst in teenagers," explained Carroll Anderson, a high school sophomore from Lawton, Oklahoma.[81] A seventeen-year-old Alabama lad insisted in 1958 that rock and roll appealed to "the side-burned, black leather jacket, prune-picker type."[82] "I never did care for rock 'n' roll. It just made me sick," said Miami high schooler John Fox.[83] A seventeen-year-old female student from Frankfort, New York, told a reporter: "Mainly it attracts those who like to get up and make fools of themselves."[84] Reinforcing these attacks were assurances by the experts that rock and roll no longer gripped youngsters the way it once did, when it was new and fresh. Declarations of rock and roll's "death" were commonplace by 1959. That year, disc jockey Ira Cook of Los Angeles radio station KMPC explained his reasons for jettisoning rock and roll from his daily music playlists: "We haven't been playing much of it because most of it is just plain junk. We're playing the middle of the road with records by such favorites as Frank Sinatra, good arrangements by Billy May, et cetera."[85]

As a DJ who loathed rock and roll, Ira Cook enjoyed plenty of company on the nation's airwaves. The songs that dominated the pop charts in the late 1950s were influenced by "mood music," which often featured large orchestras that went heavy on the string sections. The teen idols of the late 1950s and early 1960s, which included the likes of Fabian, Frankie Avalon, Bobby Vee, Bobby Darin, Ricky Nelson, and Paul Anka, among others, generally sang safe and sedate songs, nonthreatening to the parents of their fans. Still, despite adopting a mellower sound, the teen idols did not reject rock and roll. On the contrary, they embraced it, and sang their own versions of it, even though they weren't as edgy as early rockers like Little Richard or Jerry Lee Lewis. Frankie Avalon, whose hits "Venus" and "Why" shot to the number one spot on the Billboard Hot 100 in 1959, openly expressed his admiration for Elvis Presley. "I like Elvis ... We owe him a lot. I think he started the whole teenage craze," he told an interviewer.[86] Avalon's close friend and fellow Philadelphian, Fabian Forte—who simply went by Fabian—claimed he sang a "newer type" of rock and roll. "The beat isn't as raunchy as it used to be. It's more quiet.

There will always be rock 'n' roll no matter what anyone says," said the sixteen-year-old entertainer in 1959.[87] The titan of teen idols, Ricky Nelson, singer and star of television and movies, inspired the formation of 6,000 fan clubs worldwide by 1959, and received an average of 10,000 letters per week from fans. He loved rock and roll, and he did not hesitate to apply that label to his music. Nelson attributed his love of rock and roll to his father, bandleader and actor Ozzie Nelson. "Dad found that rock 'n' roll is a combination of folk music, Western music, Dixieland, and the blues, and that young people like it because it's simple, full of life, and has a contagious beat," Ricky explained. Ricky boldly attacked the oft-made charge that rock and roll contributed to juvenile delinquency, and he defended the right of fans to be expressive and loud at his concerts. "What's wrong with good healthy screaming anyway? They're just showing their enthusiasm, that's all. They're not ill-mannered or rowdy. What they're doing is a part of being young."[88]

The teen idols helped bridge rock and roll's heady early years of the mid-1950s to the sounds of the new decade in the early 1960s. They were heard on radios and hi-fis across North America, and their handsome faces appeared on colorful youth magazines. Crowds of boisterous fans gathered wherever they performed. More importantly, by embracing a newer, less raucous form of rock and roll, the teen idols fortified those venerable veterans of the music's founding cohort that enjoyed staying power into the new decade, including Elvis Presley (who had softened his image after returning from the Army), Chuck Berry, the Everly Brothers, Fats Domino, and Johnny Cash. Rock and roll during the early 1960s, thanks in part to these youthful crooners—the Frankie Avalons and Ricky Nelsons—had moved into the mainstream of American culture. Indeed, when it came to the sheer ability to stir fans into a frenzy, and generate fan club growth, the only early rock and roll star who could compete with the new teen-oriented pop celebrities was Elvis Presley. His newer songs, such as "It's Now or Never" from 1960, and "Can't Help Falling in Love" from 1961, put his more mature side on full display for the nation to see. His famous televised appearance on *The Frank Sinatra Timex Special* on May 12, 1960, signified a new chapter in his career. Frank Sinatra, Presley's former rival, now warmly welcomed the 25-year-old singer—who'd recently been honorably discharged from the Army—onto his television show, resulting in stellar ratings. The times had indeed changed. Rock and roll—once the stuff of juvenile rebellion—had gained mainstream acceptance by the early 1960s, and no longer posed a threat to the establishment. Predictions of its demise in 1958 and 1959 proved nothing more than premature wishful thinking. It was here to stay, and most sensible adult observers concluded that, like other youthful crazes in the past, it could be controlled and made safe.

A cursory glance at the covers of American teen magazines from 1963 offers clues about the collective state of mind of the nation's adolescent pop culture consumers on the eve of Beatlemania. Glossy periodicals such as *Dig, 16, Hi-Teen, Teen Time, Teen World, Teen Life, Teen Album, Hit Parader, Datebook,* and *Stardom,* all showcased the era's youthful sensations on their customer-grabbing covers, often in colorful montages with bright bursts of decorative fonts. In most issues, teen idol singers shared covers with popular movie and television stars. Many of these magazines came with foldout posters of young celebrities, suitable for hanging on bedroom walls.

Prior to the appearance of the Beatles on the *Ed Sullivan Show,* the biggest British celebrity was not a rock and roll singer, but, rather, an actress. Hayley Mills, born in London on April 18, 1946, had achieved stardom by the age of twelve, thanks to her appearance in the commercially successful British film *Tiger Bay* (1959), opposite her father, actor John Mills. Thanks to a slew of live-action Disney films, including *Pollyanna* (1960), for which she won an Academy Juvenile Award, *The Parent Trap* (1961), a major hit in which she played identical twin sisters, and *In Search of the Castaways* (1962), Mills was even more famous and beloved in the United States than she was in her native England. "Hayley Mills is only 15 and wears her hair in pigtails, but this British-born actress is known to moviegoers from Hong Kong to Hollywood," wrote American journalist Tom A. Cullen in the summer of 1961.[89] Mills remained in the spotlight for much of the decade, starring in formulaic Disney vehicles, attending movie premiers and Hollywood cocktail parties, and gracing the covers of magazines. She enjoyed a gigantic following, mostly of adolescent girls and young women, many of whom would go on to become dedicated Beatles admirers. At her height in the early 1960s, Mills received 7,500 fan letters a week. Millions of people loved her for her down-to-earth modesty and girl-next-door qualities. In the fall of 1961, she calmly reflected on her worldwide celebrity status with her usual humility:

> Reporters ask me frequently if working in films doesn't prevent me from enjoying a normal youth. I don't think it does. I still have friends I've always had. I still do things I've always done, swim, play tennis, watch my brother Jonathan play cricket. I listen to jazz and rock 'n' roll with my schoolmates. I don't think working in films has changed me much.[90]

Hayley Mills found fame at a moment in the postwar era when the youth market was coming into its own as the most thriving segment of the consumer economy. The illustrated magazines of the day that published photos of Mills, and profile stories to go along with them, were a new product of mid-century America. They could be purchased cheaply—in most cases, a quarter—at supermarkets, magazine stands, and bookstores. In addition to teen magazines, technologies that were relatively new fueled the youthful consumerism of the 1950s and 1960s. Transistor radios, which relied on transistor-based circuitry and thus rendered vacuum tubes obsolete, debuted on store shelves in the mid-1950s. But early transistor radios were expensive, often out of the price range of teens who made money from paper routes, allowances, and part-time, after-school jobs. In 1958, Masaru Ibuka, cofounder and president of Sony Corporation in Japan, explained the steep cost of transistor radios: "Price is still a problem, as a transistor is from one and a half to two times more expensive than a radio tube."[91]

By the fall of 1963, however, due to the plummeting costs of mass production, a decent handheld transistor radio, complete with a carrying strap and earphone, could be purchased for under $20. Other electronics, such as televisions, short wave radios, phonographs, high-fidelity stereo consoles, and tape players, experienced the same downward trend in prices. The introduction of the compact cassette—also referred to as the cassette tape—in the early 1960s, eliminated the need for cumbersome reel-to-reel tape decks, and by mid-decade, enabled young rock and roll fans to tape and play back their favorite songs. "It's made for fun. No reels, no threading—just drop in a cartridge, turn the dials to record or play," said a 1962 advertisement for the new RCA Victor tape cartridge recorder.[92] These electronic devices disseminated the latest in popular music to mass audiences. The music could be heard in many forms: via television variety shows, radio signals, record albums, and cassette tapes. Mail-order music clubs also flourished in the 1950s and 1960s, further expanding that reach. The most famous of these, the Columbia Record Club (later known as Columbia House), was founded in 1955 as mail-order branch of CBS/Columbia Records. Headquartered in Terre Haute, Indiana, the huge operation had millions of subscribers by the early 1960s. The Club's eye-catching advertisements in magazines, filled with rows and rows of tiny multicolored record covers with titles listed below each one, promised in 1960, "Any 5 of these $3.98 to $6.98 long-playing 12" records for only $1.97. Retail value up to $31.90." Below that, fine print stipulated: "If you join the Club now and agree to purchase as few as 5 selections from more than 200 to be offered in the coming twelve months."[93]

These innovations aided the Beatles—and their contemporaries in rock and roll—by making their music more accessible to listeners. They also contributed to a homogenization of popular culture, a process accelerated by the narrow range of television programming at the time. In most American cities, TV channels were limited to the three networks—ABC, CBS, and NBC—with scattered independent stations, usually higher on the television dial. This concentration of television's might into a trio of heavily regulated nationwide outlets resulted in The Beatles being able to draw an audience of nearly 73 million for their US debut on the *Ed Sullivan Show*—at a moment when the nation's population stood at around 192 million. And yet, despite the homogenizing effects of these new mediums of communications, popular music was diversifying in striking ways. Revivals of folk music and blues, the popularity of soul, Motown, instrumental hits, surf rock, and "girl groups," the runaway success of new types of jazz and country music, and the bold new symphonic melodies ushered in by Phil Spector's "Wall of Sound" recording techniques, resulted in a wider array of musical styles being heard on the nation's airwaves than ever before. Even with all this competition, the Beatles had achieved an unprecedented level of superstardom when they descended the stairs of Pan Am Yankee Clipper flight 101 to the tarmac at John F. Kennedy Airport on February 7, 1964. Days after they touched down, the popular trade publication *Billboard* magazine described the buzz in record stores and on radio airwaves:

> Dealers describe Beatlemania as the most virulent form of record fever since the heyday of such artists as Elvis Presley and the Everly Brothers. Even then, neither Presley nor the Everlys had more than one record going for them at a time. Currently, the Beatles have no less than four singles and three albums. Record stores are filled with different types of Beatles promotion material that often defy the imagination ... Radio stations likewise are running promotions and in all cases, playing the records like mad.[94]

Coming Together

The Beatles' landmark *Ed Sullivan Show* performance mesmerized young viewers, just as Frank Sinatra's singing had captivated bobby-soxers twenty years earlier. But it also mobilized them. In the days and weeks following the broadcast, hastily formed Beatles fan clubs sprang up in all parts of the country, with the main headquarters listing its address as P.O. Box 505, Radio City Station, New York City.[95] The national fan club—initially the creation of the well-oiled Capitol Records publicity machine—charged $2 membership dues and sent out a booklet and quarterly newsletters to joiners. It functioned as a nerve center of Beatles fandom in the United States, providing cohesion at a time when fans were starting to become more assertive and reaching out to one another. The national office established a rule that a minimum of twenty-five dues payers were necessary to start a local chapter. Larger American cities—such as New York, Philadelphia, Chicago, San Francisco, and Los Angeles—were home to numerous Beatles fan clubs, which competed for members, donations, and resources. Chicago was home to a plethora of these groups, each with different names and priorities. "Some of the clubs were school-based or neighborhood-based, while others organized on a citywide basis," explained historian John F. Lyons.[96] Detroit also contained a large population of youths who had fallen under the spell of the Beatles. Between Detroit and its neighboring city across the Canadian border, Windsor, Ontario, an astonishing 300 Beatles fan clubs had been established by the end of February 1964.[97] In Boston, a mecca of Fab Four fandom, the founders of the Massachusetts state chapter of the Beatles fan club took the bold step of renting a space in a downtown office building on Beacon Street to conduct their affairs.[98] Beatles boosters elsewhere made their presences known in dramatic ways. On the other side of the country, the founder of the local fan club in Long Beach, California, referred to herself as "the female Cassius Clay," and boldly proclaimed, "We will wear our Beatle wigs, shirts, and black capri, and then we will march with our fluorescent signs to downtown Long Beach, and I— alone, if necessary—will go to Hollywood to march for recruits."[99]

In most cases, energetic adolescents supplied the hard work that went into creating and building a chapter. Fourteen-year-old ninth grader Cindy Green, a junior high school student living in Tampa, Florida, founded that city's first Beatles fan club. She saw its membership suddenly balloon in a matter of weeks, as stamped and addressed envelopes poured into the club's P.O. box throughout the spring containing the fifty-cent joining fee. Green began producing a mimeographed newsletter to promote the group's activities and spread the latest news on the British band. "They help teenagers express themselves. It's the style of their music that does it. The mop hairdo is just a gimmick. They'd be terrific even if they were all bald," Green said.[100] The Quad Cities Beatles Fan Club—which included joiners from Davenport and Bettendorf in Iowa, and in Rock Island, Moline and East Moline, across the Mississippi River in Illinois—gathered regularly at the home of eleven-year-old club president Nancy Hatfield in Rock Island. Members ranged in age from ten to seventeen. They remained busy in the months that followed the Beatles' debut on the *Ed Sullivan Show*, recruiting new members, seeking donations, and making pin-on buttons that said, "I'm a Quad Cities Beatles Fan." "The purpose of the club," Hatfield explained, "will be to promote various money-raising events such as bake sales and car washes. We want the money so we can rent a building for our headquarters. It's kind of hard on parents meeting in homes this way you know!"[101] In many instances, civic-minded youths helmed these clubs, and they used their groups to assist charitable causes. At the American Legion Hall in Oakland, New Jersey, the local Beatles fan club held a dance that raised over $250 for the Cerebral Palsy Association.[102] Similarly, youths in Pittsburgh organized a "Beatle Hop" dance on June 6, 1964, the money from which formed a sizable donation to the city's Children's Hospital.[103] The Jackson, Mississippi, branch of the Beatles Fan Club—150 members strong—mobilized locals to attend a fashion show, and donated proceeds to the construction of a new children's ward at the local hospital.[104] A group of female club members from Belvidere, Illinois—ranging in age from twelve to eighteen—planned a series of activities to raise funds for the humanitarian relief agency CARE International.[105] In December, with the approach of the holidays, fan clubs in Wisconsin and Ohio held bake sales and other fundraisers to gather donations to assist needy families at Christmastime.[106]

Organizing a Beatles fan club in mid-1960s' America often became a family affair. In the fall of 1964, sisters Joanne and Betsy Percoski, from Somers, Connecticut, began publishing their own fan zine titled *Beatles Unlimited*. Their editorial staff consisted of members of the nearby Enfield Beatles Fan Club. They published articles, poems, and news items borrowed from "dependable" newspapers, held staff meetings, mimeographed the finished product, and sent it out in mass mailings. The earliest copies were free, but before long, the Percoski sisters began charging twelve cents an issue to cover printing costs and postage. And while they encountered occasional snags and hiccups, circulation rapidly climbed due to a growing mailing list and a dedicated army of fan writers.[107] Meantime, tolerant parents all over the United States allowed fan club meetings to take place in their homes, often serving punch and cookies to guests. For example, the mother and father of thirteen-year-old Lona Stoars of Salem, Oregon, permitted their daughter to conduct fan club meetings in her bedroom, where participants played Beatles records on Lona's portable phonograph. The group consisted of seven hardcore members, including Lona. They gathered on Saturday afternoons to listen to Beatles' songs, review their extensive photo collection, thumb through magazines, and swap bubble-gum cards and stories. "All the girls declared that their parents are just as crazy about the Beatles as they are," noted a story about the fan club in the local newspaper.[108] For some parents, listening to the Beatles was a way of bonding with their children. Songs on constant radio rotation, such as "I Want to Hold Your Hand," "She Loves You," and "Can't Buy Me Love," wore down even the most resistant grownups. Margaret Hansen, one of the organizers of the Beatles Fan Club in Reno, Nevada, asserted, "My mother likes the Beatles, too, and so does my sister and brother-in-law."[109] Some parents simply felt overwhelmed by the deluge of Beatles items in their children's lives. Jim Reid, a father of two adoring female Beatles boosters from Oklahoma City, could've been speaking for innumerable parents in the spring of 1964 when he wearily proclaimed, "Fact is, we've got wall-to-wall Beatlemania. We are knee-deep in Beatle phonograph albums, Beatle magazines, and Beatle photographs. Our radio blares Beatle tunes constantly … We've also become headquarters for a Beatle fan club whose members all wear black slacks and sweatshirts with you-know-who on them."[110]

* * *

By the time the Beatles returned in mid-August 1964 to tour the United States and Canada, fan communities had formed in every state. Fans established clubs in cities, small towns, and rural areas, in all parts of the country. The coming of Beatlemania caught adults off guard with its breadth and the sheer excitement it aroused. It flourished on a massive scale, drawing adherents from a broad sweep of backgrounds. The band's young admirers were more vocal, passionate, and engaged when it came to their idols than earlier constituencies of postwar fandom, such as the bobby-soxers of the 1940s and early 1950s, and rock and roll-loving youths present at that genre's creation.

But the dedication of Beatles fans to their heroes encountered resistance on multiple fronts. Young women and girls who gathered in public places to cheer The Beatles were often dismissed as hysterical, while boys who loved them saw their masculinity questioned. At various points, Beatles' fans—like their favorite rock and roll band—ended up on the receiving end of verbal assaults by pundits, politicians, clergy, prominent cultural figures, and assorted champions of morality. For their part, Beatlemania's foes relied on heavy doses of cynicism, dehumanization, and hyperbole in their attacks.

But they did not anticipate relentless pushback by the band's stalwart defenders. Battle lines had been drawn. Debates about the band's talent, appearance, and far-reaching influence could take unexpectedly fierce turns. The Beatles, it turns out, were more polarizing upon their arrival in North America than the mythic, revered band they would become in popular memory. The fissures they helped to create in 1964 anticipated similar, yet deeper, divisions in the closing years of the tumultuous 1960s.

2

Hysterical Girls and Long-Haired Boys

The enormity of Beatlemania in the United States owed to gatherings of fans across the country. They were impossible to miss in the mid-1960s. Enthusiasts—mostly teenagers—purchased Beatles albums, listened to their music on transistors and turntables, formed fan clubs, plastered their walls with Beatles posters, voraciously consumed Beatles-themed merchandise, and wrote fan letters to band members. Beatles fans also challenged conventional norms, particularly the band's zealous male followers, who began to grow their hair out in violation of nationwide school district bans on long hair on male students. Some intrepid souls even ventured out of their homes and neighborhoods in pursuit of the elusive goal of meeting the Fab Four. The fans, in short, sustained Beatlemania, energized by the band's creativity, and the connections they made with each other. Indeed, for many youthful first-generation Beatles lovers, their experiences in the heady early months of Beatlemania would influence them—their values, beliefs, worldviews—in meaningful ways, for the rest of their lives.

"The Pied Pipers of This Century"

On September 17, 1964, Martha Schendel and Janice Hawkins, both sixteen years of age, disappeared from their homes in Cleveland Heights, Ohio. Prior to vanishing, Martha had withdrawn $1,980—money she'd been gradually tucking away for her college education—from her bank account, without informing her parents. The police quickly pieced together that the girls had left Cleveland's Hopkins Airport that day on a Trans World Airlines (TWA) flight bound for London, with a stop in New York City, a fact confirmed by airline officials.[1] Cleveland Heights police chief Edward Gaffney informed the press that the girls had gone to England to attempt to find the Beatles, departing two days after the wildly popular English rock band had performed at Cleveland's Public Auditorium. For three weeks, millions of Americans followed the latest news updates about Schendel and Hawkins, waiting for a break in the case. Within days of their disappearance, a United Press International wire service story reported that the duo had been found in Liverpool, but it was a false alarm.[2]

Each passing day brought new developments. At the beginning of October, police found torn-up letters in Janice Hawkins's wastebasket—one written to Beatles manager Brian Epstein, the other to an English girl named Annabelle Smith—spelling out Hawkins's and Schendel's plans to run away to England to meet the Beatles.[3] Detectives from London's Scotland Yard contacted Annabelle Smith, pen pal to Hawkins and Schendel, but she claimed she had tossed out letters she received from them, and she insisted the American teens hadn't gotten in touch with her. "I'm rather surprised," she said, "that the girls haven't called on me yet."[4] Police in London, aware the girls had become a media sensation back in the United States, intensified their search, expanding it to Liverpool. Authorities asked the Beatles to issue a statement calling on the girls to return home, but the band refused, fearing such a move would spawn copycats galore.[5]

Meantime, eyewitnesses reported seeing girls who matched the descriptions of the missing teens. The police redoubled their efforts, following leads, interviewing witnesses, retracing footsteps. The search paid off. A police officer—or a "bobby," as they were popularly known—nabbed Janice Hawkins on Oxford Street on Wednesday, October 7. Hawkins led the police to the West End apartment that the girls had rented, and they apprehended Schendel. They then transported the pair to the US embassy. "The girls were similarly attired in short black boots and black woolen tights. They wore dark glasses and sweaters," reported the *Los Angeles Times*.[6] Schendel and Hawkins assured authorities they'd been having a wonderful time in England, and they praised Brits for their hospitality. It pleased them both especially that they were able to visit the Merseyside port city of Liverpool, the Beatles' hometown, to sightsee. By the time the police found Schendel and Hawkins, they still had over $1,100 of the money they'd withdrawn from Martha's college fund.[7] The press covered the journey of the two teenagers from London back to Cleveland in detail. When Janice Hawkins's legal guardian, Margaret Klein—who was also Janice's great aunt—heard the girls were coming home, she remarked: "I don't think a girl sixteen should be left alone in this country, let alone in a strange country. It is very strange that they left in the first place with no reason at all except those silly old Beatles."[8] The actions of Schendel and Hawkins irked the Cleveland Heights police, who'd grown frustrated in their efforts to track them down. They interrogated the girls at length upon their return, and angrily rebuked them for running away.[9] Meantime, authorities sought to make a cautionary tale of the two. When promoters for the Rolling Stones sent complimentary tickets to the girls to attend the band's November 3 concert at Cleveland's Public Hall, Juvenile Court Judge Angelo J. Gagliardo balked. He imposed an order banning the girls from going to the Stones' show, and angrily denounced parents who allowed their children to attend rock concerts unsupervised. "It's like feeding narcotics to teenagers. It's very dangerous. It could very well lead to riots," declared Gagliardo.[10]

But Schendel and Hawkins had their own reasons for traveling to England, and they returned to the United States unrepentant. While Martha never publicly spoke of their journey after returning to Cleveland Heights, Janice would go on to write a detailed account of it, published in 2021. Janice revealed in her narrative that she'd been best friends with Martha—Marty, she called her—for years before they boarded a TWA jet airplane that would fly them to New York City, on the way to London Heathrow. Janice's deeply troubled biological parents had abandoned her, leaving her in the care of distant relatives, which was a mixed experience for her. She grew up in the relative comfort of Cleveland Heights' leafy residential neighborhoods and received a good education at local Catholic schools. But her legal guardians could often be emotionally distant, and Janice yearned for a more cohesive family life. One of her most important adolescent relationships was with Martha, who lived with her mother and stepfather in a spacious, middle-class home nearby. In her 2021 account, Janice Hawkins—a retired former federal investigator, her last name by now changed to Mitchell—reflected on the deeper meanings of the journey, sharing vivid details about her time in England with her best friend.[11]

The story of Martha Schendel and Janice Hawkins captured the attention of millions of Americans—and, indeed, people outside the country—because it revealed the lengths to which young Beatles fans would go for a meeting, even a fleeting one, with the band they loved so dearly. That the two sojourners were teenage females only served to heighten interest in their expedition. They fled their homes at a time when youths running away from home was increasingly seen by adults as a national crisis. In Miami Beach, Florida, where seventy-five children vanished from their homes in the month of April 1964 alone, Leona Trexler, a matronly secretary for the Miami Police Department's Juvenile and Missing Persons Detail, gave voice to widespread parental fears when she proclaimed that runaways "are a source of great concern for us, and unless aided, they are easy prey for perverts."[12] In the early postwar period, parents tended to take a benign view of running away. Children packing snacks and a change of clothes and hitting the road for greener pastures was usually regarded as a harmless rite of passage by mothers and fathers. Sgt. Robert E. Burke, head of the Juvenile Division of the Los Angeles Department, gave credence to this view in the fall of 1962 when he stated: "Not having broken any laws or being criminal offenders in any way other than that they have wandered away from their homes, runaway children shouldn't be a police problem at all ... Within 24 hours, we locate 99 percent of them."[13] But something had changed by the mid-1960s. Experts began to reject the pervasive belief that running away was simply a battle of wills between parents and obstinate children. Instead, they insisted that youths who resort to such a drastic course of action needed understanding and compassion, not dismissive patronizing attitudes. Theodore Leventhal, a psychiatric expert with the Youth Guidance Center in Worcester, Massachusetts, advocated this view in the fall of 1963 when he insisted that most runaways were sensitive adolescents that felt unhappy with some aspect of home life, or feared harsh discipline at the hands of parents, and regarded running away as a means of escaping such difficulties at home. "If they have the physical means, which children progressively do they older they become, they will remove themselves physically—hence, running away."[14]

A rash of Beatlemaniacs running away from home brought this issue to the fore in the United States. Schendel and Hawkins, it turns out, weren't alone. Coincidentally, at the time the pair of Cleveland Heights teens boarded an airplane for the first leg of the trip to London, two twelve-year-old girls living in nearby Rocky River—a suburb of Cleveland—ran away from home, leaving behind a note saying they were "going to find the Beatles." The Rocky River runaways only had $6 between them, so their journey was short-lived. Two other Cleveland-area youths, a brother and sister in their mid-teens, left around the same time, also in pursuit of the Fab Four. They, too, returned home within days.[15] Elsewhere in America, young people lit out in pursuit of the Beatles, with mixed success. The first highly publicized case of Beatlemaniacs running away from home occurred on Tuesday, May 26, 1964, when fifteen-year-old Carole Pantas and twelve-year-old Alison Lynn Moore left their homes in Warrenton, Virginia, bound for England. Before setting out, Pantas and Moore "cut their hair in Beatle style," and began speaking in "British accents," with Alison adopting the name Paul and Carole going by Ringo.[16] Homemade decals on their luggage declared, "Liverpool or Bust."[17] They were missing for days. Police in Philadelphia caught the girls on Sunday, May 31, and returned them to their parents.[18]

Some runaway Beatles fans went missing for days, unseen by police or eyewitnesses, resulting in mothers and fathers panicking. On October 16, four girls—Shirley Best, Carroll Hubbell, Dixie Jo McEnery, and Suzanne Moser—all age thirteen, all from San Rafael, California, about 20 miles north of San Francisco—disappeared from their homes. Their parents put up a rigorous search for their daughters, and the police released a statement to the press announcing the girls "are trying to reach New York to go to England," to meet the Beatles.[19] Without any communication from their children, the alarmed parents feared the worst. Suzanne's father, Kenneth, expressed his frustration when he told reporters: "Suzie's schoolwork has been losing out to the Beatles lately. She's been driving us practically crazy with the Beatles. The Beatles have taken over to the point where everything else has gone out the window."[20] An all-points bulletin went out to police departments across Northern California, and rumors swirled that the four travelers were holed up in Sacramento for days. Police eventually apprehended the girls near Lake Tahoe after they'd been gone nearly a week, and promptly returned them to their homes.[21]

In terms of sheer dramatic punch, all these cases paled in comparison to the experiences of thirteen-year-old Elizabeth Freedman from Newton, Massachusetts, whose quest to find the Beatles generated headlines far and wide. After successfully applying for a passport in Boston, Freedman withdrew $405 from her personal account at Newton Savings Bank—money her grandparents had given her—and bought a TWA airlines ticket to London. Departing for England on Sunday, October 18, 1964, she disappeared from contact. "Elizabeth was described as 5 feet 7 inches tall, 125 pounds, with long blonde hair and looks older than she is," noted the *Boston Globe*, days after she went missing.[22] Freedman's maturity—her mother likened her in appearance to a full-grown woman—enabled her to travel freely without raising suspicions. Scotland Yard detectives, fresh off the hunt for Schendel and Hawkins, assured their counterparts in Newton, Massachusetts: "Don't worry, we'll find her."[23] But theirs was a difficult undertaking. London was a vast city, and Elizabeth managed to evade the police for nearly two weeks. Meanwhile, her mother, Barbara Freedman, arrived in the country to take part in the search. She knew London well, being a native of England. She had married an American serviceman shortly after the Second World War and moved with him to the United States. They settled in Newton, and he died soon after Elizabeth was born, leaving Barbara to raise their daughter on her own.[24]

Flying to London days after Elizabeth's left, Barbara Freedman met with Scotland Yard detectives, who alerted the press about the missing girl. A teenage boy who'd gotten to know Elizabeth in recent days noticed a story about her in a local paper. He tipped off the police, who found her staying in a rooming house in the Brixton district of London, owned by the aunt of a Beatles fan whom she'd met at a coffee house.[25] Like Martha Schendel and Janice Hawkins, Elizabeth Freedman's trip to England had been eventful. She'd gone dancing, visited jazz clubs, and caught a triple bill at the Palladium of Cilla Black, Petula Clark, and Cliff Richard. "I had a good time. I went to clubs, I went to the theater, I went out to eat. At that time the dollar was pretty strong, so my money went a long way," she later recalled.[26] Barbara Freedman, relieved to be reunited with her daughter, booked their flight back to the United States. Before they flew home, Brian Epstein, manager of the Beatles, arranged for the teenage tourist and her mother to be given backstage passes to the Astoria Theatre in Finsbury Park, London. The Beatles performed a concert there on the night of November 1, and Elizabeth was beside herself with excitement when it came time to meet them. The four band members greeted her with quips and instantly made her feel comfortable. "So, this is the little girl we've been reading about," chimed in Ringo Starr. George said, "I don't think we've been to Boston." To which Paul responded: "We have. That's where we had the tea party."[27] Giddy Elizabeth brought two albums along with her, *A Hard Day's Night* and *With the Beatles*, which the Beatles autographed. She recalled:

> They were very charming. I remember that John took the pen that he used to sign my albums and pretended that it was a gun and went, "Bang, bang, bang," at the cameraman, which is kind of ironic now. And I remember there was a bowl of grapes in the dressing room, and George said, "Here, take the whole bunch." We ate hot dogs. They were all very sweet and very charming and joked around a lot.[28]

A media frenzy awaited Elizabeth upon her return to the United States. A mob of reporters and cameras pounced on her and her mother as they descended the airplane steps and crossed the tarmac. Headlines told of a remarkable girl pulling the wool over people's eyes, fooling them into believing she was twice her age. For the briefest of moments, Elizabeth Freedman became a celebrity. But her fame did not last. Her life promptly returned to normal. A *Boston Globe* headline following her return said it all: "Beatle Fan Back in Dullsville."[29]

But the impact of the young female fans who ventured out into the world, without parental approval, in search of the Beatles, was far-reaching. Even though most fans did not make that attempt, the ones who did helped to heighten the anxieties of parents, who felt like they were losing control of their Beatlemaniac children, especially their daughters. Despite humor-laced stories in the press, this was no laughing matter to the mothers and fathers of the runaways. If these intrepid young women and girls could leave home in pursuit of the Beatles, what was to stop others from following in their footsteps? Harold Moore of Warrenton, Virginia, father of twelve-year-old runaway Alison Moore, likened the Beatles to the Pied Piper of Hamelin, the legendary character of German lore from the Middle Ages, who used his magic pipe to lure children out of the village when he wasn't compensated for doing the same thing to the community's rat population. "The Beatles,"

Moore warned, "are the pied pipers of this century, but they're piping the children away from their homes and into England. You can't believe it until you've been a parent and seen it in your own house."[30]

Parents of most Beatles' fans—the majority that didn't run away—could imagine their children resorting to such extreme actions. Especially when one remembers that the runaways were, in the main, modest, intelligent girls who did relatively well in school and showed little interest in rebelling or nonconformity. Suddenly, they went missing, typically leaving few clues as to their whereabouts. The frightened plea of the mother of one of the missing teens from San Rafael, California, resonated with adults: "We want her to call her mother or her grandmother in Nevada if she needs help. We want her home."[31] Some critics blamed permissive parents for the rash of runaways. Conservatives like Judge Angelo J. Gagliardo, who forbade Martha Schendel and Janice Hawkins from attending a Rolling Stones concert after their return from London, chastised mothers and fathers who let their sons and daughters go to such raucous events without adult chaperones. "The parents of Cleveland should hang their heads in shame that they allow their children to attend such a performance unsupervised," he said.[32] Regardless of where the blame lay, the rising incidents of girls running away from home to meet the Beatles came at a time when American society was in transition, with greater numbers of women entering the paid labor force, and a shrinking percentage aspiring to be wives and homemakers. Against this backdrop, parents feared the loss of control over their children, especially their daughters. Fervent expressions of love for the Beatles by young fans—including mass demonstrations of public enthusiasm, deep plunges into fandom, and letting oneself be swept away by the music—coincided with teens transitioning into adulthood. This compounded insecurities among certain parents, who looked on helplessly as their children fell deeper and deeper under the spell of the Beatles and their music.

* * *

Becoming the Beatles

Beatlemania made a grand entrance into North America in the spring and summer of 1964. Eruptions of fan mayhem drew ample newspaper and magazine coverage, making it impossible to ignore. Mass adoration played out in footage for TV news viewers. Radio stations conveyed the excitement through live, on-the-spot broadcasts. The grand spectacle of it all held a nation in rapt attention. Giant throngs of screaming fans appeared wherever the Beatles went, particularly during their February 1964 visit, and when the

FIGURE 2.1 *A group of Beatles fans—accompanied by an amused adult chaperone—reacts enthusiastically to the Beatles playing at the Boston Garden in Boston, Massachusetts, September 12, 1964. Scenes such as this one were common at Beatles concerts during the band's 1964 North American Tour.*
Source: *Photo by Bob Dean/The Boston Globe via Getty Images.*

band returned to tour the United States and Canada three times, in the late summers of 1964, 1965, and 1966.

After the Beatles' opening concert of their 1964 tour, performed at the Cow Palace near San Francisco, a high school teacher who chaperoned his three nieces left the show astonished by the levels of enthusiasm he witnessed. "No one will ever believe this. There is nothing you can write that could make anyone believe what happened here," he said (see Figure 2.1).[33] At Chicago's International Amphitheater, the deafening screams of 25,000 fans left a lasting impression on *Chicago Tribune* reporter Thomas Fitzpatrick. "Everything you've heard about the effect the Beatles have on teenagers is true," Fitzpatrick wrote. "Confusion reigns when they appear. Teenagers, and even adults, reach an uncontrollable state."[34]

Early on, Beatlemania in the United States became closely associated with female fans—the multitudes of girls and young women whose memorable public appearances at Beatles events seared into the collective memory of the American public. On the night of the band's *Ed Sullivan Show* debut, according to one account at the time, "the virtually all-girl studio audience rocked, bounced, whistled, screamed and some wept with joy when the mop-topped Britons opened the show."[35] The *Ed Sullivan Show* appearance set the tone for American Beatlemania for the next three years. Subsequent television footage and newspaper photographs showed shrieking, wide-eyed teenage females, holding placards, waving arms, tearing at their hair, leaping up and down. They cheered on the Beatles at airports, hotels, and venues where the band played. Fans surged against police lines like a crashing tide. They stood in long lines at record stores upon the release of Beatles albums. They loudly proclaimed their love for band members, each of whom assumed distinctive traits among fans. John became the "witty one," Paul the "handsome one," George the "quiet one," and Ringo the "funny one." Such descriptions were not static, and varied among American Beatlemaniacs. In 1964, Los Angeles-based Petersen Publishing Company released a magazine titled *The Original Beatles Book*, one of countless one-off glossy publications aimed at Beatles fans. It characterized George as "The Playboy," Paul as "Handsome and Serious," John as "The Married One," and Ringo as "The Quiet One" (a designation typically given to George).[36]

Meantime, girls and young women played a vital role in forging a nationwide Beatles fan culture in mid-1960s' America. They founded Beatles fan clubs, creating these groups with friends and serving as club officers. Doing so enabled them to forge friendships, some lifelong. For adolescent females, embracing Beatles fandom often entailed an odyssey of self-discovery. "I was becoming my own person and [the Beatles] were a part of me becoming my own person," a fan later recalled.[37] Adoration of the Beatles among young women and girls had reached ubiquity. As sociologist Christine Feldman-Barrett observed: "Female fans often wore Mod clothing, which they associated with the Beatles and their romantic partners—or they might sport a John Lennon cap or an 'I love Ringo' button. American Beatlemaniacs often adopted the band's British slang ('fab,' 'gear,' 'grotty') to feel culturally closer to them."[38]

Additionally, becoming pen pals with Fab Four fans living abroad gave Beatles enthusiasts in different parts of the world an important means of connecting with each other. Pen pals did not simply inhabit the United States and Great Britain. They could be found in Canada, Latin America, across Europe, in Australia, New Zealand, and Japan. With Beatlemania going global, fans increasingly dotted a wide swath of the planet. In the United States, teen magazines, specialized one-off Beatles periodicals, fan newsletters, and even some daily newspapers functioned as meeting places for pen pals, often printing pictures, addresses, and short descriptions of participants. In the pages of *16* magazine, Beatles fan Barbara Boggiano, from New York, found the address of a girl named Elizabeth, from Liverpool. The two struck up a pen pal correspondence and exchanged numerous letters. "That was exciting because I could actually write to someone who had been in the Cavern. All I could do was look at pictures, but she could write to me and tell me about just being down there, and experiencing that. And that to me was just fabulous," recalled Boggiano.[39] Beatles fans also gravitated to *Dig* magazine, which featured a page titled "Paper Mates." "My friends call me 'George,' but I forgive them. I like drag races, lasagna, dancing, and don't faint now! I want to become a teacher! I'm fourteen," wrote teen pen pal seeker Linda McKeegan, of Northridge, California.[40] Sometimes, pen pal relationships led to unexpected outcomes, such as the experience of Laura Tarrish, a teenage fan from Phoenix, Arizona. "I had a pen pal in England, and we'd send each other news about the band. One letter very earnestly told me that she was sending me a surprise but was not at liberty to tell me how she got it. An autographed photo of the Beatles arrived soon after. In my fervor for the group, I chose to believe it was authentic," Tarrish remembered.[41]

During the golden age of American Beatlemania, the band's zealous lovers shared the common goal of getting as close to the Beatles as possible. They accomplished this in a variety of ways. Running away to search for the Beatles, as we have seen, was an extreme approach to achieving this goal. Most Beatlemaniacs settled for less dramatic ways—closer to home—of bonding with band members. The cover of a 1964 fan magazine *Best of the Beatles*—the "Largest Ever Published," it claimed—promised readers an article enticingly titled "63 Ways to Meet the Beatles." Alas, the cynical piece—written by a condescending adult—offered such useless pointers as "Move next door to Ringo's mom and dad," "Marry Paul's father," and "Have your father buy Capitol Records."[42] Beatles fans weren't stupid. They knew the prospects of meeting the band were, at best, dim. Thus, they turned inward, incorporating the Beatles into their day-to-day lives. Diehard devotees, for instance, converted their bedrooms into shrines, papered their walls with pictures, filled scrapbooks with collector's trading cards and cutout images and ticket stubs, and acquired stacks of Beatles magazine and fan club newsletters. For many American teens, snapping up all things Beatles represented a newfound form of independence that felt safe yet bold. High school student Sandra Roland, from Nashville, Tennessee, articulated this concept in an award-winning essay she wrote in the spring of 1965:

> Teens must feel like something in this society belongs to them and no one else. Beatle music serves this purpose. It symbolizes a freedom to teens, and they have a strong desire to exercise their freedom. They exercise it by a strong imitation of the Beatles in hairstyles and actions. They support them fully by wearing Beatle pins and collecting Beatle pictures.[43]

Raymond Olmsted, the father of two dedicated teenage female Beatles fans living in Fort Dodge, Iowa, supported his daughters when they founded a Beatles Fan Club in 1964, which consisted "of about 12 or 14 members." He even allowed them to convert one of the rooms in the house into a meeting space. "Their clubroom had Beatle calendars, Beatle posters, and hundreds of Beatle scrapbooks and souvenirs decorating the walls," he noted. Olmsted found no harm in his daughters' love of the band, and he even came to enjoy some of the Beatles' songs. "It's not all my kind of music, but then I'm not so young anymore," he reflected.[44]

For dedicated followers, Beatles shrines offered a setting that immersed the observer with all things Fab Four. Another way fans got closer to the Beatles was by imitating their appearance. Band members' hairstyles loomed large, not merely atop their heads, but in American popular culture itself. The demand for Beatles wigs was especially high. Judy Haenel, a saleswoman in a Tampa, Florida, department store that ordered a shipment of "10 dozen of the shaggy Beatle wigs," witnessed the hairy items sell faster than she could stock the shelves. "It's the kids who buy most of them," Haenel confirmed.[45] In Columbia, South Carolina, a "usually sedate Southern capital," a rampaging stampede of customers converged on a Beatles' wig sales display in Belk's Department Store, which "reported selling more than 100 wigs in the first two hours they were on the counters."[46] In San Francisco, California, an airplane delivered a shipment of 28,000 Beatles wigs within days of the first *Ed Sullivan Show* performance, which went out to stores all over the Bay Area. "It is the biggest thing since hula-hoops," declared Lou Saunders, head of the Lowell Toy Manufacturing Company, which mass produced the wigs. The giddy toy exec added: "When the fad's over, you can shine your shoes with them."[47] Most Beatles wigs were tacky, cheaply made novelties that smelled of chemicals and bore no resemblance to the band members' hairstyles. It didn't take long for the excitement to wear off—usually within moments of their removal from the package. Inevitably, the shaggy-headed wearer bore a stronger resemblance to a porcupine, or Moe Howard of the Three Stooges. English satirist Craig Brown, seven at the time he received his first Beatles wig for Christmas 1964, remembered the uncomfortable wigs did not "look at all like hair. In fact, they could have doubled as Frisbees."[48]

A more fulfilling way of getting closer to the Beatles involved fans blessed with ample heads of hair opting for a hairstyle that resembled their favorite band member. Countless Beatlemaniacs considered this approach more satisfying than briefly donning a cheap, synthetic wig. Beatles magazines in the mid-1960s featured pictorial essays encouraging young women and girls to style their hair like the Fab Four. "Give Yourself a Beatle Bob," cried a headline in a glossy 1964 magazine titled *All About the Beatles* (see Figure 2.2). "The most swingin' hair style you can sport these days is the Beatle Bob. Our version, designed by Mark Traynor for Hess Department Store in Allentown, Pa., is hip but still feminine," said an article below the headline, accompanied by black-and-white photos of a young woman getting her hair styled like the

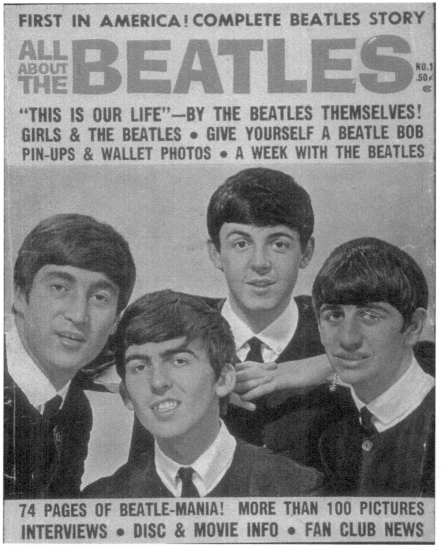

FIGURE 2.2 *American fan magazines such as* All About the Beatles, *published at the height of the Beatlemania craze in 1964, were widely circulated among fans and often contained articles encouraging young men and women to style their hair like the band members.*
Source: Photo by Michael Ochs Archives via Getty Images.

Beatles.[49] A similar article in *Beatle Mania* magazine, coincidentally published around the same time, showed step-by-step pictures of a woman in a barber's chair having her hair transformed by stylist Gene Shacove of Beverly Hills, California, into "the Beatle cut." This hairdo, the magazine proclaimed, "is so simple the girls just set on five rollers and comb out."[50] Patricia Gallo, who grew up in southwest Philadelphia, kept a detailed diary documenting her experiences with other Beatles fans in her neighborhood, all of them young women. "Diane is our Beatle leader. She is dedicated to John and was the first one of us to get a Beatle haircut," Patricia wrote in her diary entry of April 2, 1964.[51] Gradually, Patricia and her friends cultivated the Beatles hairstyle, and they began assuming characteristics of the Fab Four. Patricia noted:

> A true Beatles fan takes on the personality and traits of her favorite member of the group. Diane wears a cap like John, Grace loves lots of rings just like Ringo, and Jean is diligently learning to play the guitar like George. It makes us feel closer to them. So far, I have not met a Beatles fan who does not have a favorite, and not one of them claims more than one. So one Beatle per fan is the norm,.[52]

As Gallo's diary entries indicate, merely styling one's hair to look like the Beatles did not suffice. The Beatles had a distinctive style and manner that fans far and wide sought to emulate. A slick fan magazine titled *The Beatles*, published in the spring of 1964, featured an article titled "How You Can Become a Beatle!." "Like they do, you have to dress for impact. If you're a girl, you'll have to get an imaginative designer to improvise for you in duplicating the Beatle look. A maroon or grey round-necked cardigan-type suit is your best bet. A velvet waistcoat and white shirt, one of their alternate outfits, is also allowed," the article explained.[53] Another pictorial fan magazine, *The Beatles Personality Annual*, which also hit newsstands with the rising tide of Beatlemania in 1964, noted: "The Beatle fans are trying to look like the singers, copying their clothes and their hair style … The girls are getting into the act, too. They're buying Beatle-style straw hats and Beatle broaches to wear, as costume jewelry."[54] Across North America, Beatles-style clothing and accoutrements became intensely sought after, selling out in stores in the spring and summer of 1964. The result was a love of all things British among the nation's youth. " 'John Lennon' caps are now big with us fans. These were called schoolboy or seaman caps and were worn around Liverpool for years and years. John is especially fond of wearing caps. Right now, you can find them in a variety of colors and fabrics—everything from basic black tool to black velvet and even denim," wrote Patricia Gallo in her diary entry dated June 6, 1964.[55] Kathy Albinder, who saw the Beatles perform a concert at the Forest Hills, New York, concert on August 28, 1964, dressed in a tie, a blue jumper, and high socks, just like "all the English girls were wearing." To accomplish the Beatles "look" more fully, she "ironed" her bobbed curly hair "so it was straight"—something she had never done before.[56]

The return of the Beatles to North American on August 19, 1964, to perform thirty-two concerts in Canada and the United States over the course a month, accelerated the immersion that many fans experienced into the world of Beatlemania. A Beatles concert was always a major event, complete with thousands of cheering youths welcoming the band at the airport, press conferences, legions of enthusiastic concertgoers funneling into venues, uniformed police everywhere, searchlights crisscrossing the night skies, and extensive coverage by local television and radio stations. The band's performances consistently made front-page news in the press, and footage from their shows kicked off the nightly news. The magnitude of the pandemonium at Cincinnati Gardens in Cincinnati, Ohio, on the night of August 27, left spectators in awe. "Veteran reporters and policemen were stuck for words to describe the demonstration of 14,000 seemingly-demented teenagers put on for their idols. 'Unbelievable' was the closest they could come to creating a word picture of the bedlam," announced a page-one story in the *Cincinnati Enquirer* the day after the concert.[57] Such scenes cemented in the collective imagination of Americans the image of the screaming female Beatlemaniac, with eyes wide, hands clapping, bouncing up and down, experiencing bouts of hysteria. The *Napa Valley Register* sent two sixteen-year-old "Beatle Correspondents"—Regina Sinnes and Carolyn Plutt—to cover the Beatles concert on August 19. The duo sent back a colorful account of "their grand performance for 17,000 anxious girls in the Cow Palace." "The screaming went on through their half hour performance in which the Beatles sang 11 songs," Sinnes and Plutt reported.[58] Fourteen-year-old Janet Pickell, who lived in Beverly, a suburb of Boston, landed a job as a Beatles correspondent for a local newspaper, the *Record American*. After the band's concert at Boston Garden on September 12, she dictated a story to a reporter at the paper, which appeared in print the following day. Years later, Janet Pickell—who became Janet Lessard—remembered: "It was just a din for those 45 minutes. Screaming, crying, between that and the amplification they had on the stage, which was very primitive compared to today's standards, it was basically just being there and watching them, cause you didn't really hear anything. But that was fine with us."[59]

Even more than attending concerts, the ultimate close encounter with the Beatles consisted of a handful of fortunate fans being allowed to go backstage to meet the band members, either before or after a concert (see Figure 2.3). The press heavily spotlighted these meetings, which typically saw contest winners and fan club officers—nearly always adolescent girls filled with wonder—presenting the Beatles with gifts and handshakes. In Indianapolis,

FIGURE 2.3 *Officer Robert Yocum informs Beatles fans Chelie Mylott and Melody Yapscott that they'll have to move from their spot in front of the Hollywood Bowl, August 23, 1964. The pair of teens had no tickets, but they hoped to purchase them from scalpers. Extensive media coverage of Beatles concertgoers in the summer of 1964 heightened excitement levels among fans eager to see the band perform live.*
Source: *This photo was published in the* Los Angeles Times, *August 24, 1964, via Getty Images.*

the local newspaper, the *Indianapolis News*, held an essay-writing contest to pick a lucky fan to meet the Beatles after their concert at the Indiana Farmers Coliseum. Fifteen-year-old Elaine May won the prize and got to meet her heroes from Liverpool. "I want to meet the Beatles because they have a special magic. When they perform, the oppressing world crisis and the other problems can be temporarily forgotten. They sing happy, swinging songs. I'd love to meet the four young men who can make everything seem a little brighter," May wrote in her winning essay.[60] Marti Whitman, age sixteen, who grew up in the leafy Chicago suburb of Park Forest, founded the Chicagoland Beatle People with five of her friends at Rich East High School. One of main reasons Whitman started the fan club was to fulfill her ambition to meet the Beatles in person. Serving as the club's president, Whitman rented a post office box to receive mail, began a corresponding back and forth with George Harrison's sister, Louise (who endorsed the club), held bake sales to raise money for charitable groups, and maintained cordial relations with disc jockeys at local radio stations to help spread the word about Chicagoland Beatle People.[61] Whitman later explained to an interviewer: "As soon as I heard [the Beatles] ... I knew that I wanted to meet them. Somehow, I would plan and reach that goal."[62] Marti appeared on a local television talk show, the Lee Phillips Show, in August, resulting in an avalanche of new joiners, swelling the membership to over 1,200. By happenstance, Marti crossed paths with Beatles publicist Derek Taylor at the Stock Yard Inn in Chicago. She introduced herself, told him about the fan club, and he arranged for her to deliver a plaque from the Chicagoland Beatle People to the band members during their preconcert press conference.[63]

Such encounters with the Beatles were always memorable. In each case, the band members instantly put the fans at ease with their genial personalities and gentle humor. Debbie Chase, age fourteen, from Auburndale, Massachusetts, met the Beatles after she managed to get into a press conference on September 12, the night they performed in Boston. After the press left the room, Derek Taylor allowed her to come to the long table where John, Paul, George and Ringo were sitting, and she met each one. Still seated, Paul held out his hand and said, "Pleased to meet you." He noticed she was shaking and hastily added, "Hey, you'll be all right." Debbie leaned down and kissed Paul, before security led her out of the room to her seat in Boston Garden.[64] Seventeen-year-old Lynn Krzmarcik, from Wausau, Wisconsin, got to meet the Beatles on August 21, 1965, the night they performed at Metropolitan Stadium near Minneapolis. Her father knew somebody involved with the band's security detail, and he managed to help arrange a meeting. The family arrived at the venue around 7 p.m. and Lynn had to wait near a rear entrance crawling with uniformed guards and policemen. Following a forty-five-minute wait, a staffer led Lynn down "several long halls ... like a maze, and I'm sure I couldn't find my way around if I went there again." She finally arrived at a dressing room where the band members were preparing for the big show. Mal Evans, the Beatles' personal assistant, introduced her to the four men. John Lennon asked her what she thought of his book and the Beatles' albums. Ringo wondered aloud how she was going to take a picture of him and be in the photo at the same time, a problem solved by Evans snapping their photo together. George showed Lynn a guitar given to him as a gift by a local music store in Minneapolis. Paul chatted with her for a few minutes and welcomed her to the show. "I was surprised I wasn't nervous meeting them. They didn't act like they were big stars. All of them were very friendly, and it was just like talking to 'regular' people," she recounted.[65] Marti Whitman was even more overawed by her meeting with the Beatles. "I must've gone into some kind of shock. I didn't scream or jump up and down, but I don't remember anything that happened," she remembered.[66]

Only a handful of Beatlemaniacs got to meet the Beatles. The masses of concertgoers weren't so lucky. They never came close to crossing paths with the band. Forced to view the musicians from afar, fans screamed, shouted, and cheered—often at eardrum-splitting levels—their collective adoration. Even before the 1964 North America tour concluded, the band's fans had acquired a reputation for being exceptionally loud and unruly. A front-page story in the *Boston Globe* told of multiple girls who "succumbed to hysteria," including one "lying face down in a pool of water overcome by hysteria." In the first aid room at Boston Gardens, the overwhelmed girl "couldn't remember her name. She complained of pain in her legs." An ambulance took the dazed fan to Massachusetts General Hospital. "At least six other girls succumbed to hysteria and were carried unconscious in the arms of policemen to first aid rooms," the *Globe* reported.[67]

The loudness of audiences was another recurring problem. Long before the infamous Shea Stadium concert in New York on August 15, 1965, where the Beatles could not be heard above the roaring din of the crowd, the screams and cries of fans routinely drowned out their music. "Beatles Came, Conquered, Sang—But Weren't Heard," said a headline in the *Philadelphia Daily News*.[68] "And when the curtains opened and the lights shone on the Beatles, everyone began to scream, including myself. I couldn't help it. It's what you did to release pent-up adrenaline," recalled Cheri Bill, who was seven when she saw the Beatles at Cincinnati Gardens on August 27, 1964.[69] Similar paroxysms of cheering erupted in Milwaukee Arena in Milwaukee, Wisconsin, on September 4, 1964. While an army of uniformed policemen surrounded the stage to keep fans back, Red Cross nurses treated multiple female fans who had fainted during the half-hour performance that opened at 9 p.m. When the Beatles began playing "I Saw Her Standing There," the audience exploded in a frenzy. "They clapped, waved, laughed, cried, shouted, groaned, kicked, held their ears, jumped up, sat down, wailed and stomped. They threw jelly beans, chocolate, hair pins, hair rollers, paper and flash bulbs," wrote an observer.[70] Such scenes repeated themselves over and over during the 1964 tour, and persisted throughout the band's 1965 and 1966 concerts as well. "A roar went up in the Coliseum and it didn't subside during the whole show," wrote teen correspondent Maureen Wheelhouse, a high school student from Jackson, Mississippi, who covered the afternoon concert at Houston's Sam Houston Coliseum for the local newspaper, the *Clarion-Ledger*, on August 19,

1965. "When the show was over, and the lights on the stage were turned off, thousands of girls passed in waves out of the doors and up the exit ramps. I saw many girls crying, and to be honest, we all were sad because the Beatles had gone," she wrote.[71]

Hair Wars

One could be forgiven in the mid-1960s for thinking that all Beatles fans were girls. The band's ardent male followers—and plenty of them existed at the height of Beatlemania—typically got overlooked, or downplayed, in the extensive media coverage. Fans who wound up in the spotlight for obtaining backstage passes to meet the Beatles, or who worked as Beatles correspondents for newspapers, or who appeared in still photos and television footage depicting big crowds—in other words, the Beatlemaniacs with the highest profiles—were nearly always adolescent females. Occasionally, boys would be lurking in the background of newspaper photos, but they were easy to miss. This was no accident. The press had fashioned a dominant narrative about Beatles fandom of public gatherings teeming with "hysterical girls."[72] This was not necessarily a false or distorted portrayal. Reflecting the norms of the day, most male fans expressed appreciation in more subdued ways that did not pack the same dramatic wallop as the behavior of their opposite-sex counterparts. Nor were most boys likely to become consumed with extreme idolatry, resorting to such extraordinary measures as converting their bedrooms into Beatles shrines packed from floor to ceiling with all things Fab Four. Despite this, young men and boys formed a vital constituency of the Beatles fan base, which was every bit as integral to the band's success as the millions of females who loved them. They, too, joined (and, in some cases, formed) fan clubs, bought albums, wrote letters to the editors of their local newspapers defending the Fab Four, trekked out to airports to cheer the band's arrival, and attended concerts. They, too, cheered and shouted and joined in on the spectacle of merrymaking with the girls, even if they didn't fling themselves as dramatically into such displays of enthusiasm.

And, yet, during the early stages of Beatlemania, being a male fan could often feel like a lonely affair. Texan Rodger Brownlee, a teenager when he and his sister saw the Beatles play at Memorial Auditorium in Dallas on September 18, 1964, recalled: "I couldn't help but notice that girls outnumbered the boys by at least three to one." Before the concert, Brownlee dressed up like the Beatles, combing his hair down over his forehead, and selecting a suit that reminded him of the four lads. "My enthusiasm knew no bounds," he said. But to his astonishment, he was the only boy dressed that way in the entire auditorium. "I was surprised that I didn't see any of the guys decked out in full

Beatle regalia, and I was more disappointed no one seemed to notice I was!"[73] Brownlee was not alone. The band's more zealous male fans often felt alienated from their less excited peers, as well as those adults who found Beatlemania perplexing. Howard Carl Rubin was a fifteen-year-old student at Nashville, Tennessee, when he discovered and came to love the music of the Beatles. A member of student council and the sports editor at the school paper at West High School in the mid-1960s, Howard became an unrepentant fan when he first listened to their songs, and he never looked back. Teenagers, he reasoned, "know more and are being taught more than our elders were" about music. He developed an early distrust of those grown-ups who tried to make him feel ashamed for buying Beatles albums. Rubin predicted in a 1965 essay: "I believe the Beatle beat is a start on the road to a revolution in music. This revolution will take place when we are adults. And you know something? I can hardly wait until it comes."[74] Critic and satirist Joe Queenan, born in 1950, raised in Philadelphia, had to contend with a father who regarded "the Beatles as tools of Satan." Despite his father's disdain for the group, Queenan fell in love with their music at age thirteen. The game changer for Queenan was hearing "She Loves You" sometime around Christmas 1963. "Until that moment," he later wrote, "I viewed music as an annoyance at best, and at worst as a punitive child-rearing device." For Queenan, the Beatles arrived in his life when he was becoming more aware of the world around him, and all its promise and perils. He thought "the Beatles helped heal America" in the aftermath of President John F. Kennedy's assassination in November 1963. "The Beatles held out hope that life might actually be worth living, that popular culture need not be gray, predictable, sappy, lethal," Queenan wrote. "To this day, what I feel toward the Beatles is not so much affection or reverence. It is gratitude."[75]

Although most Beatles fan clubs were founded by girls, a few intrepid boys and young men did their part to help launch them. Days after the Beatles' first *Ed Sullivan Show* appearance in February, two male college students at the University of Detroit Mercy, a Catholic institution in Detroit, responded to a citywide "Stamp Out the Beatles" drive by starting the National Beatles Fan Club. The ambitious young men, David Clarke and John Fencsak, rented a post office box for their new group with the goal of creating "a network of local chapters" in order to "point up the happy message of the Beatles' lyrics and sponsor the bush-haired quartet's appearance here."[76] Coincidentally, in Tampa, Florida, local newspaper columnist Patrick Kelly informed readers that "seven Oak Grove Junior High School girls—and one lone boy—have established what they believe to be the only 'official' U.S. fan club for the Beatles." The "lone boy," fourteen-year-old Bill Wilhelm, became the club's "Publicity Chairman" and event organizer. It turns out that a national fan club already existed in New York City, the creation of Capitol Records, but the newly formed National Beatle Fan Club in Tampa still attracted plenty of joiners who sent in their fifty-cent dues fees.[77] Meantime, in Salt Lake City, Roger Workman accepted the position of Beatles Fan Club treasurer with gusto. In that capacity, he raised funds for the club, helped the president, Annette Taylor, decorate the backyard of her family's suburban house for a British-themed Beatles party, and helped to arrange a visit to the wingding by a local radio disc jockey.[78]

Male fans who were open about their love for the Beatles in the initial surge of Beatlemania were keenly aware of their minority status among Beatlemaniacs. Press coverage routinely reinforced such feelings by usually ignoring them altogether. In December 1964, a profile of John Lennon written by journalist Gloria Steinem, future *Ms.* magazine founder and feminist movement leader, appeared in *Cosmopolitan* magazine. Even though Lennon—the "Beatle With a Future," as the article called him—was Steinem's main focus, she could not ignore the gigantic gatherings of Beatles fans, which she referred to as "thousands of weeping, screeching girls."[79] Steinem, who had a hard time hiding her contempt for these girls, paraphrased the former leader of the Beatles Fan Club of America, Feather Schwartz, who "described that the average Beatle fan is thirteen to seventeen years old, of middle-class background, white, Christian, a B-minus student, weighs 105 to 140 pounds, owns a transistor radio with an earplug attachment and has Beatle photographs plastered all over her room."[80] Nowhere in the portion of Steinem's article that discussed the band's zealous followers did she mention their male fans. This was typical for most media coverage of the Beatles. "They screamed and squeeled [sic] at everything, these hundreds and hundreds of girls between 13 and 18, some wearing 'Ringo, for President' buttons or carrying banners that read, 'Beatles Please Stay Here 4-Ever,' " wrote journalist Gay Talese in the *New York Times*, describing a crowd outside of New York City's Paramount Theatre on the night of September 20, 1964, cheering the Beatles as they arrived to perform a charity concert. Talese estimated the numbers at the Paramount grew to 4,000 people, all anxious to witness the foursome enter the venue. When police blocked the youths from seeing the Beatles, Talese recorded their despair: "Many girls—there were relatively few boys at the Paramount last night—were in obvious pain at having missed the Beatles' entrance: a few of them began to weep. Others just howled louder than before."[81] Sometimes, being a solitary male fan in a sea of girls worked to one's advantage. Eighteen-year-old Fred Paul, from northern California, was in the giant audience in the Cow Palace, outside of San Francisco, on August 19, to watch the Beatles' opening concert of the 1964 tour. He decided he wanted to meet the Beatles, and he went about making it happen. Immediately after the San Francisco show, he boarded an airplane for Las Vegas, to see the Beatles play at Convention Hall the following night. "I ... talked my way backstage," he said. Because most fans trying to breach security were young women, Paul found it shockingly easy to get past guards to meet his idols. At Chicago's International Amphitheater on September 5, he hired a "nine-seat chauffeured Cadillac" to drop him off at the heavily guarded rear stage door entrance. He emerged from the ostentatious vehicle appearing "natty in a collarless suit and British handwoven tie," and proceeded to walk "past the doorman without looking at him." Once again, Fred Paul managed to navigate past a line of guards on his way backstage to meet the Beatles before their concert.[82]

What ultimately brought a sizable segment of male Beatles' fans out of the shadows was when they opted to let their hair grow in the same style as the band members. Of all the controversies sparked by the Beatles during the initial wave of Beatlemania, their hairy moptops were the most incendiary. Not surprisingly, the most contentious debates zeroed in on male fans who imitated the Beatles' hairstyles. Most female fans, by contrast, escaped the hair wars unscathed, although some adolescent girls and young women faced mild rebukes for embracing the so-called "Beatle-do." Eleanor Nangle, long-time beauty and fashion reporter for the *Chicago Tribune*, warned female readers to steer clear of Beatles haircuts. "We would remind those who are tempted that the hair on the floor after a mad scissor treatment represents damage to good looks that won't be undone for months and months."[83] Addressing the matter of "the new 'Beatle Bob' for girls," Vermont fashion columnist Helen McLaughlin cautioned that the "Beatniks from Britain"—as she called the Beatles—"look as if a small saucepan had been planked over the top of the skulls and the dangling locks chewed off."[84] Despite such warnings, plenty of girls and young women strolled out of beauty salons in the mid-1960s sporting Beatle hairstyles without enduring any harassment or ridicule. It helped that the so-called experts were on hand to help parents understand their daughters' attraction to the band.

* * *

Boys with Beatles' hairstyles underwent a far worse drubbing than girls who had them. No longer invisible, these intrepid hairy male fans were met with hostility in all parts of the country. When the Beatles first touched down at New York's John F. Kennedy Airport on February 7, 1964, they had no way of knowing that the matter of men's hairstyles in the United States was deeply and inextricably bound up in notions of manliness. Since the early twentieth century, barbers had been cutting men's hair shorter and shorter in the United States. Gone were the long, wavy locks seen in so many Civil War-era photographs, or the type worn by Buffalo Bill in the 1880s, replaced instead by hair that seldom grew below the tops of ears (hence the slang idiom "getting my ears lowered," especially popular in the late 1940s and 1950s). Moreover, ample facial hair—the long beards and bushy moustaches of yesteryear—had also fallen out of style in postwar America. "Men's hairstyles [in the 1950s] were almost as standardized as their clothes, the main variation being a choice between maintaining the close-cropped 'combat cut' that had been required in the military service or returning to the longer prewar slicked-back hair held in place by large amounts of tonic or cream," observed historian Victor D. Brooks.[85]

Along the way, short hair in the United States became closely associated with masculinity. "After cleanliness and clean, neat clothes, nothing makes quite as much difference as well-kept hair," explained beautician Marian Matthews in her syndicated column "Beauty and You" in 1953. Matthews insisted that "little boys ... must have a manly haircut sometime before they are two years of age."[86] Short hair also came to be viewed as patriotic, and closely associated with Americanness. Etiquette expert Amy Vanderbilt advised recent male immigrant arrivals to the United States to hurry to their nearest barbershop for a trim. "The 'foreign look' on immigrant men," Vanderbilt wrote, "is quite often dramatically changed by an American haircut, for we do not like long hair on men in this country."[87] During the 1950s, shaved haircuts—especially the increasingly ubiquitous crew cut—became the style of choice for a growing number of American men and boys. They were easy to take care of, and they seemed to suggest rugged self-confidence and virility. When the popular television host and comedian Garry Moore grew his bristly crew cut only slightly in 1954, he "got complaints" about his longer hair, which was still closely cropped. "So we took a vote," Moore said, on whether to keep his current slicked-back look or to return to the crew cut. "The crew cut won," Moore explained. Early in 1955, Moore allowed himself to be given a crew cut on live national television by his friend, singer Perry Como.[88]

Reinforcing the close association of short hair with masculinity were the many female celebrities in the mid-1960s who asserted their preference for close-cropped men. "Long hair on a man is too effeminate," said box office sensation Elke Sommer. "I think men should be allowed to do more than part their hair and comb it to one side. Think of all the things we women do with our hair. But men's hair shouldn't get too long. I see to that by cutting my own husband's hair."[89] Added Janet Leigh, star of Alfred Hitchcock's *Pyscho*: "If I were dating, I certainly wouldn't want to go out with anyone who had longer hair than I have."[90] Echoed actress Debbie Reynolds: "With a shortage of men still prevailing, it's unfair of them to wear long hair. That makes it tougher for girls to find them."[91] And actress Patty Duke, who won an Oscar at age sixteen for her memorable performance as Helen Keller in *The Miracle Worker*, told a reporter: "I think the length of boys' hair has been carried too far. I like a long cut on small boys like John Kennedy. But on bigger boys, it just looks dirty."[92]

These attitudes about hair prevailed in the 1950s and early 1960s, to the point of becoming calcified conventional wisdom. Millions of Americans obsessed about hair and attaining the proper "look." Trade magazines and conventions showcased the latest fads. For men and women, there existed a range of acceptable hairstyles, and veering too far outside of the boundaries often presented problems. Hence, parents carefully monitored the way their sons and daughters wore their hair. For boys in particular, the standards were often quite restrictive. As late as October 1965, a Gallup poll posed the question to American adults: "Do you think schools should require boys to keep their hair cut short?" A staggering 80 percent of people polled replied "yes," while only 17 percent said "no," and the remaining 3 percent had no opinion either way. One irate respondent told the Gallup pollster: "There are enough queers around now and letting boys look like girls won't help to identify the deviates."[93] Teenagers during the early phases of Beatlemania were similarly unimpressed with the coiffures of the Fab Four. A survey of 1,375 teenagers conducted by youth pollster Eugene Gilbert in March of 1964 revealed that "24 percent of the boys and 30 percent of the girls like the shaggy-dog look of the young singers."[94] "They're kind of seedy looking. They're certainly not the clean-shaven American type," observed high school junior Nancy Storie, from Rochester, New York.[95] Veteran barber Michael Zizzamia, who ran his own shop in Camden, New Jersey, expressed the disdain that millions of Americans felt in the ensuing days after the historic *Ed Sullivan Show* broadcast: "We've had some boys come in here and ask for a Beatle-cut. But it's a fad and it can't last. Who can walk around looking like that?"[96]

By mid-February 1964, school boards across the country began banning Beatles-type haircuts and the wearing of Beatles wigs. As of Valentine's Day 1964, all high schools in Minneapolis forbade "Beatle hair-dos," and began expelling students that did not abide by the edict. "School is a place for work, not play," proclaimed West High School principal Frank Jones.[97] In North Carolina, the state attorney general's office upheld a 1964 ban on "Beatle haircuts" in school boards across the state.[98] School districts in Tulsa, Oklahoma, passed a measure prohibiting Beatles haircuts on male students. To show they meant business, Tulsa's Central High School suspended sixteen-year-old student John Stanley for his Beatles hair. But in this particular case, Stanley's parents—like countless other American moms and dads who didn't understand what all the hubbub was about—supported their son's decision. "You can just say he intends to keep his Beatle cut and that's all there is to it," said Mrs. Stanley, John's mother.[99] Alas, few American school boards in the mid-1960s shared the more open-minded attitude of John Stanley's mother and father. Even in "liberal" Massachusetts, the State Supreme Court determined that eighteen-year-old George Leonard's "shaggy mop" Beatles haircut "could disrupt and impede" school decorum. The court rejected Leonard's claim that he required the hairstyle in order to be the lead singer of a band in his hometown of Attleboro, in which he crooned under the pseudonym "George Porgie." The court ordered him to trim his hair if he wanted to get back into school. And finally, the court concluded that schools should be allowed to suspend students for transgressions such as unruly hair, otherwise they wouldn't be able to cope with the "unpredictable behavior of large groups of children."[100] In February 1965, the respected scholar, education expert, and syndicated columnist Max Rafferty weighed in the tidal wave of Beatles hair bans in schools across the United States: "A school is not a freak show, nor is it a place to indulge distracting whims and crotchets. Its purpose is to teach children enough so that in later life they will know the difference between sincere individualism and phony exhibitionism. After all, even Abe Lincoln didn't grow a beard until after he was elected president."[101]

At times, the hair wars reached the depths of absurdity. A nationwide acne scare in 1965 and 1966 led to dire warnings by authorities about the physical damage caused by long hair. Lewis Kirkham, a dermatologist from Salt Lake City, sparked nationwide headlines in September 1965 when he warned about a condition he dubbed "Beatle skin"—a term for acne on adolescent boys worsened, in his opinion, by overhanging hair. "First I make them get the hair off their face," the doctor said, when asked how he treats these lads for the condition.[102] Kirkham wasn't the only one to sound the alarm about the zit-enhancing perils of long hair. In a manner reminiscent of the legendary marijuana scare film *Reefer Madness* (1936), Linda G. Allen, research associate with the American Medical Association, announced to the press that "Beatle skin" posed a danger to the nation's youth, and she cautioned against letting hair drape over the face. "Although doctors do not agree on why overhanging hair—like the over-the-forehead style recently adopted by so many boy fans of the Beatles, and the untrimmed straight hair that falls down in the faces of so many young girls—aggravates many cases of acne, they do agree that there is a definite relationship," Allen explained.[103] Boston physician H. L. Herschensohn, a syndicated columnist and respected authority on medical matters, explained in February 1966 that the "Beatle hairdo" spawned pimples thanks to blocking out sunlight. "Exposure to the ultraviolet rays of daylight is beneficial to those who have acne. When the hair is in the way, these rays are prevented from reaching the skin," the doctor asserted. Herschensohn also insisted that the zeal among the nation's youths to conform "with everybody else's Beatle haircut" exacerbated unsightly skin conditions as well. "Since acne is also known to be aggravated by emotions," Herschensohn asserted, "your desire to be a nonconformist is motivated by an emotional upheaval which obviously is no good for your skin."[104]

In countless instances, early efforts to curtail Beatles hairstyles achieved the desired results. Male students who got suspended from school for letting their hair grow often headed straight to the barber shop for a trim to get back into school. Sometimes, offenders were able to simply comb their hair differently, as a group of male high school students did in Houston, to avoid suspension.[105] But some young men boldly defied rules and expectations and social norms. A growing number of American boys arrived at the same conclusion as high school junior Daryl Nieliwocki, from Wilmington, Delaware: "In Britain, that's not such a radical hairdo."[106] These youths posed the question: Why should this look be considered so radical or different here in the United States? Some intrepid barbers, sensing which way the wind was blowing, advertised for Beatles haircuts in newspapers, despite their misgivings about offering them. Paul Gentile, owner of Paul's Hollywood Barber Shop on Thirty-third Street in Baltimore, Maryland, did not care for the moptop hairdos. Yet his establishment was the go-to spot for young male customers who sought that look. "All they do is comb it down in front and fluff it up on top," Gentile remarked. "It looks like beatniks—that's what it is."[107]

Adolescent boys from all walks of life, inspired by the Beatles, were willing to push the boundaries by going against what was accepted in the mid-1960s, and in doing so, they contributed to a reinvention of dominant styles in the United States. Claims that this was yet another type of conformity notwithstanding, the American lads who copied the Beatles' hairstyles were making a bold statement at the time. Like the band's gigantic armies of female followers, young males loved the Beatles sufficiently—the music, the members' style, and the general feeling created by the group—to make important changes in their lives to emulate the foursome they so admired. In so doing, they helped to eventually topple the era's conventional gender norms and reinvent new spaces that girls and boys felt safe occupying. Little did they know at the time, the reinvention of gender roles to which they contributed would eventually help transform the United States into a more open, diverse, and inclusive society. By decade's end, long hair had become normal for men, and the collective expression of personal preferences by girls would become the stuff of which the nationwide second-wave feminist movement was made.

3

The Beatles for Sale

Without a close second, the Beatles were the most heavily merchandised rock band of the 1960s, and likely in the entire history of rock music itself. The Beatles inspired media-hyped rivalries with other British Invasion bands, starred in movies, appeared on television, and allowed their likenesses to be used in a popular Saturday morning cartoon. Overnight, an avalanche of Beatles merchandise lured Fab Four-hungry consumers to stores and mail-order companies. Fans went crazy for any product featuring the boys' images: dolls, stationery, lockets, wigs, songbooks, T-shirts, tie clips, photos, pins, pillows, calendars, sweaters, scrapbooks, games, lapel pins, collector's stamps, and magazines. There was Beatles bubble bath. There was Beatles wallpaper. There was a Beatles Flip Your Wig Board Game by Milton Bradley. A Beatles rug was made in Belgium. The Aladdin lunch box company, which specialized in kids-themed metal lunch boxes (featuring the likes of Hopalong Cassidy and Jetsons), released a Beatles lunch box in 1965, complete with a matching thermos. Even in the decades that followed the 1960s, the catalogue of Beatles memorabilia continued to grow. This striking proliferation buoyed the band in meaningful ways, cementing their place at the top of the so-called British Invasion, and helping to mainstream them with an American public that—with each passing month—was gradually succumbing to their charms. Yet the remarkable consumption of Beatles items was by no means a permanent state of affairs, and sales of Fab Four-themed merchandise began to decline by 1966, a trend that reflected the maturation of Beatles fans, as well as changing times in the United States.

Two, Three, Many British Invasions

"THE BRITISH ARE COMING!" cried a headline on the front page of the *Minneapolis Star*, announcing the arrival of the Beatles at New York's John F. Kennedy International Airport on February 7, 1964. "At 12:40 p.m. today the Beatles, a beat singing quartet, were to make the most-heralded British invasion of America since Paul Revere's day. New York City police were alerted to use 'as many men as needed' to avert teen-age riots, a regular thing at Beatles' appearances all over Europe," announced the article that accompanied the headline in the *Star*.[1] Everywhere else in America, radio stations, television programs, newspapers, and record stores announced the coming "British Invasion." "It's beginning to look as though our future history books will have to include three dates for British invasions of the U.S.: 1775, 1812, and 1964," wrote Hugh Stevens, editor of the *Daily Tar Heel*, the independent student newspaper of the University of North Carolina at Chapel Hill, days after the Beatles' arrival.[2] "D.C. Is Alarmed as Another British Invasion Nears," proclaimed a banner headline in the *New York Daily News* on February 11, 1964.[3] "The mop-haired Beatles were about to arrive," recounted *Life Magazine* in April of the events two months earlier, "and Washington was braced for this second and possibly more devastating British Invasion."[4] Throughout 1964, Paul Revere's historic "Midnight Ride" of April 18, 1775, to alert the American colonial militia about approaching British forces, was used interchangeably alongside the term "the British Invasion." Patricia Lloyd, who wrote the gossipy "Around the Town" column in the *News Journal* of Pensacola, Florida, was one of those who sounded the familiar hyperbolic alarm in February 1964: "Almost 200 years ago Paul Revere went riding around Boston shouting, 'The British are coming!' Now the cry is 'The Beatles are coming!' Do you think it could be the British revenge for the Boston Tea Party?"[5]

Few Americans at the time knew that the label "British Invasion," and the recurring references to the harrowing exploits of silversmith, industrialist, and patriot Paul Revere—made famous in Henry Wadsworth Longfellow's memorable 1861 poem, "Paul Revere's Ride"—were part of an unprecedented $40,000 publicity campaign by Capitol Records, the Beatles' American label. With the support of its British parent company, EMI, Capitol began to aggressively market the Fab Four in the United States in the fall of 1963 and winter of 1964.[6] Months of careful, behind-the-scenes planning went into the effective PR blitz—from thousands of albums being sent to local radio stations across America by Capitol Records, EMI's American affiliate, to the distribution of millions of Beatles-themed stickers and other novelty items. Much of the US press initially greeted the Beatles with mixed coverage ranging from lukewarm to negative. However, the slow manner in which the band was exposed to its North American audience—a smattering of news articles here, some television footage there, and a handful of intrepid radio DJs spinning Beatles singles on the air that weren't yet available in American record stores—only served to heighten the curiosity of teenagers in the United States, and added to the band's mystique. The record labels even strenuously promoted the Beatles distinctive coiffure across North America. "Capitol is pushing the Beatle hair-do prior to the British rock and roll group's arrival in the U.S. in February," announced *Billboard* magazine in early January 1964. Such efforts led to the creation of a "hair style kit" sent "to beauty editors of American newspapers."[7]

By the summer of 1964, the term "British Invasion" assumed new connotations—and much broader dimensions—as more and more English bands began following in the footsteps of the Fab Four, making their US debuts on the *Ed Sullivan Show* and on teen-oriented music variety programs like ABC's *Shindig!* and NBC's *Hullabaloo*. Suddenly, for the first time, British rock and roll bands were all the rage. Some forward-looking record stores began to feature "British Invasion" sections, and rock music from England now charted high on the Billboard Hot 100, and it could be heard on radio airwaves nationwide. By the end of 1964 and opening months of 1965, a panoply of new British rock bands and singers had become household names in the United States: the Dave Clark Five, Dusty Springfield, the Searchers, Herman's Hermits, Petula Clark, Gerry and the Pacemakers, the Rolling Stones, Marianne Faithfull, the Animals, Wayne Fontana and the Mindbenders, the Kinks, Billy J. Kramer and the Dakotas, Chad & Jeremy, the Zombies, Peter and Gordon, the Yardbirds—the list goes on. They appeared on the cover of teen magazines, inspired the creation of countless fan clubs, and the more famous of them drew screaming crowds like those at Beatles concerts. "The Beatles laid the groundwork by appearing here and by leading American teenagers to search for Beatle items in British fan magazines, which introduced them to other British performers," noted journalist Bill Whitworth in the fall of 1964. "Suddenly, almost anything British was desirable to American teenagers."[8]

During the early months of the British Invasion, the Dave Clark Five emerged as the chief rivals of the Beatles. Hailing from Tottenham, London, named for its charismatic drummer, the Dave Clark Five—or DC5, as they came to be known in the press—came on strong in the spring of 1964, appearing for two weeks in a row on the *Ed Sullivan Show* in March, the second British Invasion group to enjoy that distinction. Their first UK top ten hit, "Glad All Over," climbed to number six on the Billboard Hot 100 in April 1964. Subsequent singles, including "Bits and Pieces," "Can't You See That She's Mine," "Because," "Catch Us If You Can," and "Over and Over," led to speculation that the DC5 might eventually eclipse the Beatles in popularity.

The media deliberately fueled divisions, egged on by the record companies and the band's publicists. In the summer and fall of 1964, colorful one-off magazines with titles such as *Who Will Beat the Beatles?*, *The Beatles Meet the Dave Clark 5*, and *Dave Clark 5 vs. the Beatles* began appearing at American newsstands.[9] Most of the articles in these booklets were little more than meandering and innocuous comparisons between the two bands. A typical passage from *Dave Clark 5 vs. the Beatles* read: "The Dave Clark Five have different tunes and different faces, but what really distinguishes them from the Beatles? Have they got something all their very own that sets them apart from the Beatlemania and causes their millions of teenage British fans to have preference? They sure have!"[10]

In the push to publicize the Dave Clark Five, drummer Dave Clark often hogged the spotlight. He dominated interviews with the band, answering most questions, while the other band members quietly looked on and nodded their approval of his responses. He starred in the movie *Catch Us If You Can* (1965), directed by newcomer John Boorman, who later went on to direct such acclaimed films as *Point Blank* (1967), *Deliverance* (1972), *The Emerald Forest* (1985), and *Hope and Glory* (1987). *Catch Us If You Can*—released in April 1965 in the UK, and during the summer in the United States under the title *Having a Wild Weekend*—was meant to cash in on the recent success of the Beatles' widely hailed cinematic masterpiece *A Hard Day's Night* (1964). *Catch Us If You Can* contained a threadbare plot involving a model (Barbara Ferris) and a stunt driver (played by Dave Clark) driving off together in a Jaguar for an adventurous weekend bogged down by cumbersome subplots. Unlike *A Hard Day's Night*, which showcased all of the Beatles roughly equally, each playing himself in the movie, the other Dave Clark Five band members appeared only briefly in *Catch Us If You Can*, and they did not portray themselves. Most reviews were not kind, including one that appeared in *Time* magazine describing the film's muddled plot: "Fleeing from an evil advertising man, Dave Clark, who looks like a conscientious dropout, takes sad-faced model Barbara Ferris scuba-diving in a deserted swimming pool, tree-watching in a deserted botanical garden, and wandering through a deserted factory that turns out to be full of pot-smoking beatniks and is inexplicably attacked by the British army."[11] Although Clark repeatedly positioned himself at the center of the band, it was the DC5's lovable lead singer, Mike Smith—perpetually upbeat, always wearing a friendly grin—who became the face of the group, and won over most of its fans. "Mike Smith was always my favorite," recalled educator Sharon Liss, who was a fifteen-year-old Dave Clark Five enthusiast in Philadelphia in the mid-1960s. "He was always calm and cool. I guess he was the Paul McCartney of the Dave Clark Five."[12]

Members of the Dave Clark Five steered clear of criticizing the Beatles, and the Fab Four remained mostly silent about their "Tottenham Sound" competitors. "The boys claim that the 'feud' between them and the Beatles exists only in the imagination of some reporters; in fact, the Beatles are their close friends," explained a December 1964 profile of the DC5.[13] Despite this, the American press fanned the flames of division among fans of the two groups by prioritizing—in news stories and letters-to-the-editor sections—comments by adolescents who were polarized in their allegiances. For example, a teenage female fan from Orlando, Florida, proclaimed in June 1964: "I used to like those crummy Beatles, but now I like the Dave Clark Five. They are not trying to copy the Beatles in any way. If the Beatles don't step on it, the Dave Clark Five will beat them. Long live the Dave Clark Five!"[14] Another Dave Clark Five partisan from Altamonte Springs, Florida, remarked: "Somebody said the Dave Clark Five were copying the Beatles. They couldn't copy the Beatles because there isn't anything to copy. They are a ridiculous group ... Personally, I think the Dave Clark Five are great."[15] The Dave Clark Five energized their fan base in the United States when they toured North America twice in 1964, crisscrossing the country in May and June, and then again in November and December. To control the rambunctious throngs at their shows, the band "hired 15 special police to travel with them on their ... tour of the country."[16] The Dave Clark Five's June 2 concert at the Central Theatre in Passaic, New Jersey, drew more than 2,000 screaming fans, as well as inevitable comparisons to the Beatles. Once again, the press concentrated on remarks by fans who praised the Dave Clark Five while simultaneously critiquing the Beatles. Seventeen-year-old Maureen Boyle, who screamed with other concertgoers during the Dave Clark Five's performance, remarked after the show: "I saw them at Carnegie Hall. I saw the Beatles too. But the Five are much more dynamic. They are really terrific."[17] The Dave Clark Five, wrote music critic Nick Jones in his August 1964 Platter Potpourri column, were "the heirs apparent to the throne, should the Beatles falter."[18] A half century later, in 2014, Beatles fandom chronicler Candy Leonard explained the short-lived belief that the Dave Clark Five might eventually overshadow the Beatles: "For a brief moment, this quintet with the 'Tottenham Sound' seemed like they might be serious contenders to the Beatle throne, and unlike some of the other first wave invasion bands, they didn't try to sound like the Beatles. They had a distinctive sound, more R&B than the Beatles, with a booming drum."[19]

By the fall of 1965, the much-hyped matchup between the Beatles and the Dave Clark Five was rapidly fading in the wake of rock's most famous rivalry, that between the Beatles and the Rolling Stones. For their part, the Dave Clark Five had a remarkable run: fifteen Top 20 hits in the United States, eighteen appearances on the *Ed Sullivan Show*, and a rigorous touring schedule that took them to sold-out shows all over the United States and Canada. But lacking the versatility and the song writing talents of the Beatles, the DC5 faded in popularity starting in 1967, and eventually disbanded in 1970.[20] If the Dave Clark Five sought to portray themselves as wholesome, clean-cut alternatives to the Beatles, the Rolling Stones took the opposite approach. Their manager, Andrew Loog Oldham, was still a teenager when he went to work with the Stones in 1963. What he lacked in experience, however, he made up for in savvy, bringing to the table an astonishing knowledge of the power of public relations. He instantly helped fashion a "bad boy" image for the band, presenting them as a darker, edgier alternative to the Beatles. He hired a PR firm to sell this image to the American public, bombarding the press in the United States with tantalizing press releases. "Stones Set to Invade," one of them proclaimed, and it went on to state:

> In the tracks of the Beatles, a second wave of sheep-dog looking, angry-acting, guitar-playing Britons is on the way. They call themselves the Rolling Stones and they're due in New York Tuesday. Of the Rolling Stones, one detractor has said, "They are dirtier, streakier and more disheveled than the Beatles, and in some places they are more popular than the Beatles."[21]

Describing the Rolling Stones as shabby and unkempt came with certain risks, and indeed multiple journalists covering the band used words like "ugly" and "dirty" to describe the band's members. Typical of this appearance-shaming was an especially harsh verdict offered by veteran reporter Bill Whitworth in December 1964:

> The Stones are not handsome or even cute, in any of the senses in which those words have been understood until just recently. One of them looks like a chimpanzee. Two look like very ugly Radcliffe girls. One resembles the encyclopedia drawings of pithecanthropus erectus. The fifth is a double for Ray Bolger in the role of *Charley's Aunt* [a popular movie and play about a man who has to pose as his friend's aunt]. The Radcliffe girls and Charley's Aunt wear their hair much longer than The Beatles.[22]

Despite arriving in North America with the first wave of British Invasion acts, the Rolling Stones took months to attract a thriving fan base in the United States. A lackluster two-week-long, eight-city tour in June 1964 drew uneven-sized crowds and mixed reviews, and it did little to enhance the band's standing. But the Stones seemed to find their own unique style and groove—their mojo—by the time they debuted on the *Ed Sullivan Show* on October 25, 1964, displaying their talents to a curious nation in a manner flamboyant and memorable. Opting for the incendiary approach, Mick Jagger—in a droopy sweatshirt—moved provocatively on stage, singing "Around and Around" and "Time Is on My Side," and egging on the screaming fans in the audience. The broadcast gave the Stones an enormous boost in the United States, and it became a ratings success story for CBS. The band's appearance also touched off a firestorm of controversy, perhaps the biggest since Elvis Presley's notorious hip gyrations on the *Milton Berle Show* back on June 5, 1956. Angry letters poured into CBS headquarters by the sackful, protesting the Stones' raucous stage antics. The startling response prompted Sullivan to issue a public statement distancing himself from the Stones: "I promise you they will never be back on our show. If things can't be handled, we'll stop the whole business. We won't book any more rock 'n' roll groups and will ban teenagers from the theater. Frankly, I didn't see the group until the day before the broadcast."[23] Despite Sullivan's forceful declaration, the Rolling Stones would return to his show mere months later. More importantly, their grand entrance to the American music scene via the *Ed Sullivan Show* left a lasting impression. The episode polarized the public, resulting in many high-profile figures voicing their disgust with the Stones. Singer and nightclub entertainer Wayne Newton, who specialized in romantic mood music ballads, let his contempt for the English rock group and their followers be known. "The fans of the Rolling Stones are not my fans ... The dirty music people—the ones who need a haircut and look like they need a bath and sing dirty lyrics—are not for me," Newton declared.[24] On the other side of the heated debate, music critic Anthony DeCurtis, a teenage student at the time of the broadcast in the fall of 1964, recalled the sense of rebellious excitement that came with being an early fan of the band:

> The Rolling Stones looked tough. They looked scary. And that's what made them enticing ... I remember the first time they were on *The Ed Sullivan Show*, when Mick Jagger wore a sweatshirt. The response to that was incredible. At my Catholic school the next day, every single one of my teachers gave a lecture about the Rolling Stones and how repulsive they were. They'd pat you on the head for liking the Beatles. They got a kick out of them. They didn't get a kick out of the Rolling Stones. Liking the Rolling Stones radicalized you. It made you make a stand. Whatever my teachers had to say, that only stiffened my spine. That was the element of the Rolling Stones that was thrilling.[25]

Before long, the American press began churning out the sort of headlines that Andrew Loog Oldham desperately wanted to see: "New British Invaders Outdo Beatles"[26]; "Rolling Stones Top Beatles in Popularity"[27]; "Stones Displace Beatles"[28]; "Cleveland Beatle-Chasers Now Like Rolling Stones"[29]; Rolling Stones Replace Beatles as No. 1 Group"[30]; and "Freakier Rivals of the Beatles, 'Rolling Stones,' Coming Tuesday."[31] In the United States, the Rolling Stones and their manager repeatedly emphasized the sharp contrast between their style of music and that of the Beatles. "A lot of Americans think we imitate the Beatles," remarked Mick Jagger in April, a few months before the Stones arrived in the United States for their first tour. "But they weren't the first with long hair. Hip people had hair like this for five or ten years. And soundwise we were different."[32] In June, Andrew Loog Oldham explained the differences between the two bands to the American press: "The Stones are completely different from the Beatles, who lean toward rock 'n' roll. The boys favor country and blues music, like their hit seller here, 'Not Fade Away.'"[33] On the eve of the Stones' premiere US tour, guitarist Keith Richards, who went by the last name Richard at the time (sans "s"), assured the American public that he and his bandmates were essentially harmless, despite their gritty image in the media: "People think we're wild and unruly. But it isn't true. I would say that the most important thing about us is that we are our own best friends."[34] Still, the "outlaw" image applied to the Rolling Stones stuck, and they became widely regarded as a wilder alternative to the Beatles. Susan Allen, president of the Rolling Stones fan club in Charlotte, North Carolina, offered a rationale for why so many youthful rebels were turning to the Rolling Stones for musical inspiration: "Mother didn't like the Beatles too much. Then she got to like them. That made me not like them so much. But she still doesn't like the Stones."[35]

The long rivalry between the Beatles and the Stones—fueled by the media more aggressively and colorfully than the Beatles / Dave Clark Five schism—created a dichotomy in the minds of millions of fans, pushing them to voice a definitive preference. "Curiously enough, though most young music fans today seem able to accommodate enthusiasms for two or more groups simultaneously, a Stones fan is almost always anti-Beatle, and vice-versa," observed L.A. Times music and film critic Charles Champlin in the fall of 1965.[36] In the press-generated narrative, one could not love the two bands equally; rather, a choice had to be made, and consumers had to embrace one or the other. This split drove some frustrated fans to question why they were not allowed to listen to and appreciate both bands. "Why can't people like more than one British group?" asked a teenager from Sanford, Florida.[37] John Lennon and George Harrison confronted this issue head-on in a discussion between them that was tape recorded and transcribed and subsequently appeared in the February 1965 issue of *The Beatles Book*, the monthly fanzine published by the London-based headquarters of the Beatles Fan Club. The verbal exchange between the two band members revealed their thinking regarding the increasingly contentious matter of the Beatles versus the Stones:

GEORGE: Did you see this fan letter that came in yesterday? Look at this paragraph: "I am continually having fights with my classmates at school because they like the Rolling Stones."

JOHN:	Good for her!
GEORGE:	No, you know what I'm getting at. It's a bit soft to have fights over different groups. There's no reason why somebody who likes listening to our records shouldn't like The Stones as well. I think some fans get the Idea they're only supposed to like one group or one singer at a time.
JOHN:	That's true. One kid said to me, "I used to buy some of The Stones' records, but you needn't worry because I've stopped now."
GEORGE:	Whoever your favorites are, surely it would become boring if you played nothing else but records by one artist all the time?
JOHN:	Well, I listen to a lot of Bob Dylan albums, so I suppose I'm not allowed to be a Beatle person anymore![38]

The rivalry between the Beatles and the Rolling Stones was an invention of the media, quietly encouraged by the band's publicists. In reality, members of the two groups rarely uttered anything critical of one another in the 1960s.[39] The myth of an epic clash, nevertheless, benefited both bands by keeping them in headlines and news stories on a regular basis. Moreover, the public image the Beatles and Stones sought to project in the mid-1960s influenced the nature and extent of their fans' commitment, driving their admirers into two increasingly distinct camps. Marketing-wise, the Stones could never keep up with the Beatles, and their faces were less ubiquitous. Unlike the Beatles, the Rolling Stones failed to inspire widespread product placement, such as bobbleheads, bubble bath, bed sheets, lunch boxes, trading cards, and board games. Dedicated Stones' fans were more likely to dismiss such items as childish, and the band members were not interested in seeing their likenesses splashed all over memorabilia and other items. As far as the band's youthful followers were concerned, Stones fandom usually amounted to a more mature love of the band, free of the sort of the material trappings and innocent yearnings so common among Beatlemaniacs. Novelist and journalist Joyce Maynard was twelve in 1965 when she discovered the Rolling Stones for the first time, and she was—by her own admission—instantly hooked. "There was nothing teeny bopperish in my feeling for the Rolling Stones," she later remembered. "I didn't scream at the sight of them or paste their pictures on my walls."[40] Maynard's un-"teeny bopperish" experience was far from unique. In public, Stones fans often screamed as loud as Beatles fans, and newspapers were rife with stories about unrest at Stones concerts.[41] But in private, away from chaotic crowds, being a Rolling Stones fan was usually a more subdued and less immersive experience than being a Beatles fan. "The Rolling Stones fans must be only half as rabid as the fans of the Beatles. At a recent Dallas concert, only 50 policemen were hired to guard them as opposed to the 115 that guarded the Beatles when they played Dallas," observed Michigan music journalist Bob Talbert in 1965.[42]

It was easy for the people caught in the vortex of this rock-and-roll imbroglio—and there were millions of them—to forget this was a manufactured conflict, created to gain attention, sell more albums, and attract additional consumers. Although this rift started out as a press-concocted fabrication, there is ample evidence that fans of both bands took it seriously at the time, and that this "either/or" approach persisted within Beatles and Stones fandom long after the 1960s. The notion that one could love both bands, buy their albums, listen to their songs, and admire their members, and that there was nothing mutually exclusive about their music—though hardly a revelatory or brilliant insight—proved to be surprisingly scarce among diehard devotees of the Beatles and the Rolling Stones during the heyday of Beatlemania. Historian John McMillian captured this media-driven polarity effectively in his riveting and definitive 2013 history of rock's most famous rivalry, *Beatles vs. Stones*:

> Although the Beatles were more commercially successful than the Stones, throughout the 1960s the two groups ... competed for record sales, cultural influence and aesthetic credibility. Teens on both sides of the Atlantic defined themselves by whether they preferred the Beatles of the Stones ... It is little wonder, then, that in some respects the Beatles and the Stones simply could not help but act like rival bands.[43]

Consuming the Beatles

Of all the efforts to promote and advertise the Beatles, the kind that seemed the most alluring and the least like overt marketing were the movies they appeared in at the height of Beatlemania: *A Hard Day's Night*, released in 1964, and *Help!*, which opened in theaters the following year. Both films were musical comedies that showcased the Beatles and their latest songs. Philadelphia-born filmmaker Richard Lester (real name: Richard Lester Liebman) directed the two films back-to-back. *A Hard Day's Night* was shot in black-and-white cinéma verité style, whereas *Help!* was filmed in color, and played more like a conventional comedy, influenced by the popular James Bond films of the time. *A Hard Day's Night*, made with a modest budget, followed the foursome over the course of a day and half leading up to their appearance on a television special. "The film is in the form of a mock documentary—purporting to be a day in the life of the Beatles as they travel from one English town to another, dodge squealing fans, do a TV shot, etc.," wrote *Minneapolis Star* film critic Don Morrison in his rave review of August 1964.[44] Critics across the United States who hadn't been Beatles fans before seeing the film—like Morrison—offered glowing praise for *A Hard Day's Night*, with many singling it out as one of the best films of the year. "*A Hard Day's*

Night is not only a gay, spontaneous, inventive comedy but it is also as good cinema as I have seen for a long time," opined philosopher, activist, and film critic Dwight MacDonald in *Esquire* magazine.[45]

By contrast, the next year's *Help!* received more mixed reviews, owing to a plot that made little sense (a strange Eastern cult that wishes to sacrifice Ringo chases the Beatles to various corners of the globe), a screenplay that gave the Beatles less room to improvise, and humor that often fell flat with even the most dedicated Fab Four fans. "The Beatles' *Help!* movie strives for novelty and settles for mediocrity," declared syndicated newspaper gossip columnist and radio newsman Walter Winchell.[46] A more up rapturous verdict came from Giles M. Fowler, film review for the *Kansas City Star*, who said of the movie: "*Help!* is bigger, gaudier, crazier, faster and more excessive than anything in the first film."[47] Yet the uneven reviews that greeted *Help!* did not deter Beatlemaniacs across America from flocking to theaters and drive-ins to see it. "Despite a more lukewarm reception than was perhaps expected, the film still performed favorably at the British and American box office, doing 'about as well' as its predecessor and thrilling audiences with its inventive musical sequences," wrote Bob Neaverson in his definitive history of Beatles' movies.[48]

Showings of *A Hard Day's Night* and *Help!* in movie theaters created yet another gathering place for the band's fans to do what they loved most in groups: consuming the Beatles. "The theater management suggested that I come for an evening performance," wrote the film critic for the *Chicago Tribune*, who went by the playful pseudonym Mae Tinee. "The 'screamies,' as the Beatles refer to them, attend the movie in droves during the day time and because they don't care about hearing the dialog, can squeal to the heart's content."[49] In the summer of 1964, fourteen-year-old Christine McConnell, a student at Blair High School in Pasadena, California, was chosen by the city's local newspaper, the *Independent Star-News*, to write a movie review of *A Hard Day's Night*. The scene at the movie theater in mid-August when McConnell arrived was one of pandemonium, with a massive throng gathered on the sidewalks outside. Some fans had been waiting in line since 3:00 a.m. for an opportunity to see the film on opening night. As showtime neared, the restless crowd began chanting, "We want in! We want in!" "I was in the front of the line," McConnell wrote. "And believe me, it was stifling. Several girls almost fainted, and when the doors opened and the mobs of people closed around me, I almost fainted too."[50] Once the moviegoers took their seats in the packed, sold-out theater and the lights dimmed, frenzied screaming—which McConnell described as "unbelievably loud"—filled the theater. "My eardrums were almost popped. The screaming kept on through most of the show."[51] McConnell quickly adjusted to the noisy reaction of the audience, and she loved what she saw on the big screen. Her verdict: "It had no plot, but it really didn't need one. In general, it was about the everyday lives of the four boys. They acted just like they would in person, all with great senses of humour and utterly darling."[52] Similar scenes played out in cities and towns across North America. At the Circle Theater in Indianapolis, long lines of mainly young people eager to see *A Hard Day's Night* stretched around the block. Erwin Clumb, manager of the Circle Theater, anticipated that the opening night screening of the movie would likely be chaotic. "I've got seven or eight policemen outside. I pulled in three managers from other theaters to help, doubled the number of concession girls and cleanup people and now ... here it is," explained Clumb on the evening of the film's first showing.[53] On the West Coast, Stanley Eichelbaum, film reviewer for the *San Francisco Examiner*, admitted the film "isn't half bad," but the behavior of some of certain younger viewers in attendance troubled him. He wrote in his review:

> When I saw the movie, at a small screening room on Hyde Street, two dozen females of the Beatles Fan Club were also in attendance. They shrieked and moaned and wept for joy. They pounded their fists and pounced deliriously out of their seats. And I was stupefied, but not untouched by this phenomenal and, in a sense, heathen fervor, though I dare not look into the Freudian implications.[54]

The Beatles' mesmerizing onscreen musical performances in *A Hard Day's Night* and *Help!* energized millions of young viewers, triggering screams in movie theaters. In *A Hard Day's Night*, the Beatles were shown singing multiple songs to groups of excited listeners, including "I Should Have Known," "If I Fell," "And I Love Her," "I'm Happy Just to Dance with You," and "She Loves You," and they horsed around to the sounds of "Can't Buy Me Love."[55] Similarly, in *Help!*, the Beatles perform the title track, as well as "You're Going to Lose That Girl," "You've Got to Hide Your Love Away," "The Night Before," and "Another Girl." In the film's most memorable scene, the Beatles ski downhill, frolic in the snow, and lip sync on a grand piano in the Austrian Alps to the sounds of "Ticket to Ride."[56] For moviegoing Beatlemaniacs, these segments were akin to having a front-row seats to a Beatles concert. Indeed, for those fans not lucky enough to obtain tickets to one of the Beatles' three North American tours, watching *A Hard Day's Night* and *Help!* was the next best thing to seeing them live on stage. Fourteen-year-old Dede Lawless, of Roxbury, Massachusetts, saw *A Hard Day's Night* in Boston on August 12, 1964, and found it captivating. "I have always loved the Beatles since I first heard them, but I've seen the movie and I love them more than ever ... Seeing the Beatles in this movie is almost as good as seeing them in person. Their old songs are here and as swinging as always, and the new songs—like 'If I Fell,' 'I Should've Known Better,' and 'Tell Me Why'—are even better than the old ones," said Lawless in her front-page review of the film for the *Boston Globe*.[57] Teenage Beatlemaniac diarist Patricia Gallo patiently endured months of hype before seeing *Help!* on August 11, 1965, at the 69th Street Tower Theater in Upper Darby, Pennsylvania. "*Help!* was definitely the high point of my summer," she recorded in her diary at the time.[58] Gallo and other fans stood in a long line that extended around the block to get into the theater. The wait, she believed, was worth it. The movie did not disappoint. "My most beloved scene: Paul in his camel-colored suit and soft turtleneck singing 'The Night Before' on Salisbury Plain with the wind whipping through his black hair. I was absolutely paralyzed through that entire song."[59] An adolescent Beatles fan from Rochester, New York, explained that *Help!* "really turned me on, it was fab, gear, and wonderful. It … did more for us than any other thing in this world could do because it brought us the nearest to the Beatles we love than we've ever been, or for that matter we'll ever be."[60] Many of the band's diehard followers experienced repeated viewings of both movies, drawn mainly by the musical performances. Adolescent Beatles fan Penny Wagner happened to have an uncle who owned a movie theater in Kenosha, Wisconsin, and he allowed his niece and her friends to see the movie as frequently as they wanted without charging them admission. "We must have seen *A Hard Day's Night*—I'm not exaggerating—about a hundred times, if not more, and *Help!* about 60 times," Wagner recalled. Aware that Wagner loved the group, her uncle "let us keep going back to watch it … The music is what we went for. All we'd do is scream. Just mention the name John, Paul, George, or Ringo, and we were screaming."[61]

Ultimately, *A Hard Day's Night* and *Help!* assumed an influential place in the history of modern cinema that extended far beyond the warm reception they received within Beatles fandom. Both movies blended music performance and film in innovative ways, helping to pave the way for an onslaught of rockumentaries and motion pictures that utilized rock soundtracks. For example, film and television producer Bert Schneider credited *A Hard Day's Night* and *Help!* with being his chief influences when he cocreated, along with Bob Rafelson, the absurdist cult television series *The Monkees*, which was sold to Screen Gems Television in April 1965 and ran on NBC from 1966 to 1968. When Schneider approached songwriters Bobby Hart and Tommy Boyce to ask them to write music for his newly conceived show, he described it to them as "basically … an American Beatles on television."[62] In the fall of 1966, with *The Monkees* airing on televisions across the United States each Monday night, guitarist and bass player Michael Nesmith told an interviewer: "You'd have to say the show is very much like the Beatles' *A Hard Day's Night*. It's modern, wild and you really can't say it has any definite format."[63] *A Hard Day's Night* and *Help!* also helped birth the earliest music videos, which were referred to at the time as "promotional films." Not surprisingly, the Beatles pioneered these new forms of artistic musical expression. Early Beatles promotional films for such songs as "I Feel Fine," "Help!," and "We Can Work It Out," were filmed in black and white, and showed the band members performing playfully in studio soundstages. Later promotional films for songs like "Paperback Writer," "Rain," "Penny Lane," "Strawberry Fields Forever," "I Am the Walrus," and "Fool on the Hill" (the last two appeared in their 1967 film *Magical Mystery Tour*) were filmed in color, with the band reenacting the songs in outdoor settings, either in the city ("Paperback Writer" and "Rain" were shot at the Chiswick House in west London, "Penny Lane" was filmed in and around Liverpool) or the countryside (e.g., "I Am the Walrus," "Fool on the Hill"). Psychedelic themes and sequences often abounded in these short subjects. Beatles promotional films would be shown on television variety shows around the world, and sometimes even in movie theaters before the main attraction.[64]

The Beatles were also ubiquitous on television screens across America by the mid-1960s. Their historic debut on the *Ed Sullivan Show* on February 9, 1964, opened the floodgates for other television appearances. The Beatles also appeared on the popular teen-oriented variety shows *Shindig!* on ABC

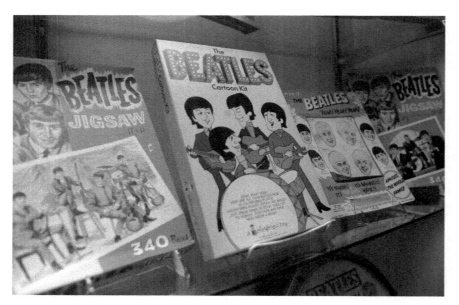

FIGURE 3.1 *These memorabilia items appeared in a 2014 CBS program called 50 Years: The Beatles, a live interactive multimedia event to mark the 50th anniversary of the Beatles' February 9, 1964, debut on the* Ed Sullivan Show. *Included here is a "Beatles Cartoon Kit," which featured an image from* The Beatles, *a popular Saturday morning cartoon on ABC in the United States.*
Source: Photo by Heather Wines/CBS via Getty Images.

(air date: October 7, 1964), and *Hullabaloo* on NBC (air date: January 3, 1966). Unlike most bands that appeared live on these programs, the Beatles' performances were taped beforehand in England, to appear at a later date. On September 25, 1965, ABC aired the first episodes of the Beatles' Saturday morning cartoon, produced for the network by King Features Syndicate (see Figure 3.1). The cartoon would run for three seasons, eventually ending on October 21, 1967. Each Saturday, two cartoons apiece appeared on ABC, produced by Al Brodax, the man responsible for the television revival of *Popeye the Sailor* in the early 1960s.[65] "The animated sing-alongs with The Beatles will be produced so that the young viewers can follow with ease," said Brodax.[66] The animation was crude, yet the characters bore a resemblance to their real-life counterparts. American actor Paul Frees, famous for his portrayal of the animated evildoer Boris Badenov on the *Adventures of Rocky and Bullwinkle and Friends*, and who furnished voiceovers in numerous cartoons, documentaries, and commercials, played both John and George on the show, while British comedian and actor Lance Percival provided the voices for Paul and Ringo. The cartoon's only connection to the Beatles were the band's songs, which were showcased on the program every week. Despite characters having voices that sounded nothing like the actual Beatles and the show's incoherent storylines (involving monsters, primitive island natives, anthropomorphized animals, and a host of other eccentrics), the cartoon was a huge ratings success, which pleased ABC network executives and surprised its creator, Al Brodax.[67] "I knew it would be a hit, but I think it has gone way past my estimates … We know from record sales and our own show's ratings that the youngsters still want to hear the music, so we can only assume that they want a new style of presentation, and we think we've got it," said a giddy Brodax in the fall of 1965.[68]

Movies, promotional films, and television offered but one means of consuming the Beatles. However, at this technological juncture in American history—coming years before the advent of videocassette recorders, cable television, and, later, DVD and Blu-ray players, the internet, and YouTube—the broadcasting of Beatles programs on TV and the showing of their films in movie theaters in the mid-1960s offered only fleeting encounters with the Fab Four. Alas, not everybody was able to tune into a television channel at a specified time or attend the screening of a Beatles motion picture. For those who sought out something more permanent, and who wished to obtain Beatles-themed material objects to remind them of the band they so deeply loved, there was a breathtaking range of consumer items flooding the marketplace by the spring and summer of 1964. This steady outpouring of Beatles merchandise would continue for the next few years.

One would think that this tsunami of all things Beatles would have resulted in a lavish fortune for the Liverpool foursome. But it didn't. One of Brian Epstein's biggest errors as a manager occurred in 1963, when his attorney, David Jacobs, agreed to let a shadowy entrepreneur named Nicky Byrne (real name: Douglas Anthony Nicholas Byrne) take over control of Beatles merchandising. Beatles chronicler John Blaney described Byrne as "a former member of The Horse Guards and a onetime nightclub manager."[69] Byrne pressured Jacobs to sign a contract giving Byrne 90 percent of profits on all Beatles merchandise, leaving a measly 10 percent for the band. Jacobs shockingly agreed to Byrne's request.[70] The results were both disastrous and fortuitous at the same time. Disastrous because the Beatles lost millions in revenues that would have gone directly to them had their merchandizing been better managed. But the absence of any meaningful control over the production of Beatles-themed products resulted in a staggering number of items being sold in stores and magazines for eager buyers. Byrne established two companies for the purpose of licensing Beatles merchandise: Stramsact, based in the UK, and Seltaeb (which was Beatles spelled backwards) in the United States. In early 1964, Byrne relocated from London to New York City with an entourage of dutiful, hardworking employees to expand the lucrative licensing business. "Nicky Byrne and his Seltaeb young men took accommodation at the elegant Drake Hotel, and offices on Fifth Avenue," explained Beatles chronicler Philip Norman. "Within hours, they were besieged by manufacturers seeking a part in what the American business world already recognized as the biggest marketing opportunity since Walt Disney had created Mickey Mouse."[71]

Byrne remained a mysterious figure, generally avoiding the press and keeping his business affairs private. As of early June 1964, the *Liverpool Echo and Evening Express* noted that Brian Epstein's NEMS (North End Music Stores) "had already granted about 150 licenses to manufacturers at home and abroad" to create Beatles merchandise, "but Seltaeb obtained a further 170 or so overseas rights on items ranging from scooters to pencils, in fact everything it could think of."[72] Yet even as Stramsact and Seltaeb enjoyed record profits from licensing Beatles products, they suffered from horrendous mismanagement under Byrne. It was only a short matter of time before Seltaeb got mired down in a host of legal battles. In the fall of 1964, a lawsuit filed in London by a group of wealthy men who controlled "30 of Seltaeb's total 100 shares," including the company's partner, Malcolm Evans, accused Byrne of reckless spending at the helm of the company. The unhappy shareholders accused Byrne of "using a chauffeured Cadillac for weeks on end at $120," and they claimed "he ran up hotel bills involving as much as $1,500 a week for girlfriends at the Drake Hotel" and "opened charge accounts for them at Saks Fifth Avenue, payable out of partnership funds."[73]

Responsibility for the Beatles merchandizing fiasco rested squarely on Brian Epstein's doorstep. His lack of interest in the entire process and his trusting nature resulted in a hemorrhaging loss of revenue for the band he managed. "The Beatles never made any money on merchandizing in the United States," said Nat Weiss, the band's American lawyer.[74] Prior to the Beatles, the most heavily merchandized rock star had been Elvis Presley, who—thanks to his shrewd manager Tom Parker—managed to inspire an array of items featuring his likeness during his heyday in the 1950s. It did not take long for the Beatles to overshadow the King in this relatively new area of promotion. "The Beatles were the first ones with little dolls coming out," recalled Larry Page, who managed The Kinks and The Troggs. "Everyone thought, 'Isn't that wonderful. Look at that. Everybody's bringing out little dolls of The Beatles'"[75] (see Figure 3.2). Because Stramsact and Seltaeb were so quick to grant licenses to companies on both sides of the Atlantic to manufacture Beatles merchandise, and they did not have the staff or resources to go after so-called "Beatleggers" (or as one account called them, "hustlers trying to use the Beatles name unlawfully"), an unregulated Wild West state of affairs abounded when it came to the production of Beatles-themed products.[76] This created, in the words of one Seltaeb executive, "an awful mess."[77]

Within less than a week of the Beatles' February 9, 1964, *Ed Sullivan Show* debut, the Reliance Manufacturing Company, based in New York—the single largest producer of Beatles items in the United States at the time—was already reporting $2.5 million in retail sales, a number that steadily climbed. The sheer demand for Beatles products manufactured by Reliance, which specialized mainly in "Beatleware" (T-shirts, pants, sweatshirts, and pajamas), left the company's president, Miles Rubin, astonished. "We had almost a tongue-in-cheek attitude when we first got into this. But it turned out to be the biggest promotion in our 60 years in business," he explained.[78] Stores across the country cashed in on the Beatles consumerism craze by taking out advertisements in newspapers for all manner of Fab Four items, transforming for a time into memorabilia dealers. For example, in Kansas City, Missouri, Woolworth's chain stores ran large display ads in the *Kansas City Star* proclaiming: "Woolworth's Headquarters for Beatle Merchandise! Remco Beatle Dolls 97c Each—All 4 for $3.77. See Our Complete Assortment of • Beatle Jewelry • Beatle Magazines • Beatle Trading Cards • Beatle Fillfolds • Beatle Musical Instruments • Records • Lp Albums."[79] Elsewhere, the Woolworth's in Greeley, Colorado, dedicated an entire section of the store to Beatles items, its aisles spilling over with dolls, guitars, jewelry, carrying bags, pictures, and albums.[80] A store owner in Macon, Georgia, who kept his establishment well-stocked with a variety of Beatles items revealed his biggest selling item to be Beatles trading cards. "There are 60 pictures in the series, and the kids often buy a whole box of bubble gum, at $1.20 a box, to try to get all the pictures," he said.[81]

FIGURE 3.2 *Carol Valentine, ten, of the Bronx, inspects Beatles dolls that were being introduced during a Toy Fair, March 9, 1964.*
Source: *Photo by Fred Morgan/New York Daily News Archive via Getty Images.*

For legions of Beatles idolizers, these consumer items made the fan experience even more all-encompassing. One young female admirer from San Francisco wrote to the band members in the summer of 1964 describing her vast collection of items: "Dearest Beatles, you should see my room. It is gorgeous. I have Beatle wallpaper, Beatle pictures, Beatle dolls, Beatle banners and Beatle wigs. My mother screams every time she walks in. Crazy for you, Debbie C."[82] In Lincoln, Nebraska, a local wallpaper dealer kept selling out of Beatles wallpaper within hours of when a new shipment would arrive at his store. He said that while some customers were purchasing entire rolls of the wallpaper, which showed scenes of John, Paul, George and Ringo in action, "mostly people are buying small pieces of it. Just enough to paper the wall behind their record player."[83] By December 1964, Beatles items topped Christmas lists across America. The board game manufacturer Milton Bradley released its Beatles Flip Your Wig game, which became a big seller during the holiday season of 1964.[84] "Fast-moving, fast-playing game starring The Beatles! Each player selects a Beatle playing piece. Hours of fun!" cried ads for the game.[85] There were Beatles alarm clocks for sale. There was Beatles bubble bath, Beatles shampoo, and Beatles wigs. A company calling itself Merit released a Beatles "magnetic hair" game, in which the player had to use a stylus with a magnet on the end of it to move black iron filings over pictures of John, Paul, George, and Ringo.[86] There were Beatles hats and necklaces, plates and cups, Beatles notebooks, bandages, and necklaces, Beatles bedsheets, Beatles pillowcases.[87] The approach of Christmas season prompted one ardent Beatles fan, ten-year-old Becky Lee Beck of Columbus, Georgia, "whose room is filled with Beatle dolls and photographs of the mop-hair group cover her walls," to write and record a Yuletide song about the Fab Four called "I Want a Beatle for Christmas." Released as a seven-inch single by the Los Angeles-based Challenge Records, "I Want a Beatle for Christmas" received airplay on radio stations during the 1964 holiday season, with one disc jockey touting it as a "real winner."[88] Becky spent the better part of three hours in a Nashville studio recording the song, along with its B-side track, "Puppy." The time and effort she put into making the single was worth it to Becky, who aspired to become a singer and considered herself a diehard Beatles fan. "I liked them immediately," Becky told a reporter, revealing that she had seen *A Hard Day's Night* "eight times."[89]

The output of Beatles' merchandise began to slow by 1966. Costly legal battles over mismanagement in Stramsact and Seltaeb, as well as efforts to curb Beatleggers "who are cashing in on the fantastic Beatles boom throughout the United States" (as the *Liverpool Echo* described them), had taken a toll on Brian Epstein and other members of the Beatles' staff.[90] "Brian was still bruised by his experience in the American legal system and, if anything, was even less keen to involve himself in merchandising, something he still considered peripheral to the essence of the Beatles, namely their music," wrote Geoffrey Ellis, an attorney who worked closely with Epstein around legal matters in the 1960s. "The Beatles themselves were also changing. Although their fan base remained huge, they were moving away from the commercialism that might have lent itself to merchandising."[91] The Beatles' evolving attitudes coincided with the shifting temperament of their fans.

Among young consumers, the novelty of Beatles-themed items was starting to wane. Things that were considered "cool" by young people in 1964 and even into 1965 came to be regarded as passé in 1966. Even as early as August 1965, Jack Dow, president of the Louis Dow Company in St. Paul, Minnesota, one of the largest manufacturers of Beatles products in the United States, grimly noted, "Resale buyers are dead as a doornail."[92]

Of course, Beatles merchandise never went away. Indeed, decades after John, Paul, George, and Ringo left the band to pursue solo careers, the production of Fab Four souvenirs, toys, keepsakes, collectibles, and other items, remained a lucrative source of revenue. But something had changed by 1966. The initial flood of things had been reduced to more of a steady stream, with the introduction of new items diminishing significantly. Moreover, immersing oneself in all things Beatles did not carry the same appeal to youthful devotees in the later years of the 1960s as it did in those exhilarating early months after the band first touched down on American soil. So why bring it up at all, this adolescent flotsam and jetsam, much of which undoubtedly ended up landfills across America? Aside from going on decades later to sale for "daft prices"—as Beatles chronicler and memorabilia collector Hunter Davies has described the astonishing cost of Fab Four collectibles by the time of the 2000s—these items served an important function in the mid-1960s.[93] These products cemented fan loyalty, demonstrating to the rest of the nation the spending power of Beatlemaniacs and their parents. Beatles-themed items gave Americans in 1964 and 1965 (and even beyond)—those who loved the band, or hated the band, and everyone in between—the sense that the Beatles were omnipresent, that everywhere you turned, there they were. It was futile to try to escape their long shadow. Most Beatles merchandise portrayed the band's members as upbeat, carefree, irreverent, and generally having a fun time, either making music or merriment. In the process, the Beatles—more heavily merchandized than any other group or performer of the day—gravitated inexorably to the mainstream of American life. Never before—and arguably, not since—had a band been so effectively marketed and promoted and transformed into innumerable items bought and sold in the marketplace. For companies that were hungry for profits, these products of Beatle capitalism were mere inanimate commodities produced for profits. But in the hands of dedicated fans, Beatles merchandise turned into objects of affection, offering yet another means of getting closer to the band they so deeply loved.

4

The Beatles and Black America

The coming of Beatlemania in early 1964 coincided with the high-water mark of the nonviolent Civil Rights Movement in the southern United States. Change was in the air when the Beatles stepped of Pan Am Flight 101 at John F. Kennedy International Airport in New York on February 7, 1964. The nation's African American population, feeling increasingly empowered by recent social and cultural developments, began to voice their views and preferences in more meaningful ways. Changes brought about by the Civil Rights Movement paralleled the striking involvement of Black men and women in American popular culture, particularly in the realm of popular music. The Beatles—who were open about Black influences on their music—became part of a vital Transatlantic cultural exchange between African American and white artists. During the height of Beatlemania, the band attracted African American fans. But Black Americans were far from monolithic in their feelings about the newly arrived foursome from Liverpool.

"Let's Us Check Them Out"

Beatlemania in general—and the Beatles, in particular—divided Black America, just as they did the rest of the country. But African Americans had their own reasons, distinct from those of whites, for holding a wide range of opinions about the famous British rock band. Some Black people—youths and musicians, in particular—loved the Beatles. Other African Americans disliked the Fab Four. And countless Blacks, caught in the vast middle, simply did not care about them. Black America at mid-decade was in a state of flux. The arrival of Beatlemania in the United States in early 1964 overlapped with the nonviolent Civil Rights Movement in the South reaching high tide. Now in a state of transition, the country was undergoing striking shifts in race relations, which would ultimately have far-reaching consequences. By the mid-1960s, African Americans were assuming more visible places in different realms of public life, including popular culture, politics, education, and business. The gradual emboldening of Blacks in the United States went hand in hand with a deepening awareness on their part of their history, cultural contributions, and political empowerment. In an influential essay published in *Show* magazine in February 1964, which went to print weeks before the Beatles appeared on the *Ed Sullivan Show*, author and political activist James Baldwin wrote of "my ancestors, who evolved the sorrow songs, the blues and jazz, and created an entirely new idiom in an overwhelmingly hostile place."[1]

The rise of positive Black role models in show business during the mid-1960s occurred at the same time as the Civil Rights Movement and what historian Clayborne Carson called "the Black awakening." Actors like Sidney Poitier, Diahann Carroll, Ruby Dee, Ivan Dixon, Bill Cosby, and others, rose to prominence in non-stereotypical roles in film and on television. While Poitier played intellectual and cosmopolitan Black men on the big screen, Cosby starred as the first Black leading actor in a major network television series, *I Spy*, which debuted on NBC's new fall lineup on September 15, 1965.[2] Meantime, African American musicians dominated jazz, blues, rhythm and blues, rock and roll, and the newly emerging genre of soul music. The likes of Miles Davis, Muddy Waters, Lena Horne, Chuck Berry, Sam Cooke, Ray Charles, and Aretha Franklin—to name a few—shattered long-standing color lines to attract sizable white audiences in addition to their Black fans.[3] At the dawn of the British Invasion in 1964, one of the few American counterinvasions to hold its own against the waves of English bands landing on US soil were the beloved Motown groups based in Detroit. The Marvelettes, Smokey Robinson and the Miracles, the Supremes, the Four Tops, the Temptations, Stevie Wonder, and other thriving acts from the Tamla label—"the Sound of Young America," as its motto went—topped charts on both sides of the Atlantic, and furnished cover songs for the Beatles during their rise to stardom.[4]

Even before traveling to the United States in February 1964, the Beatles had been ardent foes of racism, and they expressed admiration and solidarity for Black musicians. In the early 1960s, the band members insisted on sharing the stage with Joe Ankrah and the Chants, an all-Black band from Liverpool that was struggling to break into the local music scene. "It was bad enough that the modern moods [i.e., racism] never gave a Black group a chance, but if not for Paul and his friends, we would have never stayed together ... In fact, I think that meeting the Beatles changed the direction of my life ... They were very cool guys and meeting them gave us a look at real opportunity."[5] Since their earliest days as a band, the Beatles made no secret of their deep debt to African American musicians and songwriters. In interviews and press conferences, they showered praise on the figures of color that influenced them. They adored Chuck Berry, Fats Domino, Little Richard, Motown acts, and so-called "girl groups" from the United States. The Beatles cut their musical teeth by playing covers performed by these artists. The admiration was mutual. Marvin Gaye told an interviewer from *Soul* magazine in April 1966: "I think the Beatles are great. Not because they are said to be great, but because of their musicianship, writing ability, and because of their subtle originality."[6] Otis Williams, a founding member of the Temptations, who signed on with Motown in 1961, gave "credit to the Beatles" for helping Motown groups to reach white listeners in the United States: "It seemed like at that point in time white America said, 'OK, if the Beatles are checking them out, let's us check them out.'"[7] Smokey Robinson proved equally outspoken in his love of the Beatles. "The Beatles were huge. The first thing they said when you interviewed them was 'we grew up on Motown' … They were the first huge white act to admit, 'Hey, we grew up with some Black music. We love this.'"[8]

So impressed with the Beatles was Motown headliner Mary Wells—whose hit song "My Guy" shot to the top of the Billboard Hot 100 May 1964—that she spent five weeks touring with them. While in the United States during the Beatles' 1964 tour in the summer, John Lennon saw Wells singing live, and he was deeply impressed with her performance. So much so, he told the press that Wells was the Beatles' "favorite American singer," and the band's "sweetheart."[9] Wells, who was only twenty-one at the time, joined the Beatles for their fall 1964 UK tour, crisscrossing the UK, opening for the beloved Liverpool foursome. The arrangement so impressed the other artists on the Motown roster that Mary Wilson of The Supremes remarked at the time, "We were all kind of like 'whoooa!'"[10] During the tour 1964 UK tour, the British instrumental group Sounds Incorporated shared the stage with Wells, playing background music for her songs (see Figure 4.1). The drummer of Sounds Incorporated, Tony Williams, remembered that Wells excited audiences and the other musicians alike with her "unheard-of grooves," and she hit it off right away with the other musicians on the road that fall. "We were all shocked how black she was. Of course, she was equally surprised how small and white we were. But it was a great pleasure to work with her and play Motown music," said Williams.[11] On the road, Wells formed lasting friendships with John, Paul, George, and Ringo, and when she returned to the United States, she recorded an album consisting entirely of Beatles' cover songs titled *Love Songs to the Beatles*.[12] Wells also left a lasting impression on her four friends across the Atlantic, as her biographer, Peter Benjaminson, notes: "Keeping the sound of Mary's songs in mind, George believes that she might well have inspired the production of many early 'sweet and optimistic' Beatles songs, especially those sung in falsetto."[13]

FIGURE 4.1 *Twenty-one-year-old American pop singer Mary Wells (1943–1992) rehearses with members of Sounds Incorporated at the Prince Of Wales Theatre, London, in preparation for a five-week UK tour with the Beatles, October 8, 1964. The tour made Wells the first Motown artist to perform in the UK.*
Source: Photo by Chris Ware/Keystone/Hulton Archive via Getty Images.

Beyond their close relationship with Mary Wells, the Beatles routinely heaped praise on Motown, and their second studio album, *With the Beatles*, released in the UK on November 22, 1963, contained three Motown covers (The Marvelettes' "Please Mr. Postman," Smokey Robinson and the Mircacles' "You've Really Got a Hold on Me," and Barrett Strong's "Money (That's What I Want)"). The LP also included their version of Chuck Berry's beloved "Roll Over, Beethoven."[14] The multiracial, transatlantic cultural give-and-take that the Beatles participated in went both ways. A number of African American singers and groups—far too many to list here—performed Beatles songs, among them Ray Charles ("The Long and Winding Road"), Wilson Pickett ("Hey Jude"),

Aretha Franklin ("Eleanor Rigby"), James Brown ("Something"), Stevie Wonder ("We Can Work It Out"), Smokey Robinson & The Miracles ("And I Love Her"), The Four Tops ("Michelle"), Nina Simone ("Here Comes the Sun"), Jimi Hendrix ("Day Tripper"), Marvin Gaye ("Yesterday"), Otis Redding ("Day Tripper"), Al Green ("I Want to Hold Your Hand), Dionne Warwick ("A Hard Day's Night"), and Roberta Flack ("Here, There and Everywhere"). A number of noted African American jazz musicians covered Beatles songs as well, including pianist Ramsey Lewis ("Day Tripper"), guitarist Grant Green ("A Day in the Life"), and jazz singer Ella Fitzgerald ("Savoy Truffle"). In 1966, Count Basie released an entire album of Beatles covers, *Basie's Beatle Bag*, on the Verve label, followed four years later by jazz guitarist George Benson's *The Other Side of Abbey Road* (1970). Aretha Franklin, the "Queen of Soul," expressed her deep appreciation for the Beatles, explaining why she chose to perform two covers of Beatles songs on one of her albums:

> As the sixties became the seventies, soul music was still leading the field, perhaps because it expressed the raw emotion people were feeling. On my first album released in 1970, This Girl's in Love with You, I sang two Beatles songs, "Let It Be" and "Eleanor Rigby." Jerry Wexler has written that Paul McCartney and John Lennon wrote "Let It Be" expressly for me, but that was not true. The minute I heard the song, though, I loved it. Ditto for "Eleanor Rigby." Early on I recognized the Beatles' charm as showmen and their talent as writers.[15]

Aside from Black singers, musicians and songwriters, other African Americans played important roles in the Beatles' success. The first record label to promote the Beatles in the United States was Black-owned Vee-Jay Records in Chicago. Founded in 1953 by husband-and-wife partners Vivian Carter and James C. Bracken, Vee-Jay (a combination of Carter's and Bracken's first names) opened its doors in Gary, Indiana, but relocated to the nearby Windy City the following year. It developed a reputation during the 1950s as one of the most important labels in the genre of rhythm and blues in the United States, and it recorded a multitude of important soul acts in the 1960s. Vee-Jay's first non-Black group, the Four Seasons, further enhanced the label's prestige. For a fleeting moment, Vee-Jay added the Beatles to its growing and impressive roster of entertainers. It was a fluke, and a short-lived one at that, but it was still a coup for Vee-Jay. In the early months of 1963, Capitol Records executives in the United States showed no interest in promoting the Beatles, who had, by this time, been signed on to Parlophone Records, owned by Capitol's parent company, EMI, in London. Capitol Records in Canada, by contrast, began releasing Beatles' singles months before their American counterparts. South of the border, Vee-Jay moved into the void by leasing early Beatles singles from EMI, hoping to cash in on the band's growing success in the UK. Vee-Jay released two 7" Beatles 45s, the first in February 1963, "Please Please Me," with "Ask Me Why" on the B-side, followed in May by "From Me to You" and "Thank You Girl." Some radio stations in Chicago played Beatles' songs in 1963, most notably Dick Biondi's popular program on station WLS in March (making Biondi the first American disc jockey to play the Beatles on the radio in the United States).[16]

Behind the scenes, Vee-Jay employees lobbied other radio stations to play Beatles songs in the spring and summer of 1963, with little success. Radio station WVON in Chicago, owned by brothers Leonard and Phil Chess (founders of the famed Blues and R&B label Chess Records), a station aimed at an African American audience, played Beatles' singles regularly that summer. So did station WYNR (a.k.a., "Winner, Chicago's Mighty 1390" on the dial), where Vee-Jay cofounder Vivian Carter had worked years earlier as a deejay when it went by the call letters WGES. Alas, despite these fleeting early inroads, the Beatles' early Vee-Jay singles flopped.[17] Undaunted, Vee-Jay rushed to release *Introducing ... The Beatles* on January 10, 1964, mere weeks before the band's debut on the *Ed Sullivan Show*. *Introducing ... The Beatles* proved to be an important milestone: the first Beatles' studio album released in the United States. On the eve of the record's release, Vee-Jay exec Jay Lasker bragged "we have an LP that could be huge—we can get it out on the street by the end of this week—at least 30,000 LPs can be gotten out."[18] But there was a hint of desperation in Lasker's boast, for he—and others at Vee-Jay—knew the Beatles would soon be leaving their modest roster. Predictably, Capitol Records moved into the void, rushing gigantic orders of Beatles albums (LPs and singles alike) and closing off all loopholes. This resulted in Vee-Jay becoming bogged down in legal entanglements involving the album *Introducing ... The Beatles*, yet the label managed to squeeze out a second issue of the bestselling LP on February 10, 1964, the day after the Beatles' historic performance on the *Ed Sullivan Show*. The Fab Four had slipped out of their grasp, but not before earning more money for Vee-Jay than the small label had ever seen. Before going bankrupt in 1966, in fact, Vee-Jay managed to release multiple albums recycling the Beatles songs to which it had the rights.[19]

That a Black-owned record label—which specialized in jazz, soul, and R&B—played a key role in introducing the Beatles to Americans prior to and during the initial burst of Beatlemania in the United States is but one sign of the rapport that existed between the Beatles and African Americans. Once Beatlemania arrived in the country, the band's constituency of African American fans contributed richly to Beatlemania, and—in doing so—helped to diversify the band's fan base. Kitty Oliver was one of those fans. She grew up in segregated Jacksonville, Florida, in the 1950s and 1960s. Like millions of other Americans, Oliver instantly fell in love with the Beatles when she first heard their music at the beginning of 1964. It didn't matter to her that most of the Beatles fans that she knew were white. Their music resonated with her, and she bought all of their singles and LPs, and plastered her walls with pictures of the four band members.

> I was crazy about the group—swooped up in the frenzy like all the other teenaged girls I saw in the TV reports on them, on the news when I first became aware of Beatlemania! The fact that none of the girls were Black like me didn't seem to register ... [T]he Beatles were from another country which made them exotic, and they were young, fun loving, cute guys. I think, in my segregated Black community I was a bit odd. I only had one friend I shared this fascination with, but she was not as much of a fan as I turned out to be.[20]

Kitty Oliver later went on to become a respected scholar, author, oral historian, and television and radio producer. She appeared prominently in Ron Howard's acclaimed 2016 documentary *The Beatles: Eight Days a Week*, which focused on the band's eventful touring years between 1964 and 1966.[21] Her lively remembrances shine a vital light on the experiences of the band's African American fans during the early years of Beatlemania. One of the main sources of information about African American Beatlemaniacs during these early years comes from oral histories, written accounts, and reminiscences gathered decades after the fact, especially those of such luminaries as Oprah Winfrey, Whoopi Goldberg, and Dr. Oliver, all of whom counted themselves as among the band's most ardent fans. "When I was living on North Ninth Street in Milwaukee, Wisconsin, in a two-room flat, on welfare, the only decoration in a room I shared with a half brother and sister were Beatles posters," recalled Winfrey in 2010.[22]

Despite these invaluable remembrances, Black Beatles fans in the mid-1960s have often been absent from twenty-first century fan histories, nonacademic and scholarly alike.[23] Such omissions are due, at least in part, to the challenges involved with tracing the history of the band's early African American fans. Typically, the band's loyal young followers—Black and white alike—who were interviewed in the press in 1964, 1965 and 1966, or who corresponded with teen magazines and fan club newsletters, did not identify their race. This makes sense in the context of a society lurching toward greater inclusiveness at the time. Occasionally, a magazine or newspaper might identify an African American fan of the Beatles in a profile story. Such was the case with singer Carla Thomas, who had a major hit on her hands in 1964 with the soulful pop song "B-A-B-Y," on the Memphis-based Stax label. An issue of the popular African American magazine *Jet* identified her as a concertgoer at one of the Beatles' live performances at the Mid-South Coliseum in Memphis, Tennessee, on August 19, 1966 (the band put on two shows in Memphis that day). "I am a Beatle fan. I've always wanted to see them in person but was disappointed because I couldn't hear anything for all of the screaming teenagers ... I like them, especially Paul," she told *Jet* magazine.[24] In addition to press stories, photographs of cheering Beatlemania crowds from the mid-1960s often reveal the presence of Beatles enthusiasts of color. Yet much of the story of the band's African American fans has come to us in the 2000s and 2010s courtesy of oral histories. One such interview involved a Black "entertainment professional" named Paul, born in 1959, who recalled being the younger brother of a dedicated Beatles fan growing up "in a Black neighborhood." "I had a pretty wide range of influences in terms of music," Paul recalled:

> Besides whatever my peers were listening to, I was listening to whatever [my older sister] was listening to ... She was into the Beatles and the Rolling Stones and that kind of stuff ... I was a kid at that time, but I was in that kind of a progressive, political, sort of countercultural, black kind of environment. Black hippies, if you will.[25]

The most famous remembrances among African American Beatles fans come from high-profile figures as Kitty Oliver, Oprah Winfrey, and Whoopi Goldberg. It is telling that, as Beatles fans, each of these women felt unique—and, in some ways, alienated from other people of color—in their adoration of the Beatles. For example, by her own admission, Kitty Oliver regarded herself as an outsider among her Black friends when it came to her love of the Beatles.[26] Winfrey echoed this point as well: "I was the only black girl in my inner-city neighborhood who loved the Beatles."[27] Whoopi Goldberg recalled in Ron Howard's 2016 Beatles documentary *Eight Days a Week*: "People would say to me: You think you want to be white? You like those guys? I never thought of them as white guys. They were The Beatles. They were colorless, you know, and they were fucking amazing!"[28] These remembrances speak volumes about divided opinions among Blacks in the mid-1960s with regards to the Beatles. Such sentiments were also expressed by less famous African American fans at the height of Beatlemania. Cynthia Dagnal, who later enjoyed a successful career as a journalist for the *Chicago Sun-Times* and the *Arizona Daily Star*, explained what it was like to endure the lonely experience of being an eleven-year-old Beatles fan at an all-African American school on Chicago's South Side: "There was a schism. It was a real problem there. It was 'white kids' stuff, why are you doing this? Motown versus the invasion of the Brits. We used to fight about this. I mean, literally, fistfight about this stuff on the playground. I remember that very vividly because I was the 'white girl' after that."[29]

The resistance that Cynthia Dagnal faced for loving the Beatles reflected divisions among African Americans about the band and its dramatic entrance to the top tier of American popular culture. While many Blacks remained indifferent to the band and its monumental success, a handful of outspoken critics let their views be known. "We don't have to wait for the Beatles to legitimize our culture. Black intellectuals ought to come back to the community and let the community define what an intellectual is and what art is," said Black Power activist Stokely Carmichael in the pages of *Ebony* magazine in September 1966.[30] Carmichael often singled out the Beatles in his fiery public addresses. Speaking to a cheering crowd in the auditorium of Garfield High School in Seattle on April 19, 1967, Carmichael attacked the Fab Four: "The trouble is that they steal our music from us and then give it back to us and call it culture. Here come the Beatles, singing our music. They can't even harmonize and they gonna talk about culture. Yeah! Yeah!"[31] The venerable African American newspaper the *Chicago Defender*, which sponsored a contest in the summer of 1964 to give away tickets to see a special screening in the Windy City of the Beatles' debut film *A Hard Day's Night*, got bombarded with letters from readers attacking the Fab Four. "Now it's no longer the bird-brained idiots who astound me, but the Beatle brain-washed intelligentsia who go for hysterical kind of entertainment as well," wrote Doris Raynes Johnson. "My youngster, of course, says they are the 'last word.' I must be getting old, or I could agree with him ... Anyway, now that we've got English Beatles, and got 'em loaded with sugar, will somebody bring out the DDT, so we can get rid of 'em before they multiply?"[32] Meantime, some *Chicago Defender* readers referring to themselves "Theophilus and Associates" wrote a letter to the editor of the newspaper calling on the city of Chicago to "Ban the Beatles," and attacked the band members for their "moppy hair and uncouth faces (to put it mildly)."[33] Such attacks, however, often triggered sharp retorts from the band's defenders. Cynthia Jackson, an aspiring African American journalist who wrote the regular "Teen-Town Chatter" column for the *Chicago Defender*, responded to "Theophilus and Associates" with uncompromising zeal:

> You say the Beatles have a degrading influence on our nation, may I ask what is degrading about people having fun and enjoying themselves? I think the enjoyment that young people get from watching a Beatle performance is evident by the smiles that light their faces when these four handsome young men appear on stage. Since when has happiness become degrading?[34]

Impassioned defenses of the Beatles by their Black fans were countered by doubts that some African American intellectuals raised about the band. The poet, essayist, activist, music critic—man of many hats—Amiri Baraka (1934–2014, also known by his birth name, LeRoi Jones)—took a dim view of the Fab Four. As a leading literary figure of the era, Baraka exercised a great deal of influence among Black thinkers and artists alike, and his verdicts on countless matters were read widely and taken seriously. Like Stokely Carmichael, he regarded the Beatles as poachers engaged in a broader systematic campaign—along with other white singers and musicians—of appropriating Black culture. In 1968, Baraka published a book titled *Black Music*, in which he explored what he considered the theft of Black music by white artists. Baraka, a prolific author and lecturer at San Francisco State University, originally from Newark, New Jersey, was in his thirties at the time he wrote the book. In *Black Music*, Baraka utilized a form of prose that mirrored the unique style of his poetic verse, mixing history with commentary about contemporary culture in what amounted to a scathing condemnation of cultural neocolonialism. Turning his attention to the Beatles, Baraka had no kind words for the Liverpool lads, regarding them as appropriators of the basest sort. At one point in the book, Baraka wrote:

> So-called "pop," which is a citified version of Rock 'n' Roll (just as the Detroit-Motown Sound is a slick citified version of older R&B-Gospel influenced forms) also sees to it that those TV jobs, indeed that dollar-popularity, remains white. Not only the Beatles, but any group of Myddle-class white boys who need a haircut and male hormones can be a pop group. That's what pop means. Which is exactly what "cool" was, and even clearer, exactly what Dixieland was, complete with funny hats and funny names ... white boys, in lieu of the initial passion, will always make it about funny hats ... which be their constant minstrel need, the derogation of the real, come out again. Stealing Music ... stealing energy (lives): with their own concerns and lives finally, making it White Music (like influenzaing a shrill rites group). From anyplace, anytime to "We all live in a yellow submarine," with all their fiends, etc., the exclusive white ... exclusive meaning isolated from the rest of humanity ... in the yellow submarine, which shoots nuclear weapons ... They steals, minstrelizes (but here a minstrelsy that "hippens" with cats like Stones and Beatles saying, "Yeh, I got everything I know from Chuck Berry," is a scream dropping the final ... "But I got all the dough ...") ... Actually, the more intelligent the white, the more the realization he has to steal from niggers. They take from us all the way up the line. Finally, what is the difference between Beatles, Stones, etc., and Minstrelsey. Minstrels never convinced anybody they were Black either.[35]

Amiri Baraka's emphasis on appropriation dovetailed with a rising Black Power sentiment in America, especially among younger radicals. The same year Bakara published *Black Music*, 1968, radical activist Eldridge Cleaver's *Soul on Ice*—a combination memoir and essay collection—was published, and it went on to become one of the most influential Black Power books of the decade. Cleaver (1935–1998) had been in and out of prisons for years for a variety of alleged crimes, including petty theft, drug possession, and sexual assault. When he finally emerged from prison in 1966, he went to work for the radical leftist *Ramparts* magazine in San Francisco, which first published the essays that appeared in *Soul on Ice*. Like Amiri Baraka, Cleaver possessed a Beatles fixation, bringing up the band multiple times in his book. He attacked the band for their familiar " 'Yeah! Yeah, Yeah!" refrain from "She Loves You," a form of cultural theft that Cleaver insisted "the Beatles highjacked from Ray Charles." He painted a series of unflattering portraits of the band, claiming "the Beatles were on the scene, injecting Negritude by the ton into whites, in this post-Elvis Presley-beatnik era." He accused "the Beatles of Liverpool" of driving "their hordes of Ultrafeminine fans into catatonia and hysteria. For Beatle fans, having been alienated from their own Bodies so long and so deeply, the effect of these potent, erotic rhythms is electric." Cleaver's closing verdict on the Beatles presented the band as sacrificing African Americans at the altar of rock and roll in order to make the experience of listening to music more holistic one. "The Beatles, the four long-haired lads from Liverpool, are offering up as their gift the Negro's Body, and in so doing establish a rhythmic communication between the listener's own Mind and Body."[36]

For Amiri Baraka and Eldridge Cleaver, the Beatles were not only among the most recent in a long line of cultural appropriators, they were also arguably the most successful. But such arguments were far from the last word on the Beatles among African American intellectuals. A more humanistic perspective came from author, musician, and leftist activist Julius Lester (1939–2018), a writer who possessed a deep understanding of the long history of Black oppression in America without embracing Baraka's incendiary nationalism. Lester adopted a more inclusive form of multiculturalism that emphasized racial harmony. Yet, like Baraka, his perspective was informed by an in-depth knowledge of long history of Black oppression in America. Focusing more on the differing experiences of Black and white Beatles fans, Lester placed fandom itself in the broader historical context of how the two races had interacted with public figures in the United States across the decades. Lester understood that he was writing at a moment in history—in 1967 and 1968—when the masses of African Americans were starting to feel the earliest stirrings of Black Pride for the first time in their long and painful collective history. "These two very different cultures [Black and white] met under what cannot be considered auspicious circumstances," Lester wrote. "The dominant culture sought to destroy the new one. It did not totally succeed, but through slavery, intimidation, and murder it did create in the members of the minority culture a desire to deny that culture and assume the characteristics and ways of the dominant one."[37]

Lester criticized the pervasive white-dominant culture in the United States for reducing "art" to something that "to be commented upon, studied, and understood," rather than something that was to be experienced directly.[38] African Americans, on the other hand, regarded art and music and politics as something more interactive, in which the main participant and the observer were engaged in a conversation that involved a meaningful back-and-forth dialogue. This resulted in forms of cultural expression that were subjected to meaningful verbal exchanges among the men and women and children that consumed them, as opposed to music, art, film and writing that was passively consumed by spectators. Lester perceptively placed Beatles fandom within this understanding of Black culture:

> The black man knows the inherent irrationality of life. Thus, black culture is aimed at the experience. The congregation responds to the preaching by patting the foot and shouting. The blues singer's audience yells back at him, "Take your time, now. Tell it." The audience demands that the performer (preacher, singer, or what have you) relate to them at this level. It is his responsibility. White teen-agers go to hear the Beatles and scream through their entire performance. It isn't because of the music. Their screams obliterate it. It is because of an involvement with the singers. Yet, you never hear a black teen-ager gush over the Temptations like whites do over the Beatles. You will hear black teen-agers sing every line of the Temptations' current song and all their past ones. You will see them imitate every movement the performers make on stage. You can sit in restaurants in the black community and if a particularly meaningful record is played on the jukebox, every person in the place will suddenly start singing.[39]

In the end, there was no uniform opinion among Black intellectuals when it came to the Beatles and their cultural impact on US society. More importantly, the Beatles seldom gravitated to the center of most Black intellectual's radars. Writing at an eventful time of social transformation, upheavals, assassination, and Civil Rights legislation being signed into law in Washington DC, most prominent figures in the Black American intelligentsia paid little attention to the Beatles. They faced concerns in the mid- to late-1960s that they considered more pressing than an English band and their musical influences, and the sounds they—in turn—helped to shape.

Music and the Movement

Two weeks before the Beatles embarked on their historic 1964 North American tour, the bodies of three slain Civil Rights activists—James Chaney, Michael

"Mickey" Schwerner, and Andrew Goodman—were found in a shallow grave in an earthen dam on a farm outside of Philadelphia, Mississippi. This grim discovery came at the end of a massive search throughout the summer of 1964 involving Navy divers and teams of agents from the Federal Bureau of Investigation.[40] Combing the woods and farmlands of rural Mississippi, FBI men unearthed the bodies of two African American teenagers, Charles Eddie Moore and Henry Hezekiah Dee, both of whom disappeared in May. Both young men were victims of Ku Klux Klan violence.[41] The murders of Schwerner, Chaney, and Goodman—three Civil Rights activists who were registering Blacks to vote in Mississippi—generated national and worldwide headlines, due partly to the sheer savagery of the murders, but also because Goodman and Schwerner were white. "It took the deaths of two white men to wake up white America what Black America in the South particularly knew—that you could get murdered for your opinion or wanting to vote," recalled David Goodman, the younger brother of Andrew Goodman.[42]

The Deep South—Mississippi, in particular—seethed with violence in the summer of 1964. Terrorism in the form of bombings, shootings and violence exploded as the Civil Rights Movement launched its most ambitious voter registration drive yet. Spearheaded by the Council of Federated Organizations (COFO)—a coalition consisting of the Southern Christian Leadership Conference (SCLC), the Student Nonviolent Coordinating Committee (SNCC), the Congress of Racial Equality (CORE), and the National Association for the Advancement of Colored People (NAACP)—the epic drive saw armies of volunteers go out and crisscross the state, registering African Americans, old and young, to vote. Participants idealistically referred to their mission as the Mississippi Freedom Summer Project. Countless Black Mississippians who'd never been to a ballot box filled out the requisite paperwork to participate for the first time in American democracy. Tragically, enfranchisement came at an extremely high price. Day after day during that sweltering summer, bombs ripped through churches, bullets shattered windows, and idealistic volunteers from the North—Black and white alike—tasted for the first time the fear and dread that millions of Southern African Americans had known all their lives.[43] The disappearance of the three volunteers in June—and the discovery of their horrifying deaths a few months later—occurred against the backdrop of these explosive tensions, and at the apex of the nonviolent movement to topple Jim Crow segregation.

Beatlemania reached the United States amid these tensions, at the apex of the nonviolent struggle to topple Jim Crow segregation. As it happened, the three murdered Civil Rights workers who became the focus of so much media attention that summer were contemporaries of the Beatles. Andrew Goodman and James Chaney, both born in 1943, were George Harrison's age. Michael "Mickey" Schwerner wasn't quite a year older than Ringo Starr and John Lennon. When the Beatles arrived in America to begin their 1964 tour, stories of the slain Civil Rights workers still appeared on front pages of newspapers, while television network news played grainy footage of the tense voter registration drives across Mississippi. The Beatles paid attention to events in the South during their North American tours, and they sympathized with the Civil Rights Movement.[44] Upon discovering that their September 11 concert at the Gator Bowl in Jacksonville, Florida, was going to be segregated, the Beatles famously threatened to cancel the show. A statement issued five days before the show proclaimed: "We will not appear unless Negroes are allowed to sit anywhere."[45] At the time, a disgusted John Lennon famously remarked: "We never play to segregated audiences and we aren't going to start now. I'd sooner lose our appearance money."[46] Larry Kane, a 21-year-old journalist starting his career at the Top 40 music station WFUN Miami, traveled extensively with the Beatles during their 1964 and 1965 North American tours. He recalled the moment he informed them about the situation in Jacksonville:

> When we were traveling on August 20, 1964, in Las Vegas, I advised them that the Gator Bowl, where they were going to entertain in Jacksonville, Florida, on September 11, 1964, was going to be segregated. So they said, to a man, we're not going to do it. And that gave me a big story. I broke that story and said they would not entertain in the Gator Bowl. That went right up to the wire, and two days before the Gator Bowl, management basically succumbed and said we're not going to segregate people. And for the first time ever, blacks and whites sat together in the Gator Bowl. To make history like that, and to insist on it ... I thought that was pretty amazing.[47]

Ever cautious, Brian Epstein urged John, Paul, George, and Ringo to refrain from discussing racism in public. He feared the issue could potentially be explosive. But unlike most famous musical acts of the day, the Beatles showed no fear when it came to wading into the middle of contentious matters. Indeed, during the golden age of Beatlemania, they were more outspoken when it came to political controversies than any other rock band or singer of the time. More importantly, the Beatles matched their words with their actions by refusing to play in Jim Crow venues. According to historian Kenneth Campbell: "The standard copy of the Beatles' performance contract devised by Brian Epstein stipulated that the Beatles 'not be required to perform in front of a segregated audience.'"[48] Despite their willingness to take risks and speak out, the band members encountered no hostility or resistance when they walked out on the stage at Jacksonville's 32,000-seat Gator Bowl Stadium. The concert was sold out, yet some 9,000 ticket holders did not attend due to damage by Hurricane Dora, and storm winds still blowing up to 45 miles per hour. Ringo Starr's drumkit had to be bolted down to the stage to prevent it from being blown away by the heavy gusts.[49]

The Beatles made history by being the first band to play for a desegregated audience in Jacksonville. Nobody knows how many Black concertgoers were in the audience that day, but this breakthrough still represented a symbolic victory for Civil Rights. Of equal importance, the band toured with two African American acts: singer Clarence "Frogman" Henry, a young rhythm and blues singer and pianist, and a pop music group from Queens, New York, called the Exciters, a quartet of vocalists, three women and one man. Thus, the September 11 concert marked the first time that Blacks performed at the Gator Bowl Stadium. This was no accident. The Beatles approved of the singers and groups that opened for them on their maiden North American tour. The Righteous Brothers, Jackie DeShannon, the Bill Black Combo and the Exciters were all on the opening roster.[50]

Clarence Henry, best known for his 1956 hit "Ain't Got No Home," was 27 in the summer of 1964 when he joined the Beatles on their tour. Henry replaced the Righteous Brothers, who departed from the tour after bitterly complaining about the deafening crowds cheering for the Fab Four while they were singing. For years, Clarence Henry had been performing in local clubs, fairs, and dances in and around New Orleans, joining Bobby Mitchell & the Toppers at age fifteen as a saxophonist and pianist. His familiar croak, which could be heard in several of his songs, earned him the nickname "Frogman."[51] He first encountered the Beatles in 1961, while visiting England. A music promoter he knew "took me to an upstairs club in Piccadilly Circus where they were playing and introduced me to them."[52] By the time he joined the Beatles on their '64 tour, Henry had enjoyed an enormously successful career as a singer, songwriter, and musician, selling more than 4 million albums.[53] The main thing that stood out in Henry's memory about the historic Jacksonville concerts were the sprawling crowds of screaming young females trying to smash through police lines to get to the Beatles. "It really was like a football game. I mean, they were running from the policemen and the policemen were tackling them. I really enjoyed it because it was so comical. And those policemen, man, they were laughing the whole time," Henry recalled.[54]

Five days later, on September 16, the Beatles performed at the City Park Stadium in New Orleans, another southern city that had recently experienced waves of Civil Rights demonstrations against segregation. Following Clarence "Frogman" Henry and the other opening acts, the Beatles walked out on stage and played a half hour of music to thunderous cheers. One of the people in the audience that night was Deacon John Moore, an African American musician specializing in rock, blues, and R&B. He was twenty-three at the time, and already beloved in the community. Moore counted himself among the most enthusiastic fans of the Beatles. He watched them jam with rapt attention, cheering with the crowds, enjoying an evening of memorable music. Decades later, he described his reaction to seeing the Beatles in concert in New Orleans:

> I'd heard the Beatles before they got on *Ed Sullivan,* and I thought they were really refreshing because they incorporated rhythm and blues as well as pop elements and so much of the old and the new. It was totally unique and seeing it during my formative years as a musician, I embraced it. I didn't look at it as a threat to what I was doing, I looked at it as something I could add onto … I didn't look at the Beatles as a fad. I looked at them as a band who revolutionized popular music. I saw it firsthand when I saw the hysteria in the crowd at City Park. I knew right then and there that this was gonna be one of the biggest things ever to hit the music scene.[55]

The Beatles performed the final show of their 1964 North American tour at the Paramount Theater in New York City on September 20. It was a charity concert, the proceeds from which went to support the United Cerebral Palsy of New York City and Retarded Infants Services. The following day, according to a journalist, "the shaggy-maned rock 'n' roll quartet from Liverpool flies back to England, taking approximately $1 million with them from their American tour."[56] Little did the unsuspecting band members know, activists in the SNCC—the organization that played a key role in many important voter registration campaigns in the southern Civil Rights Movement, including the Mississippi Freedom Summer Project—were busily working behind the scenes toward the goal of staging a Beatles benefit concert, similar to the big affair at the Paramount Theater, to raise funds for their organization and elevate its profile.

SNCC was founded by April 1960 by mostly young people, yet they received mentoring from the revered elder Civil Rights activist Ella Baker, by then in her fifties.[57] Like so many Civil Rights organizations, SNCC sought out the support and endorsements of famous people—movie and television stars, musicians, authors, politicians, and so forth—which they hoped would make the public more aware of their struggle, and add contributions to their meager war chest. A flurry of letters and memos went back and forth between various SNCC offices, addressing the possibility of a Beatles fundraising concert. A SNCC fundraising manual from 1964 suggested an approach to such an undertaking:

> If the New York SNCC office wanted to reach a large audience of students and young adults … they might decide to have a rock and roll show, since discotheque is very "in" at the moment. To pull in more people, James Brown or the Beatles could be added; to enhance ticket sales even more,

all volunteer ticket sellers could be invited to meet the star at a party after the show.[58]

Constancia Romilly, a tireless SNCC organizer, partner of activist James Forman and daughter of British socialist Esmond Romilly and author Jessica Mitford, was determined to organize a Beatles benefit concert for SNCC. On July 9, 1965, Romilly wrote to her friend Joan Baez, asking for help in lining up the Fab Four for a fundraiser show: "For some time there has been a rumor floating around that the Beatles might be willing to do something for SNCC ... We have let this drift so long that it has now become urgent, as the Beatles are expected in the U.S. shortly."[59] Upon receiving Brian Epstein's contact information from Manuel Greenhill, Baez's manager, Romilly wrote back requesting an alternative approach. "We had hoped that there might be a more personal way to contact the Beatles than through Mr. Epstein. We had heard through various people that the Beatles (which one I don't know) had indicated that they might be willing to do something for SNCC."[60] Meantime, in Atlanta, full-time SNCC worker Betty Garman Robinson wrote to her SNCC comrades in the New York office in early August suggesting a more aggressive effort to recruit the Beatles. "It seems to me that we missed our chance to get the Beatles to do a benefit this time around, but that we can do several things immediately," Robinson wrote. "First we need to establish contact with them ... Then we must some way get to them so that SNCC people can meet with them to talk—if nothing else. We might pull off a quick reception in some city ... or (am I dreaming) they might even make some kind of press statement. It just seems that there are possibilities if we'll just follow up."[61]

Ultimately, the SNCC Beatles benefit concert never happened. Other memos and letters circulated among SNCC workers, all suggesting that other people follow up on leads that were murky at best. The band is frequently mentioned in SNCC correspondence between the fall of 1964 and summer of 1965. One organizer issued a grim "Beatles update": "Agent is a bastard, but someone who knows him has been working on it."[62] Meantime, SNCC organizer Bobbi Jones apprised a fellow activist of the situation in August 1965: "Nothing from the Beatles yet!"[63] Later that month, Betty Garman Robinson—growing anxious in the Atlanta office—nudged Bobbi Jones: "I gather not too much came from the Beatles."[64] Alas, nothing ever materialized. Plagued by the absence of any sort of concrete plan, the limitations of poor communications, and the titanic hurdle of contacting the Beatles, even modest proposals for an intimate after-concert fundraiser were doomed from the outset. However, the very fact that high-level workers in SNCC—a major Civil Rights organization that was one of the main engines of the movement— aspired to line up the Beatles for such an event is remarkable, in and of itself. The Beatles had developed a reputation for being outspoken when it came to issues of racial equality, and committed activists regarded them as loyal allies of the Civil Rights Movement. Of how many other singers and groups in the mid-1960s could that be said?

Mixed Receptions

The Beatles returned to North America in August 1965, and again a year later, in August 1966, for two more tours before they ceased public shows to focus on recording music in London's EMI Abbey Road studios. The band made history on August 15, 1965, for their epic concert at Shea Stadium in Flushing Meadows, New York, the largest event of its kind ever held up to that point. "Over 55,000 people saw the Beatles at Shea Stadium. We took $304,000, the greatest gross ever in the history of show business," boasted music promoter Sid Bernstein.[65] The Shea Stadium concert became more famous—or infamous—for the deafening roar of its vast crowd than the performance of the Beatles, which could not be heard above the din by most of the people packed into the arena that night. Peter Simon, an eighteen-year-old photographer with a passion for taking pictures of protests and rock concerts, trekked to Shea Stadium that night with his 35 mm camera.[66]

Standing outside the immense facility, he began snapping pictures of heading into the show. One of the images he captured showed three excited African American girls moving through the crowd.[67] It was one of many pictures he snapped that night. Once developed, the photograph proved to be a poignant capture of three excited fans, one with a camera hanging around her neck, walking purposefully, sharing the experience of the Beatles' music. Simon's camera captured images of countless other ebullient young fans that night, and he took photos of the band members performing on stage. But it was his photo of the three female Black concertgoers that remind future generations that the Beatles' American fan base reflected the multicultural nature of the society from whence it emerged. Other photographs of fans taken during the height of Beatlemania—1964 to 1966—confirmed this fact (see Figure 4.2).

But African Americans have never been a monolithic population within American society, and in the mid-1960s, a range of opinions existed among them when it came to the Beatles, from enthusiasm to apathy to hostility. A vocal segment of the Black population in the United States at the time did not necessarily dislike the Beatles, but the Fab Four's music did not resonate with them. Such was the case with an unidentified African American university undergraduate who explained the difference between white and Black students to a writer for *Ebony* magazine in 1968: "They are talking about the

FIGURE 4.2 *Fans gathered outside the Delmonico Hotel in New York City to cheer for the Beatles during the band's North American tour, ahead of their concert in Forest Hills, August 28, 1964. Photographs such as this one showed African American fans, who were also part of the Beatles fan experience.*
Source: *Photo by Staff/Mirrorpix via Getty Images.*

Beatles, and we are digging James Brown. They are doing dances Harlem was doing five months ago, and we are doing dances Harlem is doing now. They are talking about reforming the system, we are talking about destroying it."[68]

Twenty years later, in 1988, author, music critic, and filmmaker Nelson George expressed a similar opinion about the Beatles, but in more detail, in his book The *Death of Rhythm & Blues*. Reflecting on the coming of rock and roll in the 1950s, with a focus on the enormously influential Chuck Berry and other pioneering early Black rock and rollers, George despaired over changes in the 1960s, and took a decidedly dismissive view of the Beatles when he wrote:

> With the coming of the Beatles, Blacks, too, in an extension of their fifties attitude, saw rock & roll as white boys' music that didn't reflect their musical taste or cultural experience. That doesn't mean no black teens or adults bought Beatles records. Nor does it mean they wouldn't eventually be influenced in some way by them. But by and large, black record buyers and black musicians were moving in another direction, one that would dominate their musical, cultural, and, to some degree, even their political style for the rest of the 1960s. In black America, R&B was about to become

"soul," a word which would in its day rival "rock & roll" for social currency and commercial exploitation ... Poor old rock & roll, like blues, swing, and even doo wop and some of the less impassioned elements of R&B, was history to Blacks.[69]

Writing a mere twenty years after the fact, Nelson George—like other chroniclers of the tumultuous 1960s from the vantage point of the 1980s—was close enough to the events he was describing to see them with clarity, but far enough away to gauge initial impacts. The sentiments he expressed in his book captured attitudes held by certain African Americans at the time about the Beatles.

And yet, like so many writers who generalize and overstate their cases, George was engaging in excessive cherry-picking to suit his own ends. In two brief yet sweeping sentences, he dismissed Black Beatles fans as insignificant and not worthy of attention. In the end, his observations say a great deal more about George's values in 1988 than what was actually happening in the United States in 1964, 1965, and 1966. In a country as complex as the United States, one need only turn the prism slightly to discover an entirely different view of the nation's remarkably varied past.

There were African Americans who fell outside of Nelson George's limited scope, and did not share his feelings about the Beatles. Bonnie Greer, a native of Chicago, was one of those diehard African American Beatles fans who defied conventional wisdom. She loved the Beatles, she collected and cherished their albums, and their influence on her was profound and shaped her life in meaningful ways. Decades later, Greer—a celebrated award-winning playwright, critic, and radio personality in the United Kingdom—looked back with fondness on a sense of empowerment she developed as a young Beatles fan in the Windy City:

> I had been a black girl growing up on the south side of Chicago, in the civil rights movement, the black student's movement, Bobby Kennedy, all of it, but then there were the Beatles. They gave me agency. I moved to the UK because of them. Weird that it took four boys from Liverpool to do that. Through all their permutations, the Beatles were like Oz or Alice in Wonderland, a passageway to another world.[70]

In her adult life, Bonnie Greer achieved the status of literary star in her newly adopted country of Great Britain. Her impressive literary achievements proved numerous and varied, and the accolades came to her steadily. Appointed to the Order of the British Empire, Greer was also appointed Fellow of the Royal Society of Literature in London. And yet, even as a celebrity author of many books who made frequent appearances on television, Greer never forgot her childhood in Chicago and her debt to the Beatles. She was but one of numerous Beatles fans who happened to be African Americans. Not all of them achieved her stature or level of fame. But it is safe to say that the famous foursome from Liverpool likely left an impression on many of them that was almost as meaningful as the one they made on Bonnie Greer.

5

Beatlemania's Discontents

In the late twentieth and early twenty-first centuries, a myriad of documentaries, books, websites, and other retrospectives about the Beatles accentuated the positive by focusing on the band's remarkable accomplishments, vibrant legacies, and enduring musical contributions. Often contained in these narratives were references—sometimes detailed, sometimes brief—to the band's dedicated and boisterous fan base. Yet these accounts overlooked a sizable portion of the American population in 1964, 1965, and 1966 that detested the band during the heyday of Beatlemania. No music is everybody's cup of tea, and the Beatles were no exception. Plenty of people who disliked the Beatles—young and old alike—simply could not stand their early music. In the days before the increasingly complex music of the Beatles' Middle and Late Periods, the feel-good Beatles tunes being heard on the radio rubbed certain listeners the wrong way. "I think the Beatles are among the worst groups I've ever heard," said John Sullivan, general manager of radio station WNEW in New York City, mere days after the group debuted on the *Ed Sullivan Show*. "But then I've got two daughters in their fan age bracket, and they think the Beatles are tremendous."[1]

But detractors had other reasons for disliking the Beatles: some hated their fashion style (particularly their hair) and their nonstop irreverence, while others despised the Beatles without really listening to their music or paying much attention to the band, merely because legions of young American women and men loved them. Coincidentally, a small yet well-organized element of the conservative movement came to regard the Beatles as enemies of right-wing values, with some extremists insisting that John, Paul, George, and Ringo were all four pawns in a communist conspiracy—extending to the Kremlin in Moscow—to control the nation's youth. Whatever animosities that detractors voiced, the deep divisions fostered by the Beatles foreshadowed the coming polarization that existed alongside the upheavals of the late 1960s and early 1970s.

"We Hate You, Beatles ..."

For a band boasting so many upbeat and catchy hits in the mid-1960s—among them, "She Loves You," "I Want to Hold Your Hand," "Love Me Do," and "I Saw Her Standing There"—the Beatles turned out to be a surprisingly polarizing force in American life during the first few years of Beatlemania. Much of the controversy surrounding the Beatles had to do with their hair, which was considered by millions of Americans at the time to be outrageously long. Grown-ups, especially older adults, thought the Beatles appeared unkempt, and were long overdue to visit the barbershop. "My father thinks their haircuts are against society," said thirteen-year-old Linda Zimmerman, head of the World Wide Beatle Fan Club and a student at L. J. Hauser Junior High School in Riverside, Illinois.[2] In August 1964, a mother and self-proclaimed "Beatle hater" from Philadelphia lamented the struggle she faced trying to convince her "Beatle lover" son to visit the barber: "My son's hair hasn't been cut for six months. He is laughed at and jeered at. But does it bother him? Oh no! He just goes on his merry Beatle way ... So when I see my son on the street, I always cross over to the other side."[3]

Nationwide, bans on long hair in public schools—triggered by the success of the Beatles—led to waves of student suspensions, with countless young males being sent home for violating school rules. Donald Rogers, a thirteen-year-old student at Orange Glen Elementary School in Escondido, California, was suspended for growing his hair over his ears. The school's "student handbook" contained a rule that students must come to school with "neatly groomed hair, properly combed." Principal Ron Jahelka insisted that suspending Rogers was not excessive. "We are not looking for a close order drill in our students. We hope students will project their own personality. But there are better ways to do it," he said.[4] Donald Rogers was but one of countless adolescent boys who endured such treatment. For a time, in 1964 and 1965, the Beatles' hair turned into a national obsession. It was discussed on television, radio, in magazines and newspapers, and in press conferences and interviews with John, Paul, George, and Ringo. Grown-ups maintained a laser focus on it. Men and women alike addressed the topic, often in strident tones, in letters-to-the editor sections of newspapers across the country. "We put up with that noise from one of our own [Elvis Presley], until the Army got him to grow up. Do we have to go through it again with these fugitives from a barber shop? At least they could get haircuts and look like males, instead of sloppy, unkempt girls," wrote Vivian K. Ruby of East Hartford, Connecticut, a week after the Beatles arrived at John F. Kennedy Airport in February.[5] A rage-filled father from Cincinnati echoed Ruby's sentiments, but in a more violent manner: "I took one angry look at those sissy, degenerate Beatles and informed my son if I ever caught him with hair like that I would knock him from one end of the room to the other and give him a good swift kick into the cellar!"[6]

It would be a mistake, however, to assume that national conversations about the Beatles' hair in the months following their *Ed Sullivan Show* debut were *solely* about hair. Much more was at stake than four young lads from Liverpool sorely in need of a trim. The big hair kerfuffle of 1964—like the anti-rock and roll hysteria of the 1950s—grew out of deeper anxieties about nonconformity, eroding social norms, waning deference to authority, changing values, and the very future of the country itself. Hence, negative comments about the Beatles' hair often accompanied critiques of their style of dress, their singing, and their generally irreverent attitudes. Lucy Hagen, an infuriated Beatlephobe from Wood River, Illinois, wrote a letter to the editor of her local newspaper in late February 1964 attacking the Beatles for their hair, lyrics, and antics on stage. While she was at it, she took aim at their female fans as well:

> Other than padding the coffers from the United Kingdom, I fail to see what a bunch of gyrating, guitar-strumming, long-haired boys can do that our own kids can't—or should I say won't because of their pride. As for the Beatles singing, I've heard better voices in a hog-calling contest. Their wiggling and squirming reminded me of a woolly worm on a pin, or a boy whose teacher wouldn't let him leave the room. The silly, fainting, screaming little girls have a lot of work to do before then can be welcomed into the status of womanhood.[7]

Such over-the-top verdicts such as this one were far from unusual. In fact, the more zealous Beatlephobes did not simply dislike the Beatles. A relatively unadorned comment such as, "I don't like the Beatles' music," would never suffice for the true antagonist. An authentic anti-Beatles declaration relied on streams of hyperbole, adding layer upon layer of insults in overstated critiques, so there was absolutely no question in the mind of the impartial observer where the hater stood on the matter. William Long, a disgruntled resident of Brevard, North Carolina, best exemplified this scorched-earth approach, finding absolutely no redeeming qualities in the band. He wrote a letter to the editor of the *Asheville Citizen-Times*, attacking the Beatles for a host of reasons. "Their music (and I use the word very loosely) has rhythm and that's all it has," Long wrote. "How can one enjoy their asinine qualities is beyond me. Yet they make millions of dollars acting like imbeciles. What's worse, the ludicrous display has desecrated the great name of Carnegie Hall. Their only call to fame is their ability to capitalize on the capriciousness, immaturity, and conformity of youth."[8] Other haters placed a stronger emphasis on appearance, going after the band members for their hair, their clothes, and even their facial features. A Mississippian who went by the initials J.R. unleashed a barrage of jabs at the Fab Four's looks mere days after they took the country by storm on national television. "Anybody who thinks the Beatles are cute better have their eyes examined. Either these people are very homely and think the Beatles are cute because they look better than them, or they have never seen what they really look like under all that hair. I've seen better looking boys in *Mad Magazine*," J.R. concluded.[9] Such attitudes abounded in the pages of the mainstream press. The *Minneapolis Star*, for example, a newspaper with a sizable readership (it called itself the "Largest Daily Newspaper in the Upper Midwest") furnished a harsh verdict on the Beatles in one of its official editorials: "They could easily be mistaken for four unpasteurized fugitives from Dogpatch on the lam from the revenuers for whomping up Kickapoo juice. They cannot sing much. They aren't outstanding on guitar and drum. They aren't even particularly good muggers."[10]

Some self-proclaimed "Beatle haters" claimed in interviews with journalists that they'd formed "clubs," luring like-minded adherents to their cause. These anti-Beatles clubs set up shop all over America—in big cities and small towns alike——in the spring and summer of 1964. Disc jockey Tom Winstead, host of a program on WSSC, a Christian radio station in Sumter, South Carolina (1340 kHz on the A.M. dial), used his bully pulpit on the airwaves to start a Stamp Out the Beatles Club. Unfortunately for Winstead, his plan backfired. Rather than attracting new members, he provoked the ire of Beatles fans across the state, leading to a flood of hostile letters.[11] In San Francisco, local youths launched a Beatles Haters Association that "carried anti-Beatle signs and an American flag" to local Beatles events. At one such gathering, held in September in San Francisco's Union Square, association members clashed with Beatles fans (see Figure 5.1). "Tomatoes flew and signs were trampled, as awed adults watched the performance without budging, except to sidestep a tomato now and then," noted one account. Greatly outnumbered, the few members of the Beatles Haters Association that bothered to show up quickly fled the scene, learning the hard way that large crowds of irate Fab Four fans could be a fearsome spectacle.[12]

The first known Beatle Haters Club, formed at St. Mary's Grade School in Bismarck, North Dakota, the day after the historic *Ed Sullivan Show* performance, garnered much press coverage, and spawned countless imitators.[13] Around the same time, brothers Don and Robert Engelhardt of Massillon, Ohio, started their own Anti-Beatles Club, insisting the lads from Liverpool were "just ruining the reputation of their own country" and "wasting their time, and the time of the teenagers who watch them."[14] An Anti-Beatles Club sprang

FIGURE 5.1 *Beatles fan club members, Helena Rand, Linda Schooley, Danielle Anderson, and Lee McGurr at the Hilton Hotel in San Francisco, looking forward to the Beatles' arrival, August 14, 1964. San Francisco was but one city where Beatles fans clashed with Beatles haters, with the former outnumbering the latter. Source: Photo by John McBride/San Francisco Chronicle via Getty Images.*

up in Chicago under the motto: "We hate you, Beatles, O, yes we dooo."[15] In Pittsburgh, nineteen-year-old Tom Buschek and his chums formed an Anti-Beatles Association that "offered membership cards to anyone interested by writing to Box 1722, Pittsburgh."[16] In Oakland, California, the television editor at the *Oakland Tribune*, Bob MacKenzie, boasted that he organized "STAB"—the Society To Abolish Beatles. "The members," he wrote, "shave themselves bald and wear pants so fat that two people can stand in each leg."[17]

The Beatle haters clubs were nothing more than short-lived publicity stunts, aimed at generating provocative headlines. There is no evidence of any of them lasting beyond a few months, at the longest. Unlike Beatles fan clubs, they had no elected officers, they did not meet regularly, nobody paid dues or kept membership rolls, no one produced any newsletters, and nothing even vaguely resembling a sense of community was established. These were "clubs" in name only, fueled by the misanthropy of people who despised the Beatles and the extensive coverage afforded to them by a press that was overtly hostile to the band in the early months of Beatlemania. But the Beatle haters clubs did serve one purpose: they triggered a lot of Beatles fans, incurring their wrath far and wide, which was a goal of the people who organized them.

Almost without exception, press coverage of anti-Beatles groups led to avalanches of outraged letters, mostly from teens who adored the Liverpool foursome. In the 1960s—indeed, throughout much of the twentieth century—letters to the editor sections of newspapers in the United States functioned as the most important form of pre-internet social media. They were vital public forums—robust hubs of community commentary—in which citizens weighed in on a host of issues, from local concerns to global events. The wars of words that frequently erupted in the pages of newspapers at this time assumed a significance beyond that of Beatles fans overreacting to jabs at their idols. Newspapers were one of the few arenas of debate in which citizens representing a wide spectrum of opinions could make their opinions known to other people. When the Beatle haters clubs sprang up and began contacting their local media outlets, the fans nearly always took the bait, and clashes ensued. And nowhere were deep cultural rifts over the Beatles in the United States more apparent than in the letters to the editor sections of newspapers. The band's defenders struck back against critics with a ferocity that was uncompromising. When a student at Langley High School in Pittsburgh found out about the city's newly formed Anti-Beatles Association, she put pen to paper to voice her vehement disapproval: "Boy, what a stupid club! I'm so mad I could spit. You boys are just jealous because the girls are swooning over the Beatles and not over you. Well, I think you're a bunch of eggheads and you probably won't even get girls in your club."[18]

"Unrecognizable Beings"

In addition to critiquing the Beatles, Beatlephobic Americans routinely attacked the band's screaming throngs of fans. As noted earlier in this book, communities of dedicated enthusiasts were by no means new to the American pop culture landscape in 1964. But the size, scope, and intensity of Beatlemania dwarfed all previous examples of fandom in the United States. Beatlemaniacs were plentiful across North America, and they were—by and large—steadfastly committed to defending the band. When John, Paul, George, and Ringo came under attack—in print and broadcasts—fans could be counted on to respond with decisive and resounding pushback. It was this zeal, readily evident to anyone who dared criticize the Beatles publicly, that left certain people troubled.

Within months of the Beatles' February 1964 US debut, Beatlephobia had lost the edge and newness it once had, and quirky feature stories in newspapers about Beatle haters had largely dried up by the fall of 1965. Dislike of the Beatles was soon eclipsed by deeper concerns about the ardor that countless fans—especially female fans—exhibited in public. They screamed. They chanted. They carried signs. They formed clubs. At concerts, they were known to collectively batter against police and private security guards. There were reports of female fans fainting at events. By the end of the Beatles' 1964 North American tour, there was already a narrative taking shape that the band could not be heard above the deafening roar of cheering concertgoers. Such behavior sounded alarm bells from coast to coast. Among some nervous grown-ups, there was a growing sense that the youth of the nation had fallen under the spell of the Fab Four, and that the fans themselves posed a threat to law, order, and the dominant mores of the period.

One of the people leading the charge was a prominent legal figure from Ohio, Hamilton County Juvenile Court Judge Benjamin Schwartz, who appeared in a short film shot days after the Beatles' 29-minute-long concert at Cincinnati Gardens on August 27, 1964. The judge—by then in his fifties, stern faced, with a receding hairline, and a dark suit and striped tie—appeared in stark black-and-white footage, situated between the seal of the state of Ohio on his right and an American flag to his left. He looked directly at the camera as he spoke, expressing shock and outrage about the actions of "14,000 children, a great majority being girls." Many of the "youngsters" at the concert, he said, attended without adult chaperones. Lacking proper supervision, pandemonium erupted at the concert, sweeping through the venue in an alarming manner. Judge Schwartz told the audience:

> And the whole show was based upon producing hysteria ... And then these girls went into a coma. They ranted, they fainted. Their eyes were glassy. Some pulled their hair out. Some tore their dresses. They threw notes of a very undesirable nature on the stage. Some girls after the performance kissed the stage. Some went up and kissed the very seats in which the Beatles had sat ... One father brought a child who was epileptic, and the child had an epileptic fit.[19]

Little is known about the footage of Judge Schwartz filmed after the Beatles' Cincinnati concert—how it was used, or whether it reached its intended audience. But it would later resurface on YouTube in the 2010s and become a cult favorite in the tradition of the antimarijuana scare movie *Reefer Madness* (1936). The film fit into a larger effort by Judge Schwartz to caution his fellow

Ohioans about the dangers of the Beatles. "It's a hysteria these kids go into that can have only a bad effect on their relations with other teenagers, especially in social relations," Schwartz told a mass gathering of 400 people at a public event in Cincinnati in August.[20] Because of his stature in the community, Schwartz could draw big crowds and attract ample press coverage. Certain people listened to what he had to say, and took his warnings seriously. Schwartz added his voice to a rising chorus of critics who expressed concerns about the Beatles and their fans. Not all of these concerned individuals were taken seriously. But those with expertise in matters related to the mass behavior of fans spoke with a credibility that sometimes won them wide audiences.

In the mid-1960s, experts still held sway over the American public. The Vietnam War was in its early stages, not yet a catastrophe, and the upheavals and polarization that would characterize the later decade were a few years away. Experts on nearly every topic—from relationships to automobiles, from politics to etiquette, from science to sports—shared their expertise in the pages of newspapers and magazines, and on television and radio airwaves. Previous generations of experts had been a mainstay in progressive America of the early twentieth century, and during the heyday of liberalism in the 1930s and 1940s. Their opinions, rooted in rational thought, came from their advanced education, characterized by prolonged and in-depth training in their chosen disciplines. These "experts" helped to shape what would become the conventional wisdom of their times. Describing "the expert's aspirations" as "modest," political scientist Andrew J. Taylor characterized these "practical" specialists thusly: "Though he may display a missionary's zeal to remake the world, his contribution to collective knowledge and human flourishing is limited to his field. His approach is also largely empirical."[21]

Experts who specialized in youth-related issues were especially in demand during the postwar era—those pivotal twenty-five years after the Second World War, in which the United States experienced unprecedented economic growth and the first stirrings of dramatic cultural transformations. Thanks to the baby boom, parenting experts in the 1940s, 1950s, and 1960s looked out upon a gigantic demographic of the American public looking to purchase the latest how-to advice books on child rearing, and eager to consume advice. Bestsellers such as Benjamin Spock's *The Common Sense Book of Baby and Child Care* (1946), Hilde Bruch's *Don't Be Afraid of Your Child* (1952), and John Bowlby's *Childhood and the Growth of Love* (1953) became ubiquitous in the baby boom years, luring parents to bookstores and undergoing multiple updated editions. Meantime, leading experts such as physicians, psychiatrists, social workers, politicians, and pundits debated about the most effective methods of parenting, especially the thorny issue of whether mothers and fathers were being overly permissive with their children. In the March 1960 issue of *Parents' Magazine*, Katherine Oettinger, chief of the US Children's

Bureau, warned with grim authority that "our underlying adult attitude toward youth" was contributing to the rise of juvenile delinquency across the country. "No single area of child-rearing has recently experienced such rapid pendulum swings as discipline. In trying to give children freedom to develop, parents just released the brakes. But now we hear more about the need to set limits for the child and less about the dangers of repression," Oettinger told the magazine.[22]

But there never existed a consensus among child-rearing experts about the best way to raise boys and girls. Opinions varied widely, from specialists who advocated extreme laissez-faire approaches to those arguing for parents to employ a firmer hand, including—if need be—corporal punishment, such as spankings. "It doesn't make any sense to lay down one firm rule for all kinds of 13—or 14 or 15, or any other age. Because some children grow up fast and some don't. Some kids mature physically at 12. Others don't reach this change until 16 or so," advised Gunnar Dybwad, a sociologist, father of teenagers, and director of the Child Study Association of America, a venerable New York-based parent-education organization founded in 1888.[23] By contrast, FBI director J. Edgar Hoover insisted in 1959 that what he called the "emergency of juvenile delinquency" happening in the United States was partly due to parents engaged in "pampering, overprotection, making excuses and cooing soft words when a firm hand across the seat of the trousers would be more appropriate." Hoover reserved his harshest words for "doting mothers and fathers" who could not bring themselves to firmly discipline their children, which—in his view—resulted in those youths developing "contempt for authority" and becoming "fickle, aimless and confused." The undisciplined child of today, Hoover cautioned, could well turn into the "unruly, outspoken, rock-and-roll addict" of tomorrow, who "cruises the streets in a 'souped-up' jalopy, shouting insults out the window. In appearance, he aspires to looking 'shaggy' and to leaving behind the impression that he has not been near a barber shop in weeks."[24]

This cultural divide among experts persisted into the 1960s, and it was readily apparent when the Beatles arrived in the United States. Giving voice to views that aligned closely with those of Judge Benjamin Schwartz and J. Edgar Hoover, the psychiatrist Bernard Saibel—a child guidance expert for the Washington State Division of Community Services—expressed utter horror over the behavior of concertgoers after seeing the Beatles perform at the Seattle Center Coliseum on August 21, 1964. He recorded his impressions that served as a warning to other adults to beware of the Beatles' frightening influence over their unruly followers. The band's fans—especially the "girls"— got swept away, Saibel said, by "mass hypnosis, contagious hysteria, and the blissful feeling of being mixed up in an all-embracing, orgiastic experience." Saibel wandered around the concert, squeezing his way through a packed crowd of screaming attendees, watching startling things unfold before his very eyes. "The hysteria and loss of control go far beyond the impact of the music," he wrote. "Many of those present became frantic, hostile, uncontrollable, screaming, unrecognizable beings. If this is possible—and it is—parents and adults have a lot to account for to allow this to go on." The "children," as Saibel called the predominantly youthful crowd of approximately 14,300 people, entered into "a mad, erotic world of their own without the reassuring safeguards of protection from themselves." As if those words were not vivid enough, Saibel himself slipped into a kind of possessed state while writing his memorable account of the concert, eventually arriving at the following conclusion:

> Why do the kids scream, faint, gyrate and in general look like a primeval, protoplasmic upheaval and go into ecstatic convulsions when certain identifiable and expected trademarks come forth, such as 'oh yeah!' a twist of the hips or the thrusting out of an electric guitar? Well, this music (and the bizarre, gnome-like fairy-tale characters who play it) belongs to the kids and is their own—different, they think, from anything that belongs to the adult world. Every time a teenager screams over this music he thumbs his nose with impunity and with immunity at an adult or several adults.[25]

Saibel's editorial in the *Seattle Times* was reprinted widely across the United States, appearing in the *Washington Post*, *Boston Globe*, *Hartford Courant*, and *Chicago Tribune*, among many other papers. Even in its day, it was dismissed as overblown in irate letters to the editor, including ones written by readers who weren't Beatles fans. For example, Charles H. Hapgood, a professor of History at Keene State College in Keene, New Hampshire, called Saibel's column a "lucubration" in a letter to the *Boston Globe*, and he took the psychologist to task for his views. "We all know that teenagers have more emotion than they know what to do with. It is the essential fact of adolescence. The important thing is to give this emotion a harmless outlet. The Beatles do not create the emotion. They do not make our children adolescent," Hapgood reasoned.[26]

Still, it was not hard to find prominent individuals who were as outspoken in their contempt for the Beatles, and disrespectful toward their fans, as Saibel. Inez Robb, a long-time nationally syndicated columnist and former Second World War correspondent, attended a Beatles concert—one of their early US shows, in February—and had a similar reaction to the Washington psychiatrist. The Beatles, Robb complained, could not be heard above the "mass hysteria." Taken aback by the lack of parent chaperones at the venue, Robb felt dismayed by the repeated outbursts of screaming and the unrestrained emotions she witnessed all around her that night. " 'Squalid' is the only word for it," she wrote of the event, referring to fans as "exhibitionists" who "would once have been quickly committed for certifiable lunacy and mercifully restrained some place where they could do themselves no harm. The glassy-eyed, adenoidal girl, always on the verge of knee-jerky hysteria, who comprise the Beatles' camp followers and television audience, ... were only interested in an excuse for lapsing into the squealing syndrome with its accompanying spastic movements."[27] Similarly, in an address to the International Congress of Social Psychiatry in the summer of 1964, Joost Meerloo, a professor at Columbia University and a member of the New York School of Psychiatry, likened the beat in Beatles songs to pre-Second World War "Nazi rallies." "Collective madness does exist," Joost said, in the form of the "rhythmic shouting of slogans and the urge to twist and shake ... Rhythm in one person provokes rhythm in others."[28]

Most of Beatlemania's discontents were not as apoplectic—or colorful in their choice of words—as Schwartz, Saibel, Robb, or Meerloo. Instead, they adopted a subtler tack. More moderate detractors typically opted for a dismissive and condescending tone toward Beatles fans, as if to assure parents that the pandemonium that accompanied the band's 1964 tour would soon pass into history. Case in point: New York psychiatrist Jane Vorhaus Gang, who believed the band's legions of young followers would one day outgrow their love of Fab Four. "The teenager, after all, is entitled to be young," she wrote. "You can't expect girls of 15 or 16 to have a mature set of values. They are trying their wings at this age, and hero worship is a fairly normal and harmless way to go about it. The bobby-soxer, with all her silly behaviour, often turns out to be the responsible PTA chairman of tomorrow."[29] When asked about a teenage female Beatles fan who was obsessed with the band and avidly collected Fab Four merchandise, Alvin S. Baraff, a psychologist at Emory University in Atlanta, warned that she was running the risk of missing out on finding "an exciting new boyfriend." "When a girl is raving about the Beatles, the boy she's talking to gets no feeling at all that she's likely interested in him," advised Baraff. "He isn't likely to ask her for a date when in effect she's engaged to a Beatle—or to all four of them."[30] Yet, unlike a lot of experts at the time, who preferred to emphasize the perils that went along with being too immersive in Beatles fan culture, Baraff ended his advice on a hopeful note:

> Still, the craze is probably filling a big need in this girl's life. She has the fun of collecting something, the satisfaction of belonging to a group, an excuse to scream off steam. Also, here's an area in which she can be tops—a real expert. It's nice for a person to be very enthusiastic about something. However, it's even nicer when one is very interested in many things because then he or she is a more interesting person. So as the Beatle craze diminishes, which I think it will, I hope this girl will invest her energies in several new and more constructive interests.[31]

Other prominent experts adopted a similar approach, predicting Beatlemania would be a short-lived fad, and out-of-control fans would soon reclaim their sanity. Not only would the Beatles slip into obscurity and take their place on the ash heap of pop culture history, many people "in the know" predicted, but their fans would grow up and leave their childish ways behind. Milton Senn, a pioneering child psychiatrist and director of the Child Study Center at Yale University, made that very prediction when he concluded: "Going without haircuts and baths is not a new phenomenon. It's partly rebellion against what others expect from them at school and at home. Eventually they change and will overbathe and comb hair endlessly."[32]

Not all experts held negative views of the Beatles. Widely varied opinions could be found in these increasingly divided times. Indeed, the Beatles had spirited defenders among America's high-profile public intelligentsia. A more sympathetic viewpoint came from the prominent television psychologist and advice columnist Joyce Brothers, who admitted that even though she found the Beatles "loud, vulgar, [and] ridiculous," she could understand why they were so attractive to their fans, especially adolescent girls. She chose to accentuate the androgynous qualities of the members, which—in a music genre (rock and roll) filled with masculine performers—proved to be a big draw for teenage females. "The Beatles display a few mannerisms which almost seem a shade on the feminine side, such as the tossing of their long manes of hair," Brothers observed. "These are exactly the mannerisms which very young female fans (in the 10-to-14 age group) appear to go wildest over."[33] Ralph Greenson, who gained notoriety as Marilyn Monroe's psychiatrist, arrived at a similar conclusion to Joyce Brothers. "Girls of 12, 13, 14, 15 and even 16 are fearful of getting involved with a man of 23 or 24. Whether they know it or not, these girls are using the Beatles as a compromise. The Beatles seem so young and kidlike and feminine, with their long hair and youthful ways, they pose no sexual threat. There is something of the baby about them. And that's why the teenagers are attracted."[34] Not many experts loved the Beatles during the heyday of Beatlemania, but the less adversarial ones liked to point out that the group was far from malevolent. "I don't see anything to worry about unless it gets out of control, unless we have 13- and 14-year-olds running all over town without any parental control and being destructive," said Robert Solow, a psychiatrist from Beverly Hills.[35]

Lastly, to counteract the band's harsher critics, a handful of knowledgeable figures ventured out onto a limb and insisted the Beatles might even be recording worthwhile music. A few bold souls even went so far as to suggest that adults ought to try listening to the music before passing judgment on it. University of Cincinnati psychology professor Howard Lyman had enough chutzpah to suggest that the Beatles actually possessed talent. "By and large, the Beatles are a fairly decent bunch of kids who have somehow or other caught the imagination of the teenagers," Lyman insisted. "Another thing: These youngsters (the Beatles) have a fair amount of ability. A few of their numbers are not too bad to listen to—even from the standpoint of a person my age." When asked about Saibel's controversial column arguing that a Beatles concert was an "orgiastic experience for teenagers," Lyman did not mince words in offering his opinion about the eminent psychiatrist. "He's a stuffed shirt, and you can say I said so."[36]

"Anti-Popes" and "Teen-Age Communists"

Early disagreements about the Beatles in the United States were, for the most part, relatively apolitical in nature. Arguments about the Fab Four's talents, appearance, and other qualities were not situated at easily identifiable points along a traditional left-right political spectrum. People simply did not see eye to eye about this new rock and roll sensation from England, and—at least early on—ideology had little to do with it. To be certain, when people debated the Beatles, one could find subtle undercurrents that touched on weighty issues of the day such as race, gender, religion, and class. These early clashes, however, did not pit leftists against conservatives the same way that the anti-Vietnam War movement, the counterculture, and feminism later would. However, with the passage of time, as the Beatles came to embody many of the yearnings, desires, dreams, and sensibilities of younger, more rebellious youths, they became a target of repeated attacks and vitriol coming from individuals on the right.

One of the first prominent conservatives to attack the Beatles was *National Review* editor, activist, and author Willian F. Buckley. He used his nationally syndicated column—which appeared in newspapers in all fifty states—as a platform to pillory the four lads from Liverpool. "They are so unbelievably horrible, so appallingly unmusical, so dogmatically insensitive to the magic of the art," Buckley opined, "that they qualify as the crowned heads of anti-music, even as the imposter popes went down in history as 'anti-popes.'"[37] In the same piece, Buckley belittled fans, referring to enthusiastic Beatlemaniacs around the world as an example of "international derangement."[38] On the surface, Buckley's critique did not appear to be political in nature. He merely detested the sound of their music. "In my defense I wish to say that I am tolerant beyond recognition where modern music is concerned," he wrote. "I heard the atonal Schoenberg for the first time years ago with instant appreciation."[39] But a deeper reading of Buckley's op-ed piece—brimming with invective—reveals his own anxieties about adolescent Americans lurching collectively toward rebellion. Near the close of his column, Buckley expressed his fear that "our children can listen avariciously to the Beatles," which he believed "derives from a lamentable and organic imbalance."[40]

A respected pundit, and the most instantly recognizable mainstream conservative public intellectual at the time, Buckley would soon host his own television interview program, *Firing Line*, which featured prominent guests, including politicians, writers, artists, and activists from across the wide political spectrum. Despite his personal loathing of the Beatles' music, and his concerns about the behavior of the band's zealous fans, Buckley's disdain lacked concrete ideological underpinnings. Such was not the case with a small, yet increasingly vocal coterie of right-wingers who began to regard the Beatles as symbols of the ever-expanding counterculture, and, therefore, a threat to the well-being of the nation (see Figure 5.2). It should be noted that these anti-Beatles right-wingers were always a small segment of the nation's conservative movement, which—overall—tended to ignore the Fab Four. Still, the Beatles provoked the ire of certain traditionalists for multiple reasons: they weren't Americans. They wore their hair long. They put their irreverence on full display by constantly joking during interviews and at press conferences. They embraced tolerance and inclusivity. And their anarchical sensibilities, in turn, rubbed off on the legions of youths who played their music loudly, plastered Fab Four pictures on their walls, joined fan clubs, and monitored the band's movements.

Quasi-religious elements found in Beatlemania were especially troubling to many on the American Right. The fierce dedication of fans, the treatment of lyrics and quotes by the Beatles as something akin to scripture, the rampant idolatry inside the fan base, and the creation of shrines in fans' bedrooms—these ingredients seemed to some alarmed conservatives to be the makings of a new secular religion that threatened to displace Christianity. Derek Taylor, the Beatles' flamboyant press officer, did not help matters in the summer of 1964, as the band was preparing for its North American tour, when he described them in overtly religious terms to rock journalist Alfred Aronowitz of the *Saturday Evening Post*: "Here are these four boys from Liverpool. They're rude, they're profane, they're vulgar, and they've taken over the world. It's as if they'd founded a new religion. They're completely anti-Christ. I mean, I'm anti-Christ as well, but they're so anti-Christ they shock me, which isn't an easy thing. But I'm obsessed with them. Isn't everybody?"[41]

Conservatives took notice of Taylor's comments. *Life Lines*, a weekly newspaper published in Washington, DC, by the right-wing Life Line Foundation, sounded the alarm in its November 13, 1964 issue: "There are enough immoral influences on the American youth without importing more from Liverpool. Our suggestion for the Beatles is that they go home, take a bath, get a haircut and go to work."[42] Some detractors on the right used even more alarmist rhetoric in their condemnations. In July 1965,

FIGURE 5.2 *Young Beatles fans picket with "Ringo for President" sign on July 13, 1964, at the Republican National Convention, held at the Cow Palace in Daly City, California. Ultimately, the convention chose Senator Barry Goldwater of Arizona, not Ringo Starr, as its presidential nominee. While most Conservatives ignored the Beatles, small numbers of extremists on the right regarded the band as a threat to the nation's youth.*
Source: *Courtesy of Bettmann via Getty Images.*

an anticommunist zealot from Florida insisted the Beatles were part of an insidious plot launched deep within the Kremlin walls. "These Beatles and their music record," he wrote, "are a Communist plan through their scientists, educators, and entertainers contrived by elaborate, calculating and scientific technique directed at rendering a generation of American youth useless through nerve-jamming, mental deterioration and retardation."[43] Similarly, the ultraconservative John Birch Society, founded in 1958, smeared the Beatles as agents of a global communist revolution "bent upon softening up America's younger generation for revolution and eventual Communist take-over."[44] Coincidentally, the Committee for Public Information, a right-wing group based in Hackensack, New Jersey, bombarded people across the Garden State with a three-minute robocall message saying the Beatles were part of a carefully crafted communist master plan to dominate the globe. The man in the recording insisted that "Communist scientists have discovered a broken meter in the treble played against an insistently regular beat to a frenzied pitch," which "causes hysterical effects in young people."[45] Oil tycoon H. L. Hunt, a proud rightist and supporter of ultraconservative causes, expressed concerns that a growing number of "young people," swayed by the "unwashed prophets of collectivism," might "succumb to the 'beat' upon which the Beatles rely to hypnotize youth into a frenzy."[46] But not all "young people" were falling under the spell of the Beatles. Echoing the John Birch Society, the Committee for Public Information and H. L. Hunt, high school student David Pritikin, author of the "Teen Routine" column that appeared regularly in the *Freeport Journal-Standard* in Freeport, Illinois, and a first cousin once removed of conservative columnist Robert Novak, warned his fellow adolescents that the Beatles were part of a master plan to destroy American civilization. "To accomplish this," he wrote, "the Beatles are going to record songs with the same beat as our pulse rate. After we are hypnotized by these songs, they will add Marxist lyrics. Ultimately, we will be converted into teen-age Communists and prepared for riots and revolution."[47]

But no other conservative went after the Beatles with the same fervor or singular focus as Reverend David Noebel. A pastor of Grace Bible Church in Madison, Wisconsin, and founder of a Christian leadership training organization called Summit Ministries, Noebel instantly became fixated on the Beatles when they arrived in North America in February 1964, and his obsession never abated. He dogged them with an unrelenting dedication that took many observers aback. With the support of Reverend Billy James Hargis's far-right Christian Crusade, headquartered in Tulsa, Oklahoma, Noebel embarked on a cross-country speaking tour to address what he called the "systematic plan geared to making a generation of American youth mentally ill and emotionally unstable."[48] Hargis, who fervently believed that "the beatnik crowd, represented by the Beatles, is the Communist crowd," encouraged

Noebel to create a booklet spotlighting his views on the Beatles. In 1965, the Christian Crusade published Reverend Noebel's *Communism, Hypnotism and the Beatles*, a 28-page pamphlet overflowing with the kind of lurid red-baiting and conspiracy mongering routinely spread by the John Birch Society. On the cover was a crude ink drawing of the Fab Four—each with a devilish smile—bathed in red, under the masterful watch of a hypnotic eye located directly beneath a Soviet-style hammer and sickle.[49]

Inside the booklet, Noebel placed the Beatles at the center of a nefarious plot to control the minds of American youths through their insidious form of "popular music." "The Communists," Noebel insisted, "are desperately seeking to replace classical music with popular music."[50] The massive crowds of Beatles fans appearing in public, cheering and carrying signs, Noebel warned, were forming a vanguard that threatened to overthrow capitalism and pave the way for Soviet domination. The Fab Four, he cautioned, "clearly state that they understand their kind of music ... [is] capable of causing emotional instability, disorganized behavior, riot and, eventually, revolution. And since our teenagers under Beatlemania will actually riot, it is imperative to understand the basic underlying philosophy of the Beatles."[51] To give his booklet an air of authority, Noebel filled it with ample footnotes. In fact, nearly half of *Communism, Hypnotism and the Beatles* consisted of footnotes—168 total—many containing multiple citations. The booklet went through four editions in 1965, resulting in 55,000 printings total, and it sold for $1 apiece. Noebel also made a book-on-tape version, reading the booklet aloud to people who preferred to listen to it. No question about it: Noebel was his own biggest promoter. He lugged boxes of *Communism, Hypnotism and the Beatles* with him wherever he went, selling it at venues where he spoke.[52] By the late 1960s, Noebel was marketing himself as the Christian Crusade's in-house expert on the perils of rock music and its ties to Satan and the communist world (which to him were one and the same). At decade's end, he'd written two more books on the subject: *Rhythm, Riots and Revolution* and *The Beatles: A Study in Drugs, Sex, and Revolution*.[53] While out speaking on the road during the 1960s, Noebel added lurid elements to his talks that did not make it into *Communism, Hypnotism and the Beatles*. For instance, he emphasized that girls and young women were particularly vulnerable to the music of the Beatles, which he warned could "condition the sex glands of the female," causing them to "take off their clothes in Beatle concert halls."[54] "And the frightening, even fatal aspect of this mental breakdown process," Noebel cautioned his audiences, "is the fact that these teenagers in this excitatory, hypnotic state can be told to do anything—and they will."[55]

Early in his one-man crusade against the Beatles, Noebel encountered resistance from Beatles fans in the form of letters to the editor. Numerous fans wrote to their local newspapers to speak out against Noebel's claims.

A female Beatlemaniac from Akron, Ohio, proclaimed: "I can't see how the Beatles' music can 'weaken the nervous system of the teenager and cause him to suffer a case of artificial neurosis,' as said by Mr. Noebel ... I think Mr. Noebel may be tired of seeing his daughter spend her allowance on Beatle books, records and bubble bath."[56] Another admirer, from Camden, New Jersey, balked at the claim that the Beatles were Reds: "If the Beatles were Communists, then I suppose you'd think every other boss group that had come out in the past two years is Communist too."[57] The mother of a teenage fan from San Rafael, California, complained that her daughter had been getting mail from irate right-wingers criticizing her for helping to organize a pro-Beatles rally at the city's courthouse in February 1965. The adolescent girl "received several letters from the lunatic fringe," the concerned parent reported. "One in particular seems to equate adolescent love for the Beatles with Karl Marxism and an Anti-Christian movement by the youth of the world, and urges my daughter to 'give up the immoral Beatles and stand up for Jesus Christ.'"[58]

The initial backlash against the Beatles was already receding by the time Reverend David Noebel went on the warpath against the Fab Four. By this time, the early novelty of lashing out at the Beatles had lost what little edge it possessed. It was now dawning on the detractors that the Beatles were here to stay. Calling them childish names, insisting they were untalented, mocking them for their appearance, referring to fans as crazy, these protestations seemed to have no real effect. Beatles album sales remained robust. Beatles fans were as excited as ever. The Beatles, it was announced in the summer of 1965, were even getting their own animated show on ABC. A Saturday morning cartoon where little children could tune in and watch the band's zany antics to a soundtrack of their music was a sure sign of the Beatles' widespread acceptance.

But the anti-Beatles backlash was not an altogether spent force. Dying embers remained, waiting to be stoked. Events in the summer of 1966 would revive the rage, bringing haters out of hibernation. Fueling the animosity that a vocal minority of Americans felt toward the Beatles were deepening divisions within the United States. A polarized climate triggered cultural clashes on multiple fronts. And the Beatles would soon find themselves, once again, in the eye of the storm.

6

The Spirit of '66

The final year of Beatlemania's golden age, 1966, unfolded against a backdrop of increasing turmoil in the United States.[1] The atmosphere in the country had grown darker and more polarized. The Vietnam War slogged into its second bloody year, with no end in sight. Protests against the war continued to expand, with mass mobilizations drawing tens of thousands of resisters in major cities. The violence of Vietnam—escalating daily in agonizing ways—had dark parallels in the United States. On August 1, 1966, mere days before the Beatles arrived to start their US tour, a former US Marine named Charles Whitman gunned down seventeen people from a University of Texas bell tower in Austin, Texas, before he was shot and killed by authorities. The previous month, Richard Speck, a deranged loner, would single handedly murder eight student nurses in Chicago in a horrifying incident that shocked the nation in the long, hot summer of 1966. And the dark times did not end there. Tragedies kept coming. On August 3, a despair-filled Lenny Bruce, the brilliant subversive comedian who'd endured years of hounding by authorities and multiple arrests, died of a drug overdose.[2]

The racial divide in America remained potent. Across the southern states, the Civil Rights Act of 1964 and the Voting Rights Act of 1965—two sweeping, landmark pieces of legislation—had served as a double deathblow to Jim Crow segregation. But racism—both on an individual level and a larger, more systemic scale—had not been exorcised from American life. At a speech in Greenwood, Mississippi, in June 1966, militant Civil Rights activist Stokely Carmichael first popularized the term "Black Power" when he used it for the first time in an incendiary speech. Black Power served as a battle cry of a generation of disillusioned, poor African Americans in the North, Midwest, and West, who hadn't witnessed improvements in their lives as a result of the Civil Rights Movement. In cities across the United States, large-scale race riots had erupted each summer since 1964. In October 1966, Huey Newton and Bobby Seale founded the Black Panther Party for Self-Defense (BPP) in Oakland, California, which went on to become the most influential revolutionary Marxist-Leninist organization in the United States. Over the years, the BPP would go on to resist police abuse and systemic racism, and counter poverty in Black-dominant neighborhoods by introducing self-help initiatives such as their successful Free Breakfast for School Children Program.[3]

Early Beatlemania—a product of hopeful times—became increasingly out of place in a society moving toward turbulence and division at home, and a deadly war full of wanton destruction overseas. But the Beatles themselves also contributed—perhaps unwittingly—to its obsolescence. The maturation and complexity of the band's music, beginning with *Help!* (released August 6, 1965), followed by extraordinary leaps in new directions with *Rubber Soul* (released December 3, 1965) and *Revolver* (August 5, 1966), signified a distinctive break from the tracks of early Beatlemania. Nobody in the 1960s spoke of the Beatles' "early," "middle," and "later" periods—such talk would have been anachronistic at the time, and wouldn't have made sense to people—but there was no question that the Beatles were veering down a different path with their music, as was evident to anyone who listened to it.[4] During the summer of 1966, the "More Popular Than Jesus" controversy—which made the front page of newspapers and opened nightly network news broadcasts—left the fan community divided, and drained some of its zeal. The Beatles, for their part, felt exhausted and disillusioned with the eardrum-shattering screams of their audiences, which proved ultimately to be a major contribution leading the band to abandon the concert stage in favor of the studio.

"Radio Wars"

Based in New York City, *Datebook* was a magazine with a nationwide reach, aimed at an adolescent readership. It was not the biggest teen magazine in the country in 1966—it lacked the massive circulation of *Seventeen, 16, 'Teen,* or *Dig.* Even the slick, gossipy *Tiger Beat*—launched in September 1965—reached more people. But *Datebook*—a liberal publication full of rock star profiles, Q&As conducted by high school–age correspondents, and feature stories about prominent teen idols—was not afraid to shake things up with stories about previously taboo subjects, such as divorce, racial inequality, premarital sex, and teen mental health issues. The magazine's managing editor, 26-year-old Danny Fields, had read a series of lengthy profile stories on the Beatles, written by British journalist Maureen Cleave, that originally appeared in the London *Evening Standard* earlier in the year. Each band member was the subject of an in-depth article by Cleave, and the pieces ran weekly throughout the month of March. Cleave's profiles shed light on the private lives of John, Paul, George, and Ringo, and they failed to stir heated disagreements in England.[5] Back in the United States, Danny Fields, who was constantly on the lookout for something edgy and provocative to run in the pages of *Datebook*, recalled:

> My publisher at *Datebook* had bought Maureen Cleave's interviews with The Beatles from the Evening Standard, and I thought it might be a good idea to take these interviews and chop them up to use in the magazine. I found a Paul McCartney quote where he described America as "a lousy country where anyone black is a dirty nigger," and I thought "Oh, that looks like a headline to me." And then there was another quote from John Lennon saying, "I don't know which will go first, rock n' roll or Christianity," which I thought was interesting. So I ran maybe 800 words in *Datebook* from those articles. And deep in there was Lennon's quote about The Beatles being more popular than Jesus.[6]

The September 1966 issue of *Datebook* containing the excerpts of Cleave's Lennon and McCartney profiles arrived at American newsstands in late July, two weeks before the start of the Beatles' fourteen-city North American tour.[7] Danny Fields erred in assuming that McCartney's blunt words about African Americans and racism would trigger a backlash. "And it's a lousy country to be in where anyone who is black is made to seem like a dirty nigger," Paul told Maureen Cleave earlier in the year.[8] Surprisingly, almost nobody mentioned or seemed to care about McCartney's remark. It was as if McCartney's sentiment had been self-explanatory and so widely accepted that it was devoid of controversy. But Fields's instincts about Lennon's "more popular than Jesus" response were spot on. The September issue of *Datebook* ignited a firestorm in America. The offending quote read:

> Christianity will go. It will go. It will vanish and shrink. I needn't argue about that. I'm right and I will be proved right. We're more popular than Jesus now. I don't know which will go first—rock 'n' roll or Christianity. Jesus was all right, but his disciples were thick and ordinary. It's them twisting it that ruins it for me.[9]

Lennon intended the remark to be part of a longer rumination on the secularization of modern society. But ripped out of its original context, the "more popular than Jesus" quote led to waves of rage sweeping through parts of the United States. Although angry protests could be found all over the country, much of the furor occurred in the American South.[10]

An instantaneous "Ban the Beatles" movement emerged, led by Tommy Charles and Doug Layton, a pair of disc jockeys at radio station WAQY in Birmingham, Alabama. "We just felt it was so absurd and sacrilegious that something ought to be done to show them they cannot get away with this sort of thing," said Charles, who also worked as WAQY's station manager.[11] Charles and Layton encouraged listeners to toss their Beatles records, Beatles merchandise, and Fab Four pictures into a massive "Beatle Bonfire," which they scheduled for August 19, the night of the Beatles concert in Memphis (see Figure 6.1).[12] The "Beatle Ban" initiated by Charles and Layton

FIGURE 6.1 *Teenagers gather at a "Beatles Burning," staged by WAYX-AM in Georgia, where records, books, and wigs are burned in a bonfire in response to John Lennon's comment that the Beatles are more popular than Jesus Christ. Source: Courtesy of Bettmann via Getty Images.*

got nationwide attention in the press and on television, and dozens of other radio stations followed suit. On August 3, a dozen stations in North Carolina and South Carolina promptly banned the Beatles music on their broadcasts.[13] In San Angelo, Texas, KWFR was one of the first radio stations in Texas to ban the Beatles. Station manager Hi Duncan admitted that KWFR had not been playing many Beatles songs before the ban. Once a KWFR disc jockey announced the ban, Duncan claimed that teenage fans of the Fab Four wrote in saying "you just better not do that," but he insisted the ban "has the approval of our mature listeners." As for Duncan, he offered a mixed verdict on the band: "Personally, I think they are talented young men. I wish they would get a haircut though."[14]

From the studios of WAQY in Birmingham, Tommy Charles reacted to developments with interest, pleased that the protest that he and Doug Layton initiated had inspired so many other DJs to adopt a similar position. "We heard from 30 radio stations, mostly in the South, and today 50 letters poured in. Of the letters, about 70 to 80 percent were in favor of our stand," he told the *Birmingham Post-Herald*.[15] By mid-August, around twenty radio stations in the state of Texas alone had banned Beatles music.[16] Three radio stations in Florida—WONN of Lakeland, WDCF of Dade City, and WAUC of Wauchula—immediately banned Beatles songs in solidarity with the disc jockeys at WAQY, and other Florida stations would head in the same direction.[17] "Until John Lennon retracts his anti-Christ statement, KTEE will play no more Beatles records," said Johnny Midnight, a DJ at station KTEE in Idaho Falls, Idaho.[18] "We feel we are a public servant, and we cannot support or help publicize a person who holds such views," said an announcer at WEIM in Fitchburg, Massachusetts.[19] The Beatles are "off my station," insisted Donald Ballou, general manager of WSLB in Ogdensburg, New York.[20]

Lennon's comments were "not only deplorable, but an outright sacrilegious affront to almighty God," insisted the manager of WTUF in Mobile, Alabama.[21] In Shamokin, Pennsylvania, station WISL (1480 AM) banned the Beatles with the following brief announcement: "We've stopped programming their records."[22] WISL's move coincided with efforts in the Pennsylvania State Senate to ban all Beatles music from radio stations throughout the state.[23] When disc jockey Wayne Williams of WDVA in Danville, Virginia, went on the air to tell listeners that the Beatles would no longer be played on the station, he said, "The switchboard just lit up, and every caller was in favor of our stand."[24] WYSB in Rutland, Vermont, banned the Beatles in early August, but it was one of the shortest-lived bans in the country. Within days, the station lifted the ban, so DJs could play Beatles songs on their popular Saturday night rock and roll record program. Meantime, disc jockeys at Rutland's other station, WHWB, hunkered down for the duration, pulling Beatles music off the airwaves in a ban than that lasted longer than the one initiated by DJs down the street at WYSB.[25] Some stations that banned the Beatles encountered fierce resistance from fans. Such was the case with KSWO in Laston, Oklahoma. When program director Ron Kirby announced that Beatles music would no longer be played at KSWO, he received threats of

> anything from kicking down the door of the station to killing me personally. I thought that the choice should be made between the popularity of Christian religion and the popularity of the Beatles. It makes one wonder what is really happening with our youth today. Need I say, judging by the telephone calls and letters, the choice has been the Beatles.[26]

Not all radio stations leapt headlong onto the Beatles "ban wagon." Station WSAC in Fort Knox, Kentucky—which had never played Beatles records before—began playing them regularly on the air "to show our contempt for hypocrisy personified." The station also broadcast an editorial calling for tolerance, arguing that Lennon's comments deserved pondering. "Perhaps the Beatles could be more popular than Jesus. Perhaps that is what is wrong with society. And if they are, dear friends, you made them so, not Jesus, not John Lennon and not the Beatles," said an announcer on WSAC.[27] Norm Seeley, a popular disc jockey at KRUX in Phoenix, Arizona, boldly stated his agreement with Lennon's comments. "I think John Lennon is right. We have placed more emphasis on material and physical things than religion. Religion in itself is good and wholesome, but it's our fault that it's on the way out."[28] A number of DJs across the United States insisted that it was all about the music, and Lennon's comments should not determine whether Beatles music continues to play on American airwaves. Lennon was simply stating his beliefs, they argued, and he was only one member of the band. To these disc jockeys, banning the Beatles seemed both ludicrous and extreme. Sally Salisbury, a spokeswoman for KNAK in Salt Lake City, succinctly explained her station's reason for continuing to play Beatles songs, which was a common defense among managers and DJs refusing to join in the ban: "The beliefs are their own, and we have no plans to remove them from the air."[29] "We play them for their popularity with our audience and for their musical talents," reasoned Jack Gale of WAYS in Charlotte, South Carolina, "rather than their personal views."[30] The managers of two radio stations in El Paso, Texas, vowed to continue playing the Beatles on both stations, KELP and KINT. Gene Roth, manager of KELP, which was both a television and radio station in El Paso, explained: "We've had umpteen dozen calls and letters about this thing, but so far the opinions are about 50–50 … We don't have to believe in Lennon's ideas. We're only playing the music of a very talented group. As long as they're popular and talented, we'll continue to play their records."[31]

"Beatle Battle Lines"

The nationwide cultural clash over the "More Popular Than Jesus" controversy spread beyond the nation's radio stations. At public events, teenagers comprised most of the groups of angry protesters who showed up to speak out against Lennon's comments. In Alexandria, Louisiana, an estimated 500 people—handfuls of adults, but mostly youths—gathered on Saturday evening, August 6, at the city's Bringhurst Park for a "Beatle Bonfire." Forming a ring around an inferno, they began to burn "records, pictures, magazines, sweatshirts, and other items connected with the Beatles."[32] A similar rally the same day drew about 450 people in Oak Grove, Louisiana, egged on by DJs at KFNV in Ferriday, Louisiana, who boasted that their station would no longer play Beatles albums because of Lennon's remarks.[33] Approximately 100 teens assembled around a bonfire in Jackson, Mississippi, also held on August 6, to set flame to "Beatle records, books and wigs."[34] Crowds at anti-Beatles rallies across the South continued to grow. On August 11, around 2,500 people—mostly youths—took part in a "Beatle Bonfire" in Gadsden, Alabama, "tossing pictures, records and other souvenirs connected with the British signing group into a giant fire."[35] Two days later, KLUE in Longview, Texas, held a massive "Beatle Bonfire" south of the city, near the radio station, where over a thousand adults and youths gathered to burn records and all manner of Beatles merchandise.[36] Not all resisters who took to the streets to protest were adolescents. In Chester, South Carolina, Bob Scoggin, the Grand Dragon of the South Carolina Ku Klux Klan, tossed Beatles records and other Fab Four–themed items into "the flames of a fiery cross." Before lowering a flaming torch to a stack of albums spread around the foot of a towering cross, Scoggin proclaimed, "God is first, country second, and the Beatles last." Nobody bothered questioning how the Klan—not generally regarded as a significant part of the Beatles fan demographic in the United States—had obtained so many Beatles albums. That odd fact aside, participants at the Klan event wanted to share in the ecstatic moment of seeing Beatles' records go up in flames, which prompted cheers from the rage-filled crowd. Aglow from nearby flames, Chester Country KKK leader Steve Sloan went on to call the Beatles "an immoral and paganistic group."[37]

Elsewhere, some Fab Four foes opted for quieter, less dramatic forms of protest. Teenager David Breazele, a resident of Greenwood, Mississippi, marched straight into the barber shop—along with a photographer from the *Greenwood Commonwealth*—and asked for his Beatles-inspired long hair to be hacked off with clippers in protest against Lennon's "more popular than Jesus" remark.[38] Eleven-year-old John J. Carvalho, who lived in Pawtucket, Rhode Island, visited his barbershop to have his locks cut off and he vowed to destroy his Beatles albums once the barber was done.[39] In Eau Gallie, a suburb on the north side of Melbourne, Florida, some teenage ex-Beatles fans quietly donated their albums to members of the Cavalry Baptist Church Youth Fellowship so the zealous teenage Christians could light them on fire.[40] Meantime, bestselling author Norman Vincent Peale—guru of "positive thinking"—used the bully pulpit of his syndicated column to go after the Beatles in newspapers from coast to coast. "So, dear reader," he wrote, "don't let a Beatle's childish remark about Jesus worry you. Just remember how He always has a kindly feeling for his detractors. 'Father, forgive them; for they know not what they do.' And remember that they who come to scoff often remain to pray."[41]

With the 1966 US tour fast approaching, involving nineteen performances—seventeen in the United States, two in Toronto, Canada—the Beatles and their manager, Brian Epstein, monitored the gathering storm in the United States. The band released its new studio album, *Revolver*, on August 5 in the UK and August 8 in the United States, one of their most strikingly original yet, and none of them were eager to plunge into thorny, irresolvable debates about religion. Yet the Beatles had become more outspoken in recent months, not only when it came to spiritual matters, but on other weighty issues of the day, such as race relations and the Vietnam War. Despite this, Lennon felt anxious about traveling to the United States and encountering the rage and hatred of certain segments of the American public. The band's overwhelming success was on the line. But increasingly, Lennon also felt uneasy with excessive compromise and hiding his true feelings in exchange for greater acceptance. It was a dilemma Lennon struggled with for years. "He was terrified," recalled Cynthia Lennon, his wife at the time. "What he'd said had affected the whole group. Their popularity was under the microscope, but he was the one who had opened his mouth and put his foot in it. I didn't go on the tour with him, but I know he was very frightened."[42] So alarmed was Brian Epstein by the fallout from Lennon's comments that he flew to New York City days before the start of the Beatles' 1966 US tour in an effort to help ease tensions. He held a well-attended press conference at the Americana Hotel on 7th Avenue in Manhattan, at which he showed up in a suit and tie and addressed media outlets. Rising to a podium with bulbs flashing and television cameras whirring, Epstein delivered a statement:

> The quote which John Lennon made to a London columnist nearly three months ago has been quoted and misrepresented entirely out of context of the article, which was in fact highly complimentary to Lennon as a person and was understood by him to be exclusive to the Evening Standard. It was not anticipated that it would be displayed out of context and in such a manner as it was in an American teenage magazine. Lennon didn't mean

to boast about the Beatles' fame. He meant to point out that the Beatles' effect appeared to be a more immediate one upon, certainly, the younger generation. John is deeply concerned and regrets that people with certain religious beliefs should have been offended.[43]

On August 11, the Beatles departed from London Airport on a Pan Am flight that touched down in Boston hours later, for the start of their third and—unbeknownst to people at the time—final tour. Anxiety was palpable among the Beatles' UK fans about the band's safety in the United States. Bidding farewell to the Beatles at the airport with other supporters, English Beatlemaniac Lorraine Bartram proclaimed, "If the Yanks hurt the Beatles, it will be the start of World War III."[44] American press coverage of the Beatles' arrival in the United States emphasized the comparatively small size of the crowds that came out to greet them as a sign that Beatlemania was shrinking. One journalist pointed out that "only about 500 die-hard fans lined the ramps at Logan Airport to welcome their controversial idols."[45] But the fans who did show up at Logan Airport were exceptionally dedicated, and showed their love for the band with chants and signs bearing supportive statements: "We Love U Beatles"; "We Support John"; and "You're What's Happening."[46] The Beatles were still exhausted from harrowing experiences the previous month in Japan, where they received an avalanche of death threats from right-wing ultranationalists upon their arrival in Tokyo, and the Philippines, where they narrowly escaped angry mobs of heavily armed military personnel and civilians loyal to the country's strongman dictator, Ferdinand Marcos. Despite playing two giant sold-out shows at Manila's Rizal Memorial Stadium, the band members missed a state-sponsored gala event, organized by Marcos and his wife, Imelda, a no-no in a country where Marcos ruled with an iron fist. The Beatles and their entourage narrowly escaped Manila alive, and they vowed never to return there.[47]

Once on American soil, Lennon apologized—not once, not twice, but over and over again. Even vigilant Beatles watchers lost track of how many times he said sorry. "I'm sorry I said it, really. I never meant it as a lousy, anti-religious thing," Lennon announced once he was in the United States.[48] "I'm not anti-God, anti-Christ or anti-religion. I was not knocking it. I was not saying we are greater or better," Lennon told reporters at an August 11 press conference in Chicago.[49] For the most part, Lennon's bandmates stood by his side, showing their solidarity at every turn. "I know him. He believes in Christianity," assured George Harrison. "But I do agree with him that Christianity is on the wane."[50] Nobody was more astonished by the controversy than Maureen Cleave. The reaction in the United States left the journalist baffled. "I was astonished that John Lennon's quotation was taken out of context from my article and misinterpreted in that way," wrote Cleave. "John certainly wasn't comparing the Beatles to Jesus Christ. He was simply observing that, to many, the Beatles were better known."[51]

The "More Popular Than Jesus" imbroglio revealed how much the Beatles had changed in the previous few years, and not merely musically. As creative and socially engaged artists, all four of them had undergone transformations as individuals, and they were more willing to wade into controversies than they had been in 1964. Fans had changed, too. Their varied responses to their idols highlights a range of temperaments, intellect, musical preferences, and levels of maturity within Beatles fandom. Fans, like the rest of the American public, were divided about the issue. In press coverage of the Beatle Bonfires, many of the participants claimed to be former Beatles fans, showing up with LPs, 45s, and other items to toss into the flames.[52] In Albany, New York, three young women—Nancy Huislander, Mary Ann Awad, and Dee Hickey—all self-proclaimed ex-Beatles fans, tossed their Beatles photographs and magazines into a fire in a steel drum to protest Lennon's remarks.[53] Other ex-fans registered their disgust in quieter, less confrontational ways. Jessica Hendrix, a teenage high school student from Pensacola, Florida, did not attend a public demonstration or burn her Beatles albums, yet she was outspoken with a local reporter about her disappointment with Lennon. "My views on this subject are that when John Lennon said this, he degraded himself, therefore the group's popularity also. I feel that if we can ban their records, we would not correct the error that has been made," Hendrix said.[54]

On the opposite side of the divide, a segment of the Beatles' fan base redoubled their efforts to defend the band against the backlash. The loyalists who stood out the most were those that showed remarkable courage in the face of adversity, charging fearlessly into the thick of the hornet's nest to offer a contrarian point of view, occasionally at risk to themselves. Often, their acts of resistance occurred on a small scale, carried out by one—or at the most, a few—gutsy individuals. An instance of such boldness occurred at the huge Beatle Bonfire rally at Bringhurst Park in Alexandria, Louisiana, on August 6, when two stalwart Beatles defenders—one of whom had the audacity to wear an "I Love The Beatles" sweatshirt—appeared at the scene to confront the event's 500 attendees. The two lone dissenters were called "atheists" and worse by people in the crowd, yet they stood their ground, and even collected Beatles items left behind that hadn't been burned in the fire.[55] Meantime, when the Memphis city commission met on August 9 to debate whether to cancel the Beatles' two performances at the city's Mid-South Coliseum, scheduled for August 19, observers at the packed meeting cheered for eighteen-year-old Beatles fan John F. McCormack when he defended Lennon's right to free speech. "I am not of voting age, but I don't think this is the position to take—to cancel the appearance. It is not as if Lennon is right or wrong, but whether he has the right to say it," the teenager reasoned. In the end, the city commission did not cancel the Beatles' Memphis performances, despite support among some local citizens for such a move.[56] In Hopewell, Virginia, two teenage Beatles fans, Susan Dobbs and Theresa Earles, combined their money to take out a prominent display advertisement in London's *Daily Telegraph* stating their solidarity with the Beatles, and announcing a petition drive to pressure American radio stations to lift bans on them. They closed their advertisements with a plea to the band's British fans: "Please, England, help us, we love them too."[57] In some cases, the controversy exacerbated generational divides. Parents, like the rest of the nation, were divided, occupying places across a spectrum from supportive of their Beatle-loving children to the opposite position of strenuously opposing them. Barbara Boggiano, a high school student from New York, recalled that her father had "a fit and a half" after Lennon's "More Popular Than Jesus" comment came to light. He shouted at her: "Communist! You're listening to Communist records!" Boggiano experienced a period of sustained conflict with her father. "It was a clear-cut case of us, the younger people, versus people over 30, the establishment. There was really a sharp division. My father and I were always at odds at that time," Boggiano explained.[58]

The Ban-the-Beatles craze was short-lived. It had lost much of its steam—and what little direction it had—by mid-August, and it had largely dissipated by month's end. During its brief lifespan, radio stations functioned as cultural battlegrounds, where people of varying points of view staked out positions on the contentious issue of religion and its place in contemporary American life. And yet, most radio stations in the United States did not succumb to the temptation to ban the Beatles. At the height of the furor, stories in the press reported the number of radio stations that initiated Beatles bans as being in the low dozens—or around 30—in a country with more than 4,075 AM stations and 1,515 FM stations operating at the time.[59] Not all these spots on the dial played pop or rock and roll music—a good many of them, in fact, did not. But even taking into account the diversity of formats, relatively few radio stations in the United States publicly announced Beatle bans. Moreover, many stations that banned Beatles' music did so temporarily, lifting the ban within days of announcing it.[60] Public protests such as "Beatle Bonfires" were mainly confined to a region in the American South known as the Bible Belt, a swath extending from southern Virginia and the Carolinas in the east to Texas in the west. Outside of these states, resistance was sporadic and ineffectual at best. Once John Lennon apologized for his remarks, Tommy Charles and Doug Layton went on the air to call off their scheduled bonfire, insisting the Beatle had learned his lesson.[61] While some Christians forgave Lennon, others were in a less charitable mood. Reverend Thurman H. Babbs, pastor of the New Haven Baptist Church in Cleveland, Ohio, threatened to expel church members who shared Lennon's sentiments. Thurman reasoned it "doesn't matter" that the Beatle apologized for saying the Beatles were more famous than Jesus, which the reverend found abhorrent.[62]

By contrast, other American Christians advocated tolerance and understanding, and some even agreed with the spirit of Lennon's comments in the Cleeve interview. Jesus Christ, they emphasized, preached understanding and forgiveness, not mob actions and threats of violence. These less dogmatic believers saw the nationwide brouhaha as an opportunity to engage in what they regarded as a long overdue dialogue about religious values in modern America. In Madison, Wisconsin, Reverend Richard Pritchard of the Westminster Presbyterian Church, a staunch supporter of the Civil Rights Movement, exhorted his followers to stop criticizing others and look deeply inward "at their own standards and values." "There is much validity in what Lennon said. To many people today, the golf courses is also more popular than Jesus Christ," insisted Reverend Pritchard.[63] Similar sentiments could be found among Christians elsewhere in the United States. A nun from Dayton, Ohio, reacting to a ban on Beatles music on the local radio station, WONE, told a reporter: "Lennon's right. The Beatles are more popular than Jesus today. Rock 'n' roll music has found a way to deliver a message today while Christianity hasn't."[64]

The controversy had a lasting impact on the Beatles, especially Lennon, who was initially shaken by it, but later felt frustrated that reporters kept asking him to comment on it at press conferences. It overshadowed their US tour, and the releases of their seventh studio album, *Revolver*, and their new single, "Eleanor Rigby"/"Yellow Submarine." Ironically, due to the prolonged uproar, Americans overlooked comments by the Beatles that were arguably every bit as controversial and might have even touched off similar public displays of rage if Lennon had not compared the Beatles to Jesus in his interview with Maureen Cleave. Tellingly, Paul's uncompromising commentary about race relations in the United States, reprinted in the infamous issue of *Datebook* that started it all, went largely unnoticed. The four band members routinely offered potentially explosive observations of the Vietnam War, the Jim Crow South, organized religion, and what they perceived to be the pervasiveness of short-sighted greed in the United States.[65] A reporter asked John his opinion about the Vietnam War at one of the band's many press conferences. A visibly weary Lennon replied: "The war in Vietnam is wrong all the way and you know it is, but that's all we'll say in America about it. We could give our opinions in England but not here. America being larger than Britain, has more bigots who tend to twist everything you say."[66] One could plainly see at any one of the Beatles' US press conferences that the band was no longer as enamored of the United States as they had been during their whirlwind February 1964 visit. In the aftermath of hurricane "More Popular Than Jesus," the country, in their eyes at least, had lost some of its luster.

"Fans and Concerts"

What it meant to be a Beatles fan in the United States at the height of Beatlemania was also in a state of flux. Being a Beatles fan looked and felt different in 1966 than it did in 1964. Maturation often expanded one's taste in all things, particularly music. Thinking among Beatles fans had shifted. In 1966, one could listen to multiple bands and still be a dedicated Beatles fan. One could love John, Paul, George, and Ringo without plastering pictures of them over all the bedroom walls. A devotee might disagree with the assertion that the Beatles were "more popular than Jesus," but still be loyal the band. Diversified interests led to more nuanced reasoning among Beatlemaniacs. In her "Open Letter to Beatle Fans," teenager Karen Call of Millbrae, California, wrote a candid essay about her changing feelings toward the Beatles. Her reflections appeared in December 1965 in the pages of *KRLA Beat*, a popular teen-oriented rock music and youth culture newspaper published weekly in Los Angles, sponsored by local radio station KRLA ("*Eleven-ten on the A.M. dial!*"). With an engaging, conversational approach, Call insisted that it was normal for Beatles fans to have wide-ranging preferences, and to buy the records and see the concerts of other singers and bands. "We got to admit it. We Beatle fans ARE letting our thoughts wander from just George, John, Ringo and Paul," she wrote. "Think back. Haven't you during the past week thought about how yummy Herman is? Maybe it isn't Herman—perhaps it was Donovan (or Dave Clark, or Mick Jagger)."[67] Call revealed that she no longer screamed at the Beatles most recent concert at San Francisco's Candlestick Park—"I just sat and listened to them," she admitted—which was a significant change for her from the previous year, when she was "more than a bit more hysterical."[68] Call gently nudged her fellow fans to be more aware of their expanding interests, and not to feel guilty or apologetic about them. "We've all grown up a bit, too," she concluded. "But all the same, deep down inside, we'll always be Beatle fans, even if right now we're beginning to wonder (and wander). Just remember, Beatles 4 Ever!"[69]

The release of the groundbreaking *Revolver* album in early August 1966 only added to the confusion of those fans who were questioning their commitment to the band. Even more than *Rubber Soul*, an album hailed by critics as a departure from the group's earlier LPs when it hit record stores the previous December, *Revolver* seemed to be a dramatic break from the Beatles' musical past. Songs tackled such heavy issues as loneliness and despair ("Eleanor Rigby"), LSD use ("Doctor Robert"), and Eastern philosophy ("Tomorrow Never Knows"), and the album contained richly layered songs shaped by such varied influences as Hindustani classical music ("Love To You"), Motown and Stax songs ("Got to Get You Into My Life"), children's sea shanties ("Yellow

Submarine"), Lovin' spoonful tunes ("Good Day, Sunshine"), and psychedelic drugs ("I'm Only Sleeping," "Tomorrow Never Knows").[70] The album's trippy cover art, drawn by German artist Klaus Voormann, the Beatles' close chum from the Hamburg days earlier in the decade, combined drawings and photos in a collage that was nothing like any other Beatles' record cover before.[71] The youthful Beatle lovers who bought the album instantly understood that it was radically different from anything they had ever known, prompting some of them to question their loyalty to the band. Carol Cox, a teenage Beatles fan from northern California in 1966, briefly turned away from the Beatles around the time of *Revolver's* release. "I hated 'Eleanor Rigby' at first. I was like, 'What's happened to my Beatles? Why are they doing it?' And at that point I was also into other groups like the Monkees, Paul Revere and the Raiders, and some other bands," she recalled.[72] Similarly, Wendi Tisland, from northern Minnesota, became temporarily disenchanted with the Beatles around the same time, describing herself as "upset." She was unable to understand the new turn they were taking artistically. "I didn't really care for it," she later explained. "They were changing from the Beatles we knew, their appearances were changing, the music was changing, but I never wrote them off. I still listened."[73] Lena Marroletti was twelve when *Revolver* was released. The album left her mystified. She did not know how to react to it. She recounted: "By 1966, the Beatles' music began to evolve dramatically, and I admit that they were progressing further than my twelve-year-old mind could comprehend. This was the time when the Monkees were coming of age and, for a time my devotion shifted to that group because they were better suited to my teenybopper mentality."[74] Beatles fandom chronicler Candy Leonard explained that "many young Beatles fans ... took a 'Beatle Break'" after the release of *Revolver*. "Fans were still listening to earlier Beatle music and were intrigued with the warm sound and grown-up lyrics of Rubber Soul, but *Revolver* was more than many fans were ready for," she observed.[75]

Despite mixed reactions from adolescent Beatlemaniacs, *Revolver* was a runaway commercial and critical success, soaring to the coveted number one spot on US charts by late August, a sign that in the Beatles had emerged from the "More Popular Than Jesus" controversy mostly unscathed.[76] Far more Americans were buying Beatles' albums than burning them. But the Beatles had grown tired of touring. Increasingly, the experience left them feeling depleted and demoralized. A famous, oft-repeated story among Beatles chroniclers is when a relieved George Harrison settled into his seat on the airplane that took the band members away from their final concert in San Francisco on August 29, he proclaimed, "Right—that's it. I'm not a Beatle anymore."[77]

That fateful decision—finalized once the Beatles got back to England—ended up being the death knell of Beatlemania's golden age in the United

States. New technologies in recording studios opened a myriad of doors to experiment with sounds, and the Beatles sought to make music that could not be easily reproduced on the concert stage. "We'd finished touring in '66 to go into the studio where we could hear each other ... and create any fantasy that came out of anybody's brain," explained Ringo Starr.[78] However, game-changing innovations in studio recording were but one reason behind the change in the Beatles' approach to making music. Touring, in their eyes, had lost its magic. The Beatles could not compete with the noise levels of their shrieking audiences. Even in the 1966 US tour, which some observers in the press insisted had been more subdued than in previous years, Beatles shows were awash in waves of blaring screams. The concerts that comprised the Beatles last hurrah were, if anything, even wilder affairs than they had been in the past. Concertgoer Bonni Granato was all of fifteen when she was nearly trampled to death at a Beatles concert in Cleveland on August 14, 1966. When a chain-link fence near the stage collapsed, the crowd in the Cleveland Municipal Stadium surged forward like a giant tide, threatening to stomp on anyone in the way. As Granato later recalled: "You could barely breathe due to the pushing and shoving. It was mass hysteria. My leg was caught between other fans' legs, and kids were actually climbing and standing on our legs for a better view. Some of the guys were grabbing girls' breasts because they could get away with it."[79]

Other accounts of the final tour were rife with tales of screaming, chaos, concertgoers throwing objects, and the inability of people in the audience to hear the band (see Figure 6.2). "I saw them in Washington, D.C. in 1966, just before they stopped touring for good," recalled Beth Kaplan. "And for good reason—it was a terrible experience, a vast football stadium and so much noise. It was hideous and deafening, impossible to hear anything."[80] Fletcher Terry, from Cleveland, Mississippi, got to go to the concert at the Mid-South Coliseum in Memphis to see the Beatle, a gift for his tenth birthday from his mother, who drove him to the show. "The Beatles took the stage at 10:30 p.m.," he recalled. "The audience started screaming at the top of their lungs ... You would not believe how loud it was." At some point during the concert, a loud pop came from the stage, startling Terry and others in the audience. Luckily, it was a false alarm—a firework thrown by a concertgoer. "The kid who threw the cherry bomb was arrested," Terry remembered. "Apparently he was trying to impress his date and, needless to say, she wasn't impressed."[81] In Los Angeles, teen Beatles fans Patti Pjerrou and Arcelia Saenz took on the job of junior correspondents for their local newspaper, the *San Bernadino County Sun*, to cover the Beatles' August 28 performance at Dodger Stadium. Around 45,000 people (up from 36,000 at the previous year's Hollywood Bowl show) had gathered in the venue to hear the Beatles give their penultimate live concert. "Everyone was dressed in what she considered her most modish gear," the

FIGURE 6.2 *St. Louis—August 21: Scores of young female fans scream in sheer delight as the Beatles play at Busch Stadium, August 21, 1966, in St. Louis, Missouri.*
Source: Photo by Jeff Hochberg via Getty Images.

writers observed. "Some girls wore pants suits with turtleneck sweaters, while others were adorned with suede suits, long hair and caps to match. Most of the boys seemed just as interested in the concert as we were."[82] The audience waited through three other acts—the Remains, an obscure garage rock band from Boston, Bobby Hebb, a smooth-voiced R&B singer with a soulful hit on the charts called "Sunny," and the Ronettes, one of the country's most beloved girl groups—before the Beatles picked up their instruments and sang. The show dazzled Pjerrou and Saenz, who immediately wrote their impressions to share with readers. "At exactly 9:32, as the Beatles ran from the dugout in left field, cameras flashed all over the Stadium, while every person ... screamed with wild excitement. For about thirty minutes, masses of emotion poured forth while the Beatles sang at the top of their voices."[83]

The Beatles hid their exhaustion well. But these events invariably left them drained. Concerts had not always been painful endurance tests for them. A mere two and a half years earlier, they were eager to conquer the United States. During the Beatles' hectic February 1964 visit to the country, New York radio personality Ed Rudy asked the band members about their ambitions. Paul responded: "We used to have lots of ambitions. You know like, number one records, *Sunday Night at The Palladium*, the *Ed Sullivan Show*, go to America, you know. All kinds of ambitions like that. I can't really think of any more. We've done an awful lot of them."[84] The Beatles played their first concert in the United States on February 11, 1964, two days after their *Ed Sullivan Show* appearance, to a sold-out audience of 8,000 screaming fans at the Coliseum in Washington, DC. It was a joyous and triumphant concert debut for the four lads from Liverpool. A correspondent with the *Liverpool Echo* covering the DC concert noted that the Beatles "looked smart and spry in neat grey suits, black velvet collars, immaculate white shirts and black ties," and the people watching the concert in the Coliseum "screamed, whistled, cheered, yelled and danced up and own in their seats."[85] The Beatles' two 35-minute concerts at New York City's Carnegie Hall, on February 12, 1964, were equally riveting. Reviewing the concert for the Associated Press wire service, journalist Henrietta Leith thought the Beatles delivered an "awesome performance," yet she lamented that "no one, especially the screaming little girls, actually heard the Beatles."[86]

The Beatles brought this infectious enthusiasm to their summer tour in 1964, which was by far the largest and most ambitious of their three North American tours. They performed thirty-two shows in twenty-five cities in the United States and Canada in the span of a month. One could not possibly miss their ebullience, which shined through in every show. The Beatles seemed to draw energy from the excitement of their crowds. At their press conferences they would answer "each question with a joke," recounted a *Tampa Tribune* staff writer covering a press conference in Jacksonville, Florida.[87] A reporter at the Seattle press conference on August 21 asked band members—seated at a long table in front of the room, under the glare of bright lights—about the staggering audience noise levels. "Do you wish they'd be quiet and let you sing sometimes?" he said. Three of the Beatles instantly chimed in, "Why? They've got the records," said John. "No, you know, if they've paid to come in and if they wanna scream, great," replied Paul. "And it's part of the atmosphere now," responded George.[88] If the screaming bothered the Beatles during their first North American tour, they never let on. At each concert, they spent their half hour on stage breezing through a setlist familiar to anyone who had her or his transistor radio tuned to pop stations: "Twist and Shout," "You Can't Do That," "All My Loving," "Can't Buy Me Love," "A Hard Day's Night," and other familiar hits.[89] The Beatles used the same approach in their tours that they did in their Cavern Club gigs in Liverpool and their residencies in Hamburg. They played music they could just as easily reproduce live as in the studio. During the 1965 US tour, journalist and news anchor Larry Kane posed the question, "Did the Beatles have problems perfecting a stage sound?"

George Harrison responded:

No. We've never had much trouble, because right from the beginning when we started recording, we'd just record in one take. You know, things like

"Twist and Shout" and "Saw Her Standing There," which were all on our first album in England—we just turned the recorder on. We got a sound balance in the studio—just put the tape on and did it like that. So we never did any of this overdubbing or adding orchestras or anything like that. It's only recently where we've been using a bit of overdub stuff. We've added things like tambourine, which you don't notice, you know. Because we still like to think we can get basically the same sound on stage.[90]

The Beatles' desire to create more complex music—involving techniques they tended to avoid in the past—led them in new directions, even as Harrison spoke those words. However, it would be too simplistic to insist that this was the sole reason the Beatles ceased touring. The causes were manifold and complicated. The behavior of their audiences in the tours—particularly the screaming—took a toll on all four men. This was the case everywhere they performed, not just in the United States. At press conferences during the first tour, the Beatles claimed they didn't mind the steady din. But privately it bothered them. What fans regarded as a spirited show of appreciation, the Beatles saw more as an assault. Playing at larger venues—stadiums and arenas—during their 1965 US tour, the noise reached new heights. The madness was most visible at the Beatles' famous Shea Stadium concert on August 15, 1965 (see Figure 6.3). At the 56,000-seat, horseshoe-shaped venue where the Mets played baseball, located in Flushing Meadows, Queens, the fifty 100-watt amplifiers used by the Beatles were drowned out by the unrelenting assault of screams. *New York Times* reporter Murray Schumach, observing the event from the press box, was hardly peddling hyperbole when he offered the following verdict: "Their immature lungs produced a sound so staggering, so massive, so shrill and sustained that it quickly crossed the line from enthusiasm into hysteria and was soon in the area of the classic Greek meaning of the word pandemonium—the region of all demons."[91]

The passage of time brought even harsher verdicts about Shea '65. "It was ridiculous! We couldn't hear ourselves sing," John later said of the show, which became a model for future stadium rock concerts.[92] In the *Beatles Anthology* documentary (1995), George Harrison also used the word "ridiculous" to describe the event, as well as other troubling aspects of Beatlemania. "It was nice to be popular, but … it felt dangerous because everybody was out of hand and out of line … They were all caught up in the mania. It was as if they were all in a big movie and we were the ones trapped in the middle of it. It was a very strange feeling."[93] Ringo Starr admitted in 1969 that Beatlemania had been filled with "turmoil," and he had had enough. "No sleep, no proper meals, living out of a suitcase, being torn to bits mentally and physically … Oh, never again!"[94]

FIGURE 6.3 *Beatles fans at Shea Stadium display their enthusiasm for the band, August 15, 1965. The deafening screams of fans at Shea Stadium that night were but one factor that helped to push the Beatles away from concert tours and into the studio.*
Source: *Photo by Jim Hughes/New York Daily News Archive via Getty Images.*

During the 1966 tour, the screaming never abated. Countless stories in the press reported that concert attendance had dropped, and the Beatles were not playing sold-out shows. At San Francisco's Candlestick Park, 25,000 tickets were sold for a venue that had a seating capacity of 42,000. *Variety* magazine reported a slump in ticket sales for the third tour, even before the "More Popular Than Jesus" furor.[95] But ticket sales steadily climbed, and while Candlestick Park was not full, other venues had sold out. Ultimately, the 1966 North American tour was the band's most profitable tour.[96] And by all accounts, the 1966 concerts were every bit as deafening as past seasons. Nancy Ellis, a recent high school graduate from Concord, Massachusetts, had the unique experience of seeing four of the Beatles performances in the 1966 tour—in Washington, DC, Philadelphia, Boston, and New York City. Ellis was a lifelong music lover. In fact, she was a classically trained pianist who received a prominent scholarship to go to Vassar College in Poughkeepsie, New York, one of the nation's most elite women's colleges. She attended each concert fully expecting—based on news coverage of the "More Popular Than Jesus" story that she had been following—to see diminished crowd sizes. "Newspapers, radio and television told eagerly of the diminished crowds at the airports, hotels and concerts themselves," said Ellis. This media-generated narrative, according to Ellis, left people at the time believing "that Beatle popularity is on the wane."[97] After attending the four concerts, Ellis arrived at the opposite conclusion: the Beatles were more popular than ever, and their shows were every bit as packed and loud and buzzing with excitement as in past tours, and the Beatles exhibited great showmanship on the stage. Being a veteran of Beatles' performances, Ellis spoke with credibility about the experience of seeing them in concert, and being among the screaming fans. To Ellis, their screams and cries and shrieks made perfect sense. It was a natural and understandable, even predictable, reaction to being so close to the band that had enriched their lives so meaningfully. The response of the "typical" screaming Beatles fan, she said, was due to pent-up emotions, feelings, and desires that lurk not very far beneath the surface—and sometimes they burst forth, no longer repressible. Surveying the vast throng of screaming fans at all four shows (which she called "marvelous, crazy events"), Ellis was able to see—firsthand—the collective energy of youthful Beatles fans gathered in the same place to come as close to the band as they ever will. Reflecting on the sights and sounds at the four concerts, Ellis wrote of the typical energetic concertgoer: "She has listened to the music all year. But she hasn't seen the Beatles all year and tonight—concert night—tonight only, and for a half hour only, the four funny, handsome young men who make all this fabulous music are going to be here a hundred feet away instead of 3000 miles away."[98]

Nancy Ellis had discovered the Beatles when she was a junior in high school. She watched them on the *Ed Sullivan Show*, like tens of millions of other Americans, and she loved what she saw. In the summer of 1966, on the verge of leaving home to go to college, Ellis deliberately purchased tickets to the four Beatles concerts as a sort of farewell to her childhood. Now ready to move on to the next chapter of her life, Ellis understood that the Beatles were ready for a similar transition in their lives. They were evolving, growing, changing. They, too, were moving on. Going to four Beatles' concerts was Ellis's way of letting go. Unbeknownst to her, the Beatles were also letting go. And yet, even though Ellis had no way of looking into the future, her parting words in an essay she wrote for the *Boston Globe* in September of 1966 seem—in hindsight—to be a bittersweet farewell to the vibrant and immersive world of Beatle fandom, which had sustained communities of fans for the past few years.

She concluded with poignant observations:

> Probably the concert tours are not as much fun for the Beatles as they used to be. With three of them married, two of them fathers, and all of them settled in their own homes, chances are they would rather be at home. I have a feeling that when the time actually does come, the first people to admit that Beatlemania is on the wane will be the Beatles themselves—gladly, in weary relief ... It will be a sad day when the era of the Beatle concert ends. Never have so many people been made so very ecstatically happy in so little time.[99]

Not with a Bang

The Beatles never announced to the public that they were going to stop touring. There is no evidence of any long-term planning on their part. Nobody in the fall of 1966—not even the Liverpool foursome—could predict what the future held in store. For all anybody knew at this point, the band could be around for decades. Or years. Or months. As for tours, maybe dozens of tours were in the works. Or perhaps the last one had passed. Uncertainty gave rise to speculation about prospects for another tour—among journalists, disc jockeys, fans, and even the Beatles and their management. Tantalizing stories routinely appeared in the press, nearly always the result of rumors or vague comments made by band members.

Throughout the rest of 1966 and well into 1967, the editors of the *Beatles Monthly Book*, the official publication of the Beatles fan club headquarters in London, claimed that they had been inundated with letters inquiring about the group's future touring plans. The Beatles' press officer, Tony Barrow, using the pseudonym Frederick James, addressed the issue bluntly in the April 1967 issue of the *Beatles Monthly Book*. By way of context, he brought up the band's years of working on their stage presence at the Cavern Club and in Hamburg in the early 1960s, and how much it meant to them to perfect their craft. But the Beatles, Barrow wrote, had reached a point where neither they nor their audience could hear their live performances above the screaming. "For the Beatles," Barrow wrote, "all the challenge of gaining audience appreciation by improving their act had gone."[100] Barrow informed fans that the Beatles were hard at work in the studio, making an album that—upon its release—listeners far and wide could enjoy. In addition to an LP, the Beatles, according to Barrow, were busily recording multiple singles, and planning to appear in yet another film. "The great effort and concentration which once went into their earliest beat club programmes," Barrow wrote, "is now going into the making of their first 1967 LP album."[101]

Despite Barrow's reassurances, fans continued to circulate petitions and write letters to the Beatles pleading for another tour. Because nothing was ever confirmed or denied, ruled out or finalized, the armies of young Beatles lovers across the United States kept fan clubs going awhile longer, and communities of kindred spirits maintained their connections with each other, and their sense of excitement. Their heroes—John, Paul, George, and Ringo—had always radiated optimism, and embodied a can-do spirit that inspired their young followers to do likewise. But the passage of time began to undermine buoyancy. Even as late as April 1968, American disc jockeys were calling on fan clubs to join a petition drive pleading with the Beatles to tour again, promising that "audiences will be quiet and music appreciated" if the band "will only come back."[102]

The rumor mill kept humming. Conjecture thrived. Hopes were raised and dashed. Gossip about upcoming tours went hand in hand with warnings of an impending breakup. To the degree that the golden age of Beatlemania in the United States experienced any kind of a farewell, it occurred in November and December of 1966—months after the third (and, it turned out, final) tour. American newspapers buzzed with stories about the unraveling of the Fab Four and the end of Beatlemania. Headlines conveyed grim stories that seemed to confirm the worst fears of fans: "And It's Bye-Bye Beatles!"[103]; "Beatlemania Ending; Echo Lingers on"[104]; "Beatles Near Splitsville; Americans Invade England"[105]; "The End to Beatlemania"[106]; and "Are Beatles Really Breaking Up?"[107]

Rumors of a Beatles breakup were—to borrow from Mark Twain—greatly exaggerated. The band continued working for months at EMI Studios in London on a LP that they were keeping largely under wraps. Beatles fans, meantime, moved on with their lives. School years began anew. Fall arrived, bringing a chill in the air. Nightly news on television sets across America played grainy footage of the deepening war in Vietnam. Diarist Patricia Gallo was starting her senior year of high school. She was already thinking ahead about which universities she would apply to, deciding that nearby Temple University in Philadelphia would be the ideal choice for her. As the first member of her family to go to university, she felt a heavy responsibility had been placed on her shoulders.

She missed the long days of summer, when she saw the Beatles in concert twice—in Philadelphia and New York. She played the Beatles' *Revolver* album repeatedly on her turntable. She acknowledged that it was "different; the style was new." She could especially relate to "Eleanor Rigby." In her November 2, 1966, entry, she wrote that "the refrain sums up nicely how I feel right now." She lamented in the same entry: "Don't see the old group these days to talk about the Beatles."[108] The weeks passed. Winter came and went. Spring arrived, and Patricia got accepted into Temple University. It thrilled her to be given her high school diploma at Philadelphia's Convention Hall, where the Beatles played three years earlier, on their first North American tour.

Her last diary entry, dated November 27, 1967, was written while she was a freshman at Temple, facing the stresses of her first university exams. She mentioned hearing "Love Me Do" on the radio, a song that took her right back to that unforgettable night when she first saw the Beatles on the *Ed Sullivan Show* back in February 1964. The sound of it filled her full of warmth and contentment, and it calmed her amidst life's uncertainties. She could have been speaking for legions of fans when she closed off her diary with the following passage:

> Of course, the Beatles aren't the only focal point in my life now, but they have played an important part of my past. They actually helped me to grow up and lose my shyness. Before they emerged upon the scene, I was the perfect bookworm. During Beatlemania, I blossomed into a regular teen who loved rock 'n' roll and Paul McCartney … In the future, if someone states that 'the Beatles were good for nothing,' I'll smile, for I know the truth. They were part of a spellbinding phenomenon that pushed me out from my little corner and into the big world. For this, I shall always be thankful.[109]

For Patricia Gallo and millions of other Beatles fans, the disappearance of noisy crowds, of bedroom walls covered with Beatles posters, and of long lines around the block of moviegoers waiting to see *A Hard Day's Night* and *Help!* did not spell the end of the biggest rock group in the world. The band's dedicated followers knew that times change, eras come and go, and nothing is permanent. But long after the screams had stopped, and concert venues had fallen silent, and fan club P.O. boxes ceased to exist, and magazine stands no longer sold glossy Beatles magazines, the music would still be there. The music, fans came to understand, was the most enduring monument of all.

7

In Such a Groove

It is easy to pinpoint the date of Beatlemania's birth in America. On the night of February 9, 1964, it arrived in the form of a five-song debut on the *Ed Sullivan Show*. More challenging, however, is the task of determining the date of its demise. Did it die instantly when the Beatles rushed off the field at Candlestick Park on August 29, 1966? Tony Barrow, the Beatles' original publicist, thought it did. Barrow, who was based at Brian Epstein's artists' management company, NEMS (North End Music Stores) Enterprises, a job he held from 1963 to 1968, and who coined the nickname "Fab Four" in a press release he sent out early in their rise to fame, believed the band's decision to stop touring sealed the fate of Beatlemania and the Beatles themselves. "The Beatles," he later wrote, "actually finished being the Fab Four at the end of their touring era in 1966. From then on, they were more like a limited company trading as the Beatles."[1]

Many US news outlets—broadcast and print—concurred with Barrow, treating Beatlemania as a bygone relic by the fall of 1967. But the retreat of Beatlemania left an opening for Americans who loved the band to enter a more reflective period of quietly admiring them from afar. And fans did not disappear from the scene, either. They would continue to make their presences known, long after the band ditched live performances in favor of working in the studio. In all parts of the country, people who idolized the Beatles still gathered in public—albeit in far smaller numbers—to make their love of the band known, lining up at stores to buy the Beatles LPs and singles. Or by writing letters of support for the band that appeared in newspapers and fan magazines, and record reviews published in youth-oriented underground press publications. Tens of thousands of young men and women continued paying dues to fan clubs that lasted well into the 1970s. And small clusters of fans gathered together to listen to the Beatles' music together, and experience a very different kind of music than what they heard when they watched the *Ed Sullivan Show* on that frigid February night back in 1964. And so it was that while Beatlemania had largely evaporated from American life after August 1966, the embers of Beatle fandom still glowed brightly.

After the Screaming Stopped

The release of the Beatles eighth studio album, *Sgt. Pepper's Lonely Hearts Club Band*, on June 1, 1967, in the UK, and June 2, 1967, in the United States, assumed a significance beyond simply another LP arriving in record stores. It was a landmark event in the history of modern music. The record skyrocketed up the charts on both sides of the Atlantic, spending twenty-seven weeks at the number one spot in England, according to *Record Retailer*, and fifteen weeks perched atop the *Billboard* LP chart in the United States. A runaway commercial success, *Sgt. Pepper* was also nearly universally praised by critics. With its kaleidoscopic, multicolored cover featuring a wide range of historical and cultural figures—everybody from Bob Dylan to Stan Laurel and Oliver Hardy, Marilyn Monroe to Karl Marx, Stu Sutcliffe to Edgar Allan Poe, Shirley Temple to William Burroughs, Aleister Crowley to Mae West—and songs that were every bit as eclectic and varied as the people on the cover, *Sgt. Pepper's Lonely Hearts Club Band* proved to be as much a revolution as it was a record album.[2] "The art work alone has cost fifty times more than the art work on a normal LP," grumbled Sir Joseph Lockwood, chairman of EMI Records.[3] Paul McCartney told curious journalists that Sgt. Pepper was "a mythical band leader, and this is the record of his show, plus the sort of hand-out material he would give out."[4] Adding to the intrigue, these new Pepper-esque Beatles—now hardly recognizable, even to devoted fans—bore little resemblance to their old selves, what with their new mustaches and dressed in bright satin Boer War–style uniforms, decked out with old-time military regalia. Weighty with symbolism, *Sgt. Pepper's Lonely Hearts Club Band* grew out of the Beatles' shared desires to extricate themselves from the worldwide mania that bore their band's name. Explaining the album's genesis to author Barry Miles, Paul McCartney articulated the frustration that each of the four band members felt following years of unrelenting Beatlemania:

> We were fed up with being the Beatles. We really hated that fucking four little mop-top boys' approach. We were not boys, we were men. It was all gone, all that boy shit, all that screaming, we didn't want it anymore, plus we'd now got turned on to pot and thought of ourselves as artists rather than just performers ... I thought, let's not be ourselves. Let's develop alter

egos so we're not having to project an image which we know. It would be much more free.[5]

The release of *Sgt. Pepper's Lonely Hearts Club Band* in early June 1967 occurred at a moment when youthful experimentation with alternative lifestyles was more widespread than ever. People did not use the word "counterculture" in 1967. That word would not enter into the parlance of the times for another two more years, when historian Theodore Roszak popularized it in his influential nonfiction work, *The Making of a Counter Culture: Reflections on the Technocratic Society and Its Youthful Opposition*, in 1969.[6] Roszak was one of the first scholars to draw attention to a series of loosely aligned youthful subcultures that emerged in the middle of the decade in opposition to the so-called establishment, particularly against consumer capitalism and all forms of materialism in general, the Cold War (especially the Vietnam War), racism, sexism, and the dominant popular culture in the United States. Roszak drew attention to the process in which young people were becoming increasingly alienated by—and withdrawing from—mainstream American life and culture in the late 1960s, forming alternative communities in response. These enclaves, especially visible in big cities and college towns, Roszak wrote, contained what he called a "hip economy" consisting of their own unique "clothing, light shows, rock music and its clubs, posters, electronic strobes, jewelry, buttons, bells, beads, black-fight glasses, dope pipes, and assorted 'head equipment.'"[7]

Strolling through these hippie havens, one encountered young men and women growing their hair long, wearing psychedelic fashions of the day, and living in communal settings, including farms and Victorian homes and apartment buildings overrun with cultural rebels. Not all practitioners of the new counterculture were radicals. In fact, as Roszak pointed out, some men and women who gravitated to this lifestyle harbored a deep distrust of the more ideological "politicos" in their midst, who exhorted them to take to the streets in support of Black Power, or feminism, or to resist the war in Vietnam. But the counterculture lacked an identifiable, consistent ideology. In some cases, the absence of a well-defined worldview worked against its youthful practitioners. People of the counterculture, Roszak warned, must either locate a deeper set of unifying principles—a visionary humanistic ethos—to unify and guide them through life, or else run the risk of seeing their attempts to remake the world fade into irrelevance. "If the counter culture should bog down in a colorful morass of unexamined symbols, gestures, fashions of dress, and slogans, then it will provide little that can be turned into a lifelong commitment," wrote Roszak.[8]

The trends Roszak identified in *The Making a Counter Culture* were evident in the United States years before the book was published. By 1967, many elements of the counterculture—most prominent among them, psychedelic music—were moving from the periphery of American life to its core. Upon its release, *Sgt. Pepper's Lonely Hearts Club Band* found its way to radios, tape players, and turntables at a time when the nation in the throes of change as meaningful as what the newly reconstituted Beatles had been experiencing. Virtually every aspect of American society—from domestic life to foreign policy, from popular culture to politics and the role of government in people's lives, from masculinity to femininity, from child-rearing to consumerism—was being questioned, debated, and even reshaped in complex ways. What Theodore Roszak called the "counter culture" (which soon became one word) was but one example of rapidly changing attitudes and mores and ways of doing things in the United States in the 1960s—albeit, one of the more dramatic examples. Back when the Beatles debuted on the *Ed Sullivan Show*, nobody—not even the most forward-looking Americans—could have predicted the seismic shifts taking place in the country in 1967. "But then, all revolutionary changes are unthinkable until they happen ... and then they are understood to be 'inevitable,'" said Roszak.[9]

Some of the era's most astonishing transformations happened in music. Rock historian Andrew Grant Jackson pinpointed the year 1965 as a pivotal moment when rock and roll—with its songs about teenagers, dating, falling in love, fast cars, and having sex—morphed into rock, often characterized by a louder, harder, more enveloping and multilayered sound, which made for a more diverse and nuanced soundscape. "Nineteen sixty-five is the moment in rock history when the Technicolor butterfly burst out of its black-and-white cocoon," writes Jackson.[10] Other music scholars have pointed to the year 1966—which saw the releases of such influential albums as the Beatles' *Revolver*, Bob Dylan's *Blonde on Blonde*, the Beach Boys' *Pet Sounds*, among many others—as more of a turning point.[11] Ultimately, rock music's evolution—though it may have taken remarkable leaps forward during certain years—spanned a longer arc dating back to previous decades. However, there was something undeniably dizzying about the changes occurring in the mid-1960s. Hard rock, acid rock, psychedelic rock, progressive rock—whatever one wished to call it—the louder and more aggressive new styles of music, heavily driven by guitar, characterized many of the up-and-coming groups of 1967. The Monterey Pop Festival, a three-day outdoor rock festival held in June in the city of the same name on the Pacific Ocean, showcased some of the most original and compelling acts of the time, including Big Brother and the Holding Company (with powerful-throated blues vocalist Janis Joplin), the Who, the Jimi Hendrix Experience, Simon and Garfunkel, Otis Redding, the Byrds, the Grateful Dead, and Jefferson Airplane.[12] African Americans were at the forefront of innovations, with the likes of Aretha Franklin, Ray Charles, James Brown, Marvin Gaye, Wilson Pickett, and Sly and the Family Stone helping to elevate soul and funk to the level of fine art. The same could be said of the protest songs of Nina Simone and Mahalia Jackson, or the jazz of Miles Davis, Thelonious Monk, and Sonny Rollins, to name a few. The millions of Americans from coast to coast listening to radios or watching television variety programs such as the *Ed Sullivan Show*, the *Smothers Brothers Comedy Hour*, *The Mike Douglas Show*, and *American Bandstand* could not miss the new, amplified sounds of the late 1960s. On television, the pioneers of rock performed against backdrops of brightly colored psychedelic backgrounds. "Not everyone was listening to the same thing anymore—there were more options—Cream, Hendrix, Simon and Garfunkel, the Doors, the Monkees. But the Beatles were the common denominator regardless of what you listened to," recalled a young male Beatles devotee.[13]

Although the term "counterculture" was not in use in 1967, the word "hippie" (sometimes spelled "hippy") appeared frequently in print, and was spoken often. Hippies seemed ubiquitous in America in 1967, so much so that a backlash against them was underway. The popular syndicated advice columnist Ann Landers, responding to a "fellow" wishing to establish a "Down With Hippies Society," told him that she sympathized with his sentiment. "Unfortunately, bizarre and oddball behavior is often more fascinating than decent living," observed Landers. "So long as this is one of the unalterable facts of life, the offbeat, the kook and the wayouter is going to grab the center of the stage."[14] Even the more liberal-minded adults in the United States tended to regard hippies with puzzlement and sometimes even distrust. This movement—later named the counterculture—seemed to come out of nowhere, and it appeared to be growing every day. People often said "hippie" in the same breath as "Summer of Love," the nickname given to the spring and summer months of 1967, which saw 100,000 people—many of them teenagers or in their early twenties—arriving daily to the countercultural neighborhoods of San Francisco's Haight-Ashbury district (nicknamed "Hashberry" due to the wafting clouds of skunky pot smoke always in the air there). In mid-May, Thomas Cahill, San Francisco's alarmed police chief, warned that youths were already spilling into the city, which he predicted would prompt tourists to flock in droves to the Bay Area to "see what hippies look like."[15] The threat of a hippie invasion prompted one weary San Francisco café owner to hang a sign in his window that read: "No Bare Feet, No Blankets, No Bikinis & No Beads."[16] There were "gatherings of hippie tribes" elsewhere in the United States, but none as astounding to the "square establishment" as the one in San Francisco.[17] But not all was rosy in this brave new flower-child utopia, and by late summer, television and radio broadcasts and newspapers were full of stories about overdoses, muggings, runaway teens, and rising incidents of violence in the City by the Bay. As one lurid account read: "Sidewalks are clogged by tourists with cameras, smart-aleck teeny boppers, youths on the prowl for free sex, pickpockets, toughs and, worst of all—in the eyes of the hippies—people with whiskey bottles."[18]

While San Francisco functioned as the epicenter of hippiedom during the "Summer of Love," *Sgt. Pepper's Lonely Hearts Club Band* provided the score of the times. Millions of Americans were buying the record, keeping it at the top spot of the charts for nearly four months. Unlike past Beatles' records, the success of *Sgt. Pepper's* was not driven by radio airplay. The Beatles did not release the album's songs individually as singles, which had been a major factor in propelling earlier hits to the top of *Billboard* and *Record Retailer* charts. No, the massive sales of *Sgt. Pepper* owed to people who sought it out in its entirety, as a single, whole work, of which each track was an essential part. Not surprisingly, veterans of Beatlemania had mixed reactions to the album. Janet Pickell, a long-time Beatlemaniac from Beverly, Massachusetts—a suburb of Boston—was a senior in high school when *Sgt. Pepper* was released. She could not relate to the "flower child/hippie" style of the album's tracks, and she began to lose interest in the Beatles. "I know a lot of music in that period, when they were doing *Sgt. Pepper* and all that stuff, is praised by the critics, but I just didn't like that period. I didn't like their appearance, and I didn't like that music," Pickell recalled.[19] Sandy Johnson, an ex-Beatles fan from Des Moines, Iowa, switched allegiances after deciding the Monkees were far superior to the Fab Four. To the editor of the magazine *Teen Scoop*, Johnson wrote, "Once and for all I would like to put an end to all the Monkee-Beatle arguing. The Beatles are out and the Monkees are in. The Beatles think they're too good for their fans while the Monkees are always thinking of their loyal followers. Monkees 4-ever!"[20] Dan Bond, a Beatles fan from Fond du Lac, Wisconsin, bitterly complained about the Beatles embracing counterculture styles. "I think the Beatles have ruined themselves by wearing beards and mustaches and they look horrible. They should wake up and come to their senses and clean themselves up. Also, some of the songs they have now are the most stupidly composed," said Bond.[21] Perhaps the harshest dismissal of the "new" Beatles by a former fan came from Chicago teen Barb Haig, who had adored them during Beatlemania, but had no use for them in this phase of their career, especially their widely praised *Sgt. Pepper* LP. Writing a youth column for her local newspaper called *Serendipity*, Haig opened fire on the Beatles in print:

> A lot of people thought *Sgt. Pepper's Lonely Hearts Club Band* was such a work of genius. I thought it stunk. I bought it without even hearing it because I thought that just because the Beatles did it, it had to be fabulous. I think it's kind of sad that the Beatles have changed their image so. When they first started out in '64, they were so clean and they really appealed to teens. Now with the beards and weird clothes, they look like slobs. They

no longer want to appeal to young people, their experiments in LSD proved that. They are out to be the leaders of the "Cool Group."[22]

Other fans loved the new direction taken by the Beatles. Nine-year-old David Michaelis was at summer camp with his older brother in Vermont in the summer of 1967 when he first heard *Sgt. Pepper's Lonely Hearts Club Band* coming from the inside of a barn. Back home in New York, Michaelis had two Beatles albums in his collection, *A Hard Day's Night* and *Beatles '65*, and he and his brother owned Beatles wigs. But he had never heard anything like *Sgt. Pepper's Lonely Hearts Club Band* before, and the album cover mesmerized him. "I remember feeling pierced by the words—It was twenty years ago today," he later wrote. When he returned home at the end of the summer, to a household where his parents had recently gotten divorced, David Michaelis immersed himself in the colorful psychedelic world of *Sgt. Pepper's Lonely Hearts Club Band*. He recalled: "This new album was different, more complicated. This was no longer just a release of youthful energy; it was playful, as before, but there was now an elegiac tone in the words and music—and that was what made me feel I was entitled to the record's hidden truths."[23]

For their part, the Beatles were no longer looking to impress Beatlemania fans of yesteryear. When music journalist Ray Coleman asked John Lennon in May 1967 what he thought about the Monkees, who were riding high at the time on the success of their TV show and various radio hits, Lennon—"arms flying, Dickensian spectacles flashing"—suggested that screaming adolescents who drowned out Beatles' concerts might wish to turn the Monkees into the object of their frenzies. "Let 'em dig the Monkees. Let 'em dig their cuddly mop-tops till they change their minds," Lennon declared. "The Monkees are up there to be screamed at. We're busy now, just living, and we're in such a groove!"[24] Lennon's Monkees rant highlighted a deeper truth: The post-touring Beatles now hoped to attract listeners who could hear, and appreciate, their music on a record that had been finely crafted over a period of months. Concerts, which had been such an integral part of connecting with the fans, had become obsolete to them, and they were not hesitant to say so. Their views on the matter had changed a great deal in a short period of time. In a profile of the band that appeared in the September 1966 issue of *16 Magazine*, Ringo Starr told an interviewer: "The traveling bit isn't always enjoyable, but touring is still one of the most important things we do ... Fans want to see groups—not just listen to their records."[25] Less than a year later, in June 1967, Ringo's attitude about touring had undergone a complete reversal. "The past is past. That tour thing, for instance. We probably won't do any more tours—at least not like the old ones. We're trying to break new ground," he stated.[26] Even more succinctly, John Lennon stated, "Tours are out."[27] Well into 1968, journalists were asking the Beatles whether they would consider touring again, and if they missed the dazzle of Beatlemania. "We're not asking anyone to love us or hate us," George Harrison told a reporter in August 1968. "Who was it said we were the goody-goody fab four moptops? Not us. We're not. We're four young people going through life just like anybody else, learning all the time."[28]

Multitudes of fans from the Beatlemania period remained loyal to the band after touring ceased, transitioning with their idols into their next incarnation, and witnessing new fans entering the expanding tent. A new kind of Beatle fandom emerged in the aftermath of *Sgt. Pepper's Lonely Hearts Club Band*, one that was more sophisticated and introspective, more mature and subdued. Like David Michaelis, the new breed of Beatles fans was more committed to seeking the "hidden truths" and deeper meanings of the Beatles' multifaceted music.[29] They did not simply listen to the music. They analyzed lyrics, considered the unique style of each track, and searched for threads, for common themes, that drew the songs together. Screaming at large venues had given way to quiet reflections beside the hi-fi. An Oxford University undergraduate in 1968 could have been speaking for countless fans on the other side of the "pond" when he explained what the Beatles meant to him: "I liked the Beatles five years ago, when I was a kid. Then I started growing too old for them, and passed my records on to my kid sister. I think their latest records are great, though. I've got *Sgt. Pepper's Lonely Hearts Club Band* up at Oxford with me, and we play it a lot."[30]

Meanwhile, Beatlemania did not vanish outright, and mentions of it could still be found in the press, and heard on television and radio. As of February 1968, the Beatles Fan Club in England boasted 40,000 members, and its American counterpart still had 20,000 people on its rolls.[31] "Beatle fans are not dead. The 'mania' that was prevalent two years ago may have died a bit, but the appreciation and love is still very much alive," wrote Patti, a fan from Fresno, California, in July 1967.[32] But in these changing times, nobody could deny that Beatlemania was a fragment of its once mighty self. By confining themselves to EMI Studios on Abbey Road, the Beatles missed out on the gargantuan outdoor rock festivals that became such an integral part of the counterculture: the Monterey International Pop Festival in Monterey, California, in June 1967; the Miami Pop Festival, held in May and December 1968; and the mighty Woodstock, the leviathan of open-air gatherings, held in August 1969, where the Beatles were conspicuously absent. But in the case of the Beatles, absence made hearts grow fonder. There were still millions of individual Beatles fans in the United States. They no longer gathered in huge numbers in public places to scream and be part of mass pandemonium. But that did not make them any less dedicated. Ron Sweed, of Euclid, Ohio, age seventeen at the time of the release of *Sgt. Pepper*, had been a Beatles fan for years. He was already a veteran of the Beatles' concert circuit, having seen them play at Cleveland's Public Auditorium in 1964 (after attending the band's press conference), then again in 1965 in Toronto, and back in Cleveland once more in 1966. After touring ended, Beatles fans in Cleveland showed their love for the band in other ways. "I remember the summer of '67 when Sgt. Pepper came out," he recalled. "I would walk around downtown Cleveland or in Euclid, where I was raised and grew up, and you'd hear out of people's windows just a track from *Sgt. Pepper*. For months after it was released!"[33] Even though the throngs of screaming fans that were an essential ingredient of Beatlemania were now gone, Beatles fans still found ways to express their love for the band in public across the United States, albeit in smaller groups. "There was lots of discussion about *Sgt. Pepper*—it was a big part of our lives," remembered a sixteen-year-old fan. "My friends and I would meet and hang out in the park on a Sunday afternoon, and we'd listen to the album."[34]

By the summer of 1967, the more politicized elements of the counterculture were starting to embrace the Beatles in greater numbers. The Beatles' increasingly experimental approach to making music, and their antiauthoritarian sensibilities, dovetailed perfectly with the crystalizing agenda of countercultural politicos. No other prominent rock band of the era was as outspoken, on a host of vital issues, as the Beatles. And their statements of dissent, coupled with the poetry and surrealism of their songs, resonated with youthful insurgents. The timing was ideal for the idolization of the Beatles' by men and women in the counterculture. Events were taking a darker turn, at home and abroad. The war in Vietnam, expanding with each passing month, continued to fuel the dissent, triggering marches in streets and on campuses across the United States, and contributing to the growth of the nation's antiwar coalition. Domestic upheavals in the streets of Newark, Detroit, Birmingham, Milwaukee, Minneapolis, New York, and elsewhere supplied jarring footage on nightly network news. Talk of a so-called Long, Hot Summer of 1967—a term used to describe over 150 race riots and other disturbances across America— eclipsed references to the "Summer of Love."[35] Under these circumstances, resisters redoubled their efforts, and New Left radicals began to refer to the Beatles as harbingers of a new era. "The Beatles themselves represent the heart of a growing protest on behalf of youth against a society blatant with hypocrisy and moral bankruptcy," wrote Barry Weisberg, a Students for a Democratic Society (SDS) activist and scholar based in Berkeley, California.[36] In the fall of 1967, a New York region SDS newsletter pointed to the Beatles as a significant influence on protests that were gaining traction among the nation's high school students.

> The greatest and most exciting growth in the student has been in high schools ... It must be realized that a new, politically inarticulate, but radically

healthy, generation of students has been produced by a combination of this America, now at war for two and a half years, and those Beatles, with their message of love. Great numbers of 14-, 15- and 16-year-old people are consciously choosing to reject their country's society and create their own.[37]

Writing in a New York City–based SDS newspaper in December 1967, antiwar movement organizer, writer, and scholar Paul Wasserman attempted to explain the significance of the Beatles to his fellow radicals:

> The Beatles, for one, provide some grounds for hope, for their immense popularity has left them free to do pretty much whatever they want, on radio, in film, or on TV ... There is much to be said for discussing the Beatles. They are the most influential and most creative force in pop music today. Besides this (again, thanks to the mass media), anything they do or say in public becomes instantaneously symbolic to ... their own generation ... Thus, by discussing the Beatles, we discuss everything.[38]

In other segments of the activist left and the counterculture, the Beatles were held up as spokespeople of their generation. Abbie Hoffman, the colorful cofounder of the Youth International Party (also known as the Yippies) kept the Beatles on constant rotation while he organized bold acts of resistance.[39] He often sang their praises in speeches, and claimed they influenced Yippie actions, including their outrageous protests during the Democratic National Convention in Chicago in 1968, during which they threatened to put LSD into the city's water supply and were filmed getting arrested by the Chicago police. "There was a cultural revolution where the best and the popular were identical," Hoffman explained. "And that is a very rare occurrence in history. The effect of something like *Sgt Pepper's Lonely Hearts Club Band* ... on me and other activists, organizers and counterculture people around the world was one of incredible impact."[40] After the release of *Revolver*, which contained the beloved psychedelic track "Yellow Submarine," hippies and peace activists transformed the "yellow submarine" of the song into a symbol of their own utopian dreams and aspirations. This was evident at repeated public gatherings, especially at demonstrations. In the fall of 1966, students at the University of California in Berkeley organized antiwar protests aimed at resisting Navy recruiters on campus. They gathered by the thousands outside of Sproul Hall—the hub of student activity on campus—and sang the lyrics en masse to "Yellow Submarine." At the time, Theodore Roszak noted, the song was "the current hit on all the local high-school campuses."[41] "Yellow Submarine" even found admirers among revolutionary extremists. The radical Weather Underground, a splinter group that grew out of the SDS, engaged in a series of militant protests in the streets of Chicago during their so-called Days of Rage actions in October 1969. While causing mayhem and chaos, they could be heard singing their own "Yellow Submarine"–inspired theme song: "We all live in a Weatherman machine, Weatherman machine, Weatherman machine."[42]

Not everyone on the political left sang the Beatles' praises, or their songs, for that matter. Even though large segments of the counterculture and New Left applauded the reincarnated Beatles of *Sgt. Pepper's Lonely Hearts Club Band*, the band's controversial song "Revolution," released in 1968, upset a number of committed radicals, due to its warnings against revolutionary violence, and its assurances, "Don't you know it's gonna be all right?" The Beatles released two versions of the song: a slow, bluesy rendition ("Revolution 1"), featured on the album *The Beatles*, popularly known as the *White Album*; and a harder rocking "Revolution," released as the B-side with "Hey Jude," that was the version played most frequently on the radio. To no one's surprise, ideological purists in the New Left went after Lennon savagely in the underground press for the sin of questioning the act of revolution. Radical journalist and music critic David Lippman, writing in the Seattle-based leftist pop culture newspaper *Helix* in 1968, attacked the Beatles—John Lennon in particular (who wrote "Revolution 1")—for embracing "oppressive capitalism." "If the Beatles, feeling the thrill of exploiting their fellow youth, continue to wage a war of counterrevolution, then we will have lost them to the enemy," Lippman insisted. He acknowledged that the Beatles' latest self-titled album contained some "very interesting" tracks. Yet Lippman adopted a dark tone in his analysis of the Beatles, right down to his gloomy conclusion, mired in conspiratorial thinking: "But the fact remains that the demise of the Beatle-myth and of Beatle-worship has social implications and can have political impact if we wish to make something of it. The Beatles are gaining increased trust from the Western ruling class as they expand their exploitive capitalist dealings."[43]

A flurry of similar attacks echoed throughout the more radical publications of the underground press. The radical music critic Ralph J. Gleason, a beloved figure in the San Francisco jazz and rock scenes, offered an equally grim verdict about "Revolution" and the Beatles. Writing for the Liberation News Service (LNS) in September 1968, Gleason warned leftists that the Beatles could not be counted on by leftist activists. They were not reliable allies, he insisted, and "Revolution" was Exhibit A of their cynicism and greed. "So the Beatles say put down your flags and believe that all we need is love and say the word and you'll be free," wrote Gleason, in a piece overflowing with sarcasm. He insisted the song was aimed directly at "Americans, specifically student activists, Beatles fans all." In Gleason's analysis, "Revolution," Lennon's critique of well-documented excesses committed by revolutions in recent history, was emblematic of the entire body of Beatles' songs, in all their diversity. His reductionist review wrapped up with a harsh dismissal of well-meaning politicos who still found inspiration in the Beatles' music: "And here you have it. The answer to the questions raised by the people who wanted the Beatles to speak out against the war in Vietnam. To the people who wanted the Beatles to endorse this or endorse that cause and contribute to this campaign or to that campaign."[44]

Many ultraleft militants who thought of themselves as the vanguard of a coming revolution embraced the protest song "Street Fighting Man," by the Rolling Stones, as an alternative to what they regarded as the betrayal of "Revolution." The track was released as a single amidst the epic clashes between riot police and protesters in the streets of downtown Chicago during the Democratic National Convention in August 1968. "Street Fighting Man" appealed to young militant ideologues, many of whom failed to notice the lyrics were actually Mick Jagger's lament that he could not take part in anti–Vietnam War demonstrations in London. The singer-songwriter had participated in a protest rally at the US Embassy in London in March 1968, but hordes of fans recognized him, making the event more about Jagger than the Vietnam War. Jagger turned the experience into a song that, like "Revolution," became emblematic of its times. Despite vague lyrics, "Street Fighting Man" won praise among politico writers in the underground press, and a segment of the radical left even regarded Stones' frontman Jagger as a bona fide revolutionary, who—unlike the pacifist Lennon—recognized the historical necessity of armed struggle. "Soon after 'Street Fighting Man' was released, New York City's most militant newspaper, the *Rat*, printed its lyrics in a sidebar," noted historian John McMillian.[45] In the pages of the glossy leftist *Ramparts* magazine, radical journalist Susan Lydon cheered the Rolling Stones as "musical anarchists, harbingers of chaos." On the other hand, the Beatles, said Lydon, "have come to occupy a place in British society as structured and secure as the Queen's. Basically, they were always nice kids, a little weird maybe, but you wouldn't mind if your sister married one." Lydon critiqued "Revolution 1," which—in her view—"confirms the Beatles' process of intellectual ossification," and, worse yet, "in these troubled times, preaches counter-revolution." By contrast, with "Street Fighting Man," a song Lydon insisted was an expression of "solidarity with the street-fighters," the Rolling Stones "have created a song that is a sympathetic and symbolic representation of street fighting."[46] Lydon was far from alone in her denunciation of the Beatles and praise of the Stones. The leftist music critic Jon Landau compared the Beatles unfavorably to the Rolling Stones, who he regarded as the more principled of the two bands: "The Stones strike for realism, in contrast to the Beatles' fantasies ... The Stones may not be sure where their heads are, but their hearts are out in the streets."[47] Celebrations of the Rolling Stones as authentic revolutionaries abounded in the underground newspapers. Historian John Wiener perceptively summed up the mind-set on the far left in the United States in the stormy months following the release of "Revolution 1" and "Street Fighting Man": "By late 1968 the political significance of pop groups had become a central issue for the New Left. Almost without exception the Rolling Stones were held up as revolutionaries, in contrast to the accommodationist Beatles."[48]

The slings and arrows of far-left ideologues did not deter the Beatles any more than those coming from the extreme opposite side of the political spectrum. They continued writing songs, making music, recording albums, and reinventing themselves. In doing so, they led the way during the heyday of psychedelic rock, remaking rules, only to break them again, with their compositions. Beatlemania's demise marked the opening of a new chapter filled with fresh beginnings and exciting possibilities. Fans continued following the Beatles in the news, rushed to stores to purchase their albums on release dates, and expressed their love for the band on smaller scales.

The Last Hurrah

The Beatles maintained a relentless schedule between the release of *Sgt. Pepper's Lonely Hearts Club Band* in early June 1967 and their breakup in the spring of 1970. Constantly in and out of EMI Studios, they alternated their time between writing music and recording it. Each new Beatles milestone continued to capture the attention of the press on both sides of the Atlantic: John Lennon meeting Yoko Ono in London in the fall of 1966, and forming a relationship—both intimate and collaborative—that would disintegrate their families and send them both in new directions artistically; the Beatles' performance of "All You Need is Love" on the satellite program *Our World*, on June 25, 1967, which reached an estimated 400 million viewers worldwide; manager Brian Epstein's tragic death on August 27, 1967; the release of the *Magical Mystery Tour* LP in the United States and double EP in the UK in the late fall, and the airing of the film of the same name on the BBC on Boxing Day (December 26) 1967; the Beatles' immersion in the teachings of Maharishi Mahesh Yogi and their heavily publicized journey to India in February 1968; the release of *The Beatles*—also known as *The White Album*, for its plain white cover—in late November 1968; John Lennon's marriage to Yoko Ono, and Paul McCartney's to Linda Eastman, within a few days of each other, in March 1969; the long, arduous, troubled making of their *Get Back / Let It Be* album, and its subsequent release in early 1970; their celebrated *Abbey Road* (was it their final album or their penultimate album?), released in late September 1969; and their unraveling as a band in the early months of 1970 and all the uncertainty that went with it. Their story has been richly chronicled in books, articles, websites, documentaries, graphic novels, oral histories, and even in a videogame.[49]

But the band's influence on American society post-Beatlemania was more difficult to gauge. Beatle fandom's shift from the public realm to the private sphere removed it from the spotlight, resulting in expressions of love for the band becoming a more solitary affair. Beatles fans being increasingly out of sight, and, by extension, out of mind, sometimes created the false impression that they no longer existed. A Beatles supporter from Detroit endeavored to correct such notions in a letter to *Teen World* early in 1969: "I think it's sickening when magazines stop printing stories about really terrific people just because they don't have people jumping off roofs and screaming themselves silly anymore. Sure, maybe the Beatles don't have the kind of fans they once had, but they're still the greatest group in the whole world."[50] Teenager Elaine Svientek, a Beatle person from Chicago, expressed similar regrets: "Plenty of times I wish that Beatlemania would start all over."[51] Glowing embers of Beatlemania no doubt remained, and public gatherings of fans still happened from time to time. One obvious example were the groundswells of support that occurred when a new Beatles' album arrived in stores. Like *Sgt. Pepper's Lonely Hearts Club Band*, the release of each subsequent Beatles' record generated excitement in the United States, rising to the level of a significant historical event. Fans across America eagerly awaited Beatles' LPs and singles, sending them all to the top of the *Billboard* charts.

And there was always talk of another tour, of more concerts, and the possibility of seeing the band live again. In 1968, disc jockeys in the United States collected names on petitions for a "Bring Back the Beatles" campaign, hoping all the signatures would impress the Beatles to return for another tour of North America. "The Beatles have said that they would return to the United States for a tour if they could be sure that audiences would listen to their music quietly without screaming," noted a columnist in the July 1968 issue of *Hit Parader*. "Petitions signed by fans promising to be quiet if the Beatles come back are being started all over the country."[52] In Phoenix, DJ Phil Motta of KRIZ AM 1230 gathered 150,000 names on a petition pleading with the Beatles to come back to the United States to perform live.[53] Similar large-scale petitioning efforts took hold across the United States, especially big cities such as New York, Minneapolis, and Los Angeles.[54] Rumors swirled in 1968 that the Beatles would soon be returning for another tour. Music promoters swore that they had it on "good authority" that the band planned to play multiple concerts in North America once more after a long hiatus. During the fall, there was talk of a "farewell concert tour" which would consist of, in the words of *San Francisco Chronicle* journalist Tom Campbell, "ten open dates at $100,000 per, or a cool $1 million. It's a comfort to learn the Beatles still care about the Long Green."[55]

Hopes stayed high in 1969 that the Beatles would return to the United States for a series of concerts. In February, *16 Magazine* optimistically informed its readers: "Since over one half of the 30 new songs in the Beatles' double Apple LP—called *The Beatles*—can be adapted for stage performance, there is an excellent chance that the Fab Four will be giving a live English performance before the new year. We sure hope so!"[56] Fueling speculation were occasional comments by John, Paul, George, and Ringo containing tantalizing hints of another tour. Even as late as the summer of 1969, John Lennon told an interviewer that a tour was "a possibility," and that he had been talking with others in the band about "how we'd do it if we did."[57] "We will give several public shows this year," Lennon assured an interviewer in March 1969.[58] Asked around that same time if the Beatles ever planned to play live again, George Harrison expressed his wish to "play resident in a club." George then clarified: "Not to go touring ... because I didn't like all that traveling and playing, and all that sort of thing. But if we were to do a live show, I'd prefer to do it like at the Top Ten in Hamburg for three months, and just play in the one place for about three months."[59]

Despite such talk, another tour was not to be. Months passed, and the Beatles never returned as a band to play live in the United States. However, individual band members would come back to North American soil to entertain audiences. On September 13, 1969, John Lennon's newly formed Plastic Ono Band, with Yoko Ono providing additional vocals, Eric Clapton on guitar, artist and musician Klaus Voormann on bass, and session musician Alan White playing drums, performed in front of 20,000 people, who came to the concert from both sides of the border, at Toronto's Varsity Stadium. The Plastic Ono Band shared the stage at the Toronto Rock and Roll Revival with other acts, old and new, including the Doors, Chuck Berry, the Chicago Transit Authority (later, simply, Chicago), Jerry Lee Lewis, Little Richard, Alice Cooper, Gene Vincent, and Bo Diddley. Lennon had agreed only the day before to bring his band to the festival, making it a hastily organized affair. "We're just going to do numbers we know 'cause we've never played together before," announced John Lennon from the microphone, "looking like the White Rabbit with a full beard," according to one account.[60] The Plastic Ono Band played a version of "Yer Blues," from the *White Album*, and some familiar rock and roll standards, such as "Blue Suede Shoes," "Money (That's What I Want)" and "Dizzy Miss Lizzy." The setlist included a couple of new Lennon compositions, including "Cold Turkey" and "Give Peace a Chance." "The sound of the '50s hadn't changed but the audience was different. Long hair, bare feet, beads, beards, and way-out clothes were all around," observed a Canadian journalist.[61] An LP of the concert, on the Apple label, came out three months later, instantly soaring to number 10 on the Billboard 200.[62]

Other events drew fans out into the public eye. Beatlemaniacs flocked to see the animated feature film *Yellow Submarine* in the summer of 1968, marveling at the bizarre, colorful psychedelic images that filled the movie screen—the Blue Meanies ("who hate music, hate color, hate everything positive"), the weirdly distorted Beatles (as they might appear to someone on LSD), and a cast of eccentrics (Old Fred, the Turtle Turks, Tall Apple Bonkers, Butterfly Stompers, etc.) doing their thing against multicolored fantasy landscapes. Al Brodax, the man responsible for the Beatles' Saturday morning cartoon on ABC, produced and codirected the film, and became its most enthusiastic promoter upon its release. "It starts with a war," explained Brodax enthusiastically. "The Meanies attack with anti-music missiles and Pepperland dissolves in the sense that color goes and everything is frozen in black and white. The only way to bring it alive is music."[63] Even diehard Beatles fans did not quite know what to make of the striking psychedelic imagery of *Yellow Submarine*. At a sneak preview of the film in Boston, film critic Marjory Adams "saw several young men rapt in adulation. The strange thing is that they wore their hair Beatle style, had on the same flared pants, wore no ties. Although there were eager young girls, I could see that this particular picture had more appeal for male fans. There wasn't a single female shriek during the film."[64] The film featured several Beatles songs, including the titular "Yellow Submarine," as well as "Nowhere Man," "Eleanor Rigby," "When I'm Sixty-Four," and "Lucy in the Sky With Diamonds." The tracks "Only a Northern Song," "All Together Now," "It's All Too Much," and 'Hey Bulldog" were written and recorded for the film, but the Beatles refused to provide the voices for their animated likenesses. The band members were, according to music historian and critic Kevin Courrier, "still shaking off the brutal response to *Magical Mystery Tour*," their widely panned film from the previous year, and they kept their involvement in the animated film to a minimum.[65] Despite that, *Yellow Submarine* ended up being a respectable box office hit in 1968, winning the acclaim that eluded their perplexing cinematic fiasco *Magical Mystery Tour*. "The film is a masterpiece and it has opened up new and undreamed of horizons for animation. It bears seeing several times for its content to be fully appreciated, and it has given such an impetus to the full-length animation cinema that is already a classic," wrote filmmaker and animation scholar Bruno Edra.[66]

Aside from their forays into cinema, the individual Beatles captured the public's attention at various points in the late 1960s. Through no fault of their own, the Beatles were dragged into the media by the insane rantings of Charles Manson, the musician and head of a cult of bloodthirsty followers who murdered a number of people in California in the summer of 1969. Upon his arrest, Manson blamed the depraved acts of his "family," in part, on coded messages he insisted were contained in Beatles tracks on the *White*

FIGURE 7.1 *Newlyweds John Lennon and Yoko Ono in their bed in the presidential suite of the Hilton Hotel, Amsterdam, March 25, 1969. The couple was staging a "bed-in for peace" and intended to stay in bed for seven days "as a protest against war and violence in the world," specifically the Vietnam War. Source: Photo by Keystone/Hulton Archive via Getty Images.*

Album, especially "Helter Skelter," "Blackbird," "Revolution 1," "Revolution 9," and "Piggies." The Beatles condemned the Manson Family's horror show in no uncertain terms.[67] Around the same time, John Lennon was hogging the spotlight, thanks to the unorthodox anti–Vietnam War protests that he engaged in with partner Yoko Ono: the Bed-Ins for Peace in Montreal and Amsterdam (see Figure 7.1), their practice of wearing enormous bags over their bodies (which they called "bagism") to resist the militarism, and their decision to mail acorns to world leaders, requesting that they be planted in support of world peace.[68] By now, Lennon sported long hair and a long beard, and he, along with Yoko Ono, welcomed journalists, photographers, politicians, celebrities, and other prominent figures into their hotel rooms while they sat in bed, condemning the bloodletting in Southeast Asia and extolling the virtues of nonviolence. The couple's eccentric approach to resistance paralleled their artistic collaborations, which included the records *Unfinished Music No. 1: Two Virgins* (1968), *Unfinished Music No. 2: Life with the Lions* (1969), and

Wedding Album (1969), albums that were full of primal screams, otherworldly sound effects, dialogues about art and peace and world affairs, and avant-garde music. Their unusual approach to protest, like their experimental albums, attracted attention chiefly because of Lennon's status as one of the most prominent rock musicians in the world. Lennon's efforts won praise of antiwar activists and journalists in the underground press, including some who had soured him over the song "Revolution 1." In March 1970, the radical news collective LNS syndicated to numerous alternative press publications an interview with Creedence Clearwater Revival lead guitarist, songwriter, and singer John Forgerty, who singled out Lennon for praise for his newfound commitment to activism:

> I think John Lennon is really trying to do something. A lot of times you can, well, I won't, but a lot of people will attack, let's say, his methods. They think that it's foolish or whatever. But the fact that he's doing anything is, you know, so much more than what most people are doing. And for a guy of that stature—I mean, he's one half of the number one songwriting team in the world. He's one-quarter of the number one group in the world. Far and away number one, I mean, miles ahead of number two, whoever that is. They're like legends in their own time ... They have no other group to compare to, really.[69]

Of the four Beatles, it was Paul McCartney, not John Lennon, who inspired a brief resurgence of Beatlemania. But this was not a last hurrah of McCartney's making. Since 1967, tales had been circulating around the world, particularly in the United States, that he had died in a mysterious car crash driving his Aston Martin in November 1966. McCartney, according to the true believers, had been surreptitiously replaced by a doppelganger, a la *Invasion of the Body Snatchers*, the 1956 science fiction film (remade in 1978) in which alien "pod people" lookalikes replaced the human beings they resembled. The other Beatles—John, George, and Ringo—went along with the cover-up, to ensure a bright future for the band, welcoming the ersatz changeling "McCartney" into their band with open arms. Part conspiracy theory, part urban legend, part mass panic, part exploitive hoax, the so-called Paul Is Dead narrative spread quickly across the United States, kept alive by a mix of anxiety-filled fans fearing the worst, paranoid individuals who envisioned dark cabals, and tongue-in-cheek pranksters who found the story absurdly comical and tried to prolong its longevity. Before long, the rumor took on a labyrinthine quality, filled with arcane details. Decades before the emergence of the internet, when information was harder to come by, believers assumed the worst, while skeptics pointed to inconsistencies in the rumors. The story began in September as an article in the student newspaper at Drake University in Des

Moines, Iowa. It eventually went national on October 22, when the nightly news on ABC alluded to it, followed by a mention of it by newsman John Chancellor the following night on NBC.[70] While the "Paul Is Dead" affair captured the attention of handfuls of fans outside the United States, this was chiefly an American phenomenon that dovetailed with the country's long history of conspiracy thinking.[71]

And rapidly it spread, with tenacious Paul-is-dead theorists in all parts of the nation hunting for clues in Beatles song lyrics and on album covers, particularly *Sgt. Pepper's Lonely Hearts Club Band*, *Magical Mystery Tour*, and *Abbey Road*. Anything cryptic was seized upon as hard evidence of the conspiracy. Gossip added new dimensions to the allegations, and the story continued to snowball. Magazines packed with colorful pictures and lurid stories appeared at newsstands and in supermarkets. A spokesperson for Apple Corps, Ltd., said the company's switchboards had been "inundated by telephone calls from teenagers in the United States inquiring about the rumor."[72] Gatherings of fans—at times by the hundreds—occurred in parts of the country.[73] Some Beatlemaniacs, like eighteen-year-old Joel Glazier, from Wilmington, Delaware, dedicated endless hours to investigating potential leads and signs of deception. Glazier spent decades amassing a "Paul Is Dead" archive, filling file folders with the latest clippings. "A lot of people like conspiracy theories. And it's a mystery, too. People like mysteries," said Glazier twenty years later, in 1989, still collecting information for his unusual repository.[74] In late 1969, at the height of the nationwide fixation, the Puerto Rican composer, musician, and singer José Feliciano—under the pseudonym "Werbley Finster"—wrote a song about it titled "So Long, Paul," as did a band called Mystery Tour with their minor novelty hit, "The Ballad of Paul."[75]

The "Paul Is Dead" uproar proved to be the biggest Beatles media frenzy since the "More Popular Than Jesus" controversy three years earlier. "Rumours that Paul McCartney is dead, which have pushed the Beatles back to the top of the charts in America, are only part of a new surge of Beatlemania, which is sweeping the United States," observed journalist Victor Keegan in the *Manchester Guardian* in October 1969.[76] The "Paul Is Dead" obsession captured the imaginations of Americans from all walks of life, resonating especially deeply with fans who could not understand why Paul, in their view, had been so aloof in recent years. A Harvard university student could have been speaking for millions of young people across the country when he said, "My roommates and about 10 other guys spent the night listening to Beatles records, forward, backward, at 33 1/3, 45. It's the conversation rage here."[77] Two Detroit disc jockeys, John Small and Dan Carlisle, joined forces with rock music promoter Russ Gibb, to fan the flames of paranoia by collecting as much evidence as they could find to prove that McCartney was, indeed, deceased, or at least in very bad shape. Small told an interviewer: "We feel sure there is something to this. I mean, we've talked with top record producers who say it's inconceivable that all these things could have been coincidentally put in songs and jackets."[78]

Nobody at the time could have anticipated that talk of Paul's "death" would last for decades, with true believers recycling aging, discredited evidence, and persevering with their delusions well into the twenty-first century. McCartney himself found the allegations ludicrous and perplexing, and he denied that it was a publicity stunt originating with Apple Records. "It's all bloody stupid," Paul angrily fired back. Asked why so many people were obsessed with his nonexistent death, he shrugged and expressed his dismay about the potency of such claims. "Perhaps the rumour started because I haven't been much in the press lately," he said. "I have done enough press for a lifetime, and I don't have anything to say these days. I am happy to be with my family and I will work when I work."[79] There was no missing the bitter edge of McCartney's words. At age twenty-seven, the Liverpudlian had already given over more than a decade of his life to his music, working on it night and day, consumed by it year after year. His band mates shared his weariness. The "Paul Is Dead" craze had unleashed upon McCartney the ravings of a restless segment of the Beatles' fan community that—when going through McCartney withdrawals—turned against him by churning out a barrage of unfounded claims about his death and replacement with an imposter, merely for the sake of keeping the Beatles intact. It is little wonder that McCartney regarded the entire strange episode as a deeply insulting affront to him. While skeptics found humorous camp value in it all, Paul did not. At the height of the rampant rumormongering, McCartney pleaded with a journalist: "Can you spread it around that I am just an ordinary person and want to live in peace? We have to go now. We have two children at home."[80]

The End

The break-up of the Beatles was first announced by Paul McCartney on April 10, 1970, in the form of a press release in a Q&A format containing a statement by him which journalists interpreted to mean that the band was no more. McCartney intended the timing of the announcement to coincide with his debut solo LP, *McCartney*, scheduled for release on April 17. But news of the Beatles' disbanding overshadowed the release of McCartney's album. "The Beatles died last week, victims of that dread condition, maturity," wrote author Albert Goldman in the pages of *Life Magazine*.[81] The eyes of the world were now—at least momentarily—on the Beatles. And yet, for months, newspapers on both sides of the Atlantic had been filled with stories about discord in the band, hinting that a parting of ways was forthcoming. The break-up occurred at a time of tumult in the United States, against a backdrop of a catastrophic yet expanding American war in Southeast Asia, and a corresponding groundswell of antiwar resistance. The nation was still reeling from a decade full of upheaval, polarization, assassinations, and nonstop warfare in Vietnam, a conflict becoming increasingly unpopular with each new opinion poll. In these days of torment, with President Richard Nixon poised to expand American military personnel into Vietnam's neighbor to the west, Cambodia, and the antiwar coalition busily mobilizing for its spring offensives, the abrupt ending of a rock band seemed unworthy of front-page headlines. Nevertheless, press coverage of the Beatles' break-up was extensive in the United States, and it was widely reported on network nightly news broadcasts as well.[82]

When the end finally came for the Beatles, fan reactions in the United States ran the gamut from distraught to indifferent. "I was devastated. It was like losing a parent after your parents get divorced. We had a fear that they wouldn't make music again as individuals. And we didn't want to lose that," recalled Maryanne Laffin, a Beatles fan from New York.[83] "We're so sad, we can't stop crying," declared Mindy, Nancy, and Hortense, a trio of Beatles fans from Pasadena, California, in June 1970.[84] Looking back at the event decades later, Lena Marroletti, of Turnersville, New Jersey, remembered that she fell into a "state of depression" along with "many other fans ... following that announcement."[85] Mickey McLean of Greensboro, North Carolina, recounted that he "agonized over their breakup in 1970 and ... I longed for a reunion."[86] However, there were Beatles fans that simply did not care about the announcement. As far as they were concerned, the band had not performed live in the United States in nearly four years, and the four of them going their separate ways was hardly the end of the world. Mike Crowley, a junior at Cherry Hill High School East in Cherry Hill, New Jersey, interviewed a group of his classmates, asking them how they felt about McCartney leaving the Beatles. An aspiring journalist, Crowley wrote their reactions in the form of an article that appeared in Camden's newspaper, the *Courier-Post*. His fellow high school students felt apathetic about the break-up, and none of them seemed to be in the least bit saddened or shaken by the announcement. "Paul McCartney can do very well without the Beatles," was the consensus opinion that Crowley found in the halls of his school. Many of his classmates "were long-time Beatles fans from the group's early years," Crowley wrote. One of his fellow juniors, Connie Metzen, stated a widely held view among the students when she said, "He was smart to go off by himself. Why should he stay with them when he can well by himself?" Other students at Cherry Hill High, such as eighteen-year-old Dave Etengoff, held Paul in similarly high regard, singling him out as the most talented band member in the Beatles, a towering figure in pop music whose future was bright with hope. "Paul will be able to find more of what he wants now, and the Beatles can still grow and prosper," Etengoff told Crowley.[87]

Such apathetic reactions were more the norm than the exception in the United States in April 1970. Like the proverbial boy who cried wolf from Aesop's Fables, talk of a Beatles breakup had been the stuff of alarmist news stories for years. A survey of press headlines from as early as the fall of 1966 adds perspective to the pervasive skepticism of four years later: "Beatles Break-Up Has All England in a Fog"[88]; "Manager Refuses to Deny Rumor of Beatles Break-Up"[89]; "Rumored Beatles Break-Up Denied"[90]; "Beatles Break-Up Coming?"[91]; and "Beatles May Break Up as Top Singing Group."[92] Wire service stories about the Beatles calling it quits remained abundant for the rest of the decade, resulting in people harboring doubts about each new round of rumors and speculation. These previous false alarms, coupled with reassurances that the disbanding of the world's most famous band was not going to happen, helped bring calm to the Beatles' fan community. "The Beatles still like each other—that is part of the trouble. They do not want to split up, but the present rift seems to be part of their growing up. The split is probably temporary and not irretrievable," said Derek Taylor, publicist for the Beatles and Apple Corps, Ltd.[93] Similarly, Ringo Starr and George Harrison issued a playful statement to the press—written with soothing Beatle humor—hinting that a forever break-up was not happening. "The world is still spinning and so are we and so are you [and] when the spinning stops—that'll be the time to worry. Not before. Until then, the Beatles are alive and well and the beat goes on. The beat goes on."[94]

Whatever comfort came from those words was soon extinguished by the gathering storm of events. The month of May brought terrible news of the Vietnam War spilling into neighboring Cambodia, a development that triggered uprisings on college campuses across the United States. While round-the-clock bombing pulverized the Cambodian countryside, and US troops penetrated the country's thick jungle frontier, protesters back home shut universities down by the hundreds during the spring. The horrifying killings of students at Kent State in Ohio and Jackson State in Mississippi sent shockwaves through America. "The country is virtually on the edge of a spiritual, and perhaps even physical, breakdown. For the first time in a century, we are not sure there is a future for America."[95] So said New York mayor John Lindsay on May 6, two days after the killings at Kent State, who could have been speaking for any one of millions of Americans who felt the same way as they watched helplessly, with nervous dismay, as their country seemed to be spiraling downward into a morass of chaos and disorder before their very eyes.

Under these circumstances, the Beatles break-up became old news, a throwback to a simpler time, mere weeks before everything went so horribly wrong. When Michael Lindsay-Hogg's grim 80-minute documentary *Let It*

Be opened in scattered American theaters later in the month, it predictably failed to stir the same enthusiasm as *A Hard Day's Night* six years earlier. It wasn't simply a dark film metaphorically. It was a dark film literally, filled with poorly-lit sequences of the Beatles slogging their way through making an album tentatively titled *Get Back*, which would later be changed to *Let It Be*. Bay Area music critic Philip Elwood arrived at this terse verdict in the *San Francisco Examiner*: "The film *Let It Be* is ... a documentary of precisely nothing, except the death throes of the Beatles."[96] Many viewers who sat in darkened theaters during the turbulence of May 1970 arrived at similar conclusions while watching the friction between the Beatles unfold on the big screen. The film's director, Michael Lindsay-Hogg, admitted that his film focused on the more dramatic moments of tension in the studio during the making of the *Get Back / Let It Be* album to construct a narrative about the Beatles' final days. "You can virtually see them breaking up. There is one particularly telling shot in which Paul McCartney and George Harrison get into a heated argument," explained Lindsay-Hogg.[97]

Like the ill-fated film *Magical Mystery Tour*, the *Let It Be* documentary fell out of circulation for decades, reduced to a footnote in Beatles' history.[98] Time passed. Months turned into years. Fans moved on with their lives. Solo albums by ex-Beatles arrived in record stores each year. John, Paul, George, and Ringo—in songs such as "Imagine," "Band on the Run," "Give Me Love (Give Me Peace On Earth)," and "Photograph"—could still be heard on turntables and radio airwaves across the nation. That much had not changed. But they were on their own now, and something had undeniably been lost. The last of the Beatles fan clubs folded in 1972.

In April 1977, a musical called *Beatlemania*, made up entirely of Beatles songs, opened at Boston's Colonial Theatre, relocating to Broadway the following month, where it premiered at the Winter Garden Theatre at the end of May. For more than two years, *Beatlemania* ran for a total of 1,006 performances, grossing over $40 million, and it traveled to other cities, including Atlanta, Chicago, and Los Angeles. The musical revue involved a lavish multimedia show that projected images of the Beatles onto large screens above a stage where four cast members imitated John, Paul, George, and Ringo. The musical drew screaming fans on some nights, including an excited teenager who said, "I know it's silly, but this is probably as close as I'll ever get to the Beatles. He [actor Mitch Weissman] looks so much like Paul it gives me the chills."[99] *Beatlemania* was also turned into a film, released in 1981, but it flopped at the box office. *Beatlemania*—the musical—soon hit a series of legal snags. In 1979, Apple Corps sued Beatlemania's creator, Steve Leber, and its producers for $60 million, stating in the suit that "no one gave them any right to perform a simulated Beatle performance or to use the name of the Beatles."[100]

Beatlemania ended its Broadway run in the fall of 1979. Its demise led some cynics—who saw the musical as crass exploitation of fan nostalgia—to agree with the lyrics in "London Calling," the 1979 song by English punk rockers the Clash, in which lead vocalist Joe Strummer half sang, half wailed: "Phony Beatlemania has bitten the dust!"[101] The Clash recorded that song, which furnished the title of their most acclaimed album, at a moment when the British economy was souring and unemployment levels were rising. In some cities, working-class neighborhoods were literally crumbling, and adolescents were losing hope in the future.

A similar malaise gripped the United States in the aftermath of the Vietnam War. Runaway inflation, long lines at gas pumps, prevalent doubts about the country's future, and lingering polarization continued to beset the nation. In December 1980, the actions of a deranged assassin, standing in the shadows on a cold December night, waiting for John Lennon outside the Dakota Apartments in Manhattan, wiped out, in the briefest of muzzle flashes, long-held hopes that the Beatles might once again reunite.

By this time, Beatlemania was long gone. The giant crowds were a distant memory. But those who lived through it, and who experienced it firsthand, never forgot what it was like to stand in the middle of the vortex, screaming at the top of their lungs, bonding with fellow fans, singing songs that formed the soundtrack of their youth, their hearts and minds filled with the warm thoughts of a future they imagined to be boundless with hope.

Epilogue

The surviving veterans of Beatlemania who were still alive in the 2020s had lived through eventful times. Some of them had saved their aging Beatles scrapbooks, opening them to see yellowing clippings from newspapers and fan magazines, and pictures of the Beatles. Collectively, these men and women had witnessed numerous changes over the long arc of Beatles history. Memories of Beatlemania's jubilant days remained fresh in the minds of many people that lived through it, especially those who fully embraced its trappings in their youth.

After the breakup of the Beatles, the first generation of Beatlemaniacs lived through the solo years of the 1970s, buying the albums of John and Paul and George and Ringo, each man on his own, but occasionally sharing the recording studio with former band mates on some projects. Fans stubbornly held out hope in the 1970s that their idols might come together again for a reunion. When Lorne Michaels, producer of the comedy variety show *Saturday Night Live*, offered the Beatles $3,000 to perform on live television in April 1976, and then upped the offer to $3,200 the following month, the rumor mill shifted into high gear, and speculation was rife. It excited fans when George Harrison tantalizingly appeared on *SNL* on November 20, 1976, as the special musical guest of guest host Paul Simon, who, dressed in a turkey costume (days before Thanksgiving), performed "Still Crazy After All These Years." The episode also featured Harrison and Simon performing "Homeward Bound" and "Here Comes the Sun." As for the Beatles, they were nowhere to be found.[1]

Hopeful talk of a reunion continued for the rest of the decade, with Beatle lovers keeping vigilant about the latest developments. But not all fans wanted to see it happen. Rock journalist Mark Shipper, whose farcical 1977 novel *Paperback Writer* imagined the Beatles reuniting to be an opening act at a

Peter Frampton concert, said he wrote his book to be a cautionary tale, a warning that a Fab Four reunion would be "a disaster." Shipper had been a first-generation Beatles fan, who watched them on the *Ed Sullivan Show*, and saw them in concert as a teenager. By 1977, 27-year-old Shipper hoped the Beatles would stay disbanded. "The expectations would be so high. That's why I don't want it to happen. I want to remember the Beatles for what they were. I don't want to see them end up polluting their legend any more than they already have with their solo careers."[2] Other Beatlemaniacs disagreed with Shipper's assessment, and yearned to see the foursome back together again, instruments in hand, singing their beloved hits. In the Long Island hamlet of Merrick, New York, 28-year-old entrepreneur Alan Amron established the International Committee to Reunite the Beatles in 1976, which had the goal of raising $50 million to entice the Beatles to play live in the United States again. According to Amron, his group boasted "thousands" of supporters, and he said he met John Lennon in the lobby of Lennon's Manhattan apartment and gave the former Beatle literature from his group. Lennon, he said, just whistled and looked at him, and went on his way. "We've got some response from Paul McCartney, it's definitely not bad," Amron added. In Boulder, Colorado, a similar organization, the Beatles Reunion Foundation (or BRF for short), founded by Eric Park, son of a wealthy Korean-American scientist, in 1974, opened an office and began raising funds by selling T-shirts. Park insisted his outfit had 300 members.[3]

Meantime, music promoter, talent manager, and impresario Sid Bernstein, who played a key role in bringing the Beatles to America in 1964, and booked their Shea Stadium concert in 1965, repeatedly assured fans that a reunion was on its way. Every few years, Bernstein would make noise and appear in newspapers and on the nightly news. In September of 1979, he said the Beatles were "quite close to getting back together for an appearance." He had recently taken out a full-page advertisement in the *New York Times* encouraging the Beatles to give a benefit concert to help refugees escaping Southeast Asia on ramshackle boats. "It is my belief, in spite of denials, that a Beatles reunion will come off," Bernstein declared.[4] Coincidentally, in 1978, former wrestler and millionaire Rocky Aoki, owner of the popular Benihana restaurant chain, told the press that he was paying $45 million to the Beatles to gather together for a reunion concert. Around the same time, Los Angeles–based filmmaker and actor Dirk Summers said he was on the verge of persuading the Beatles to perform a benefit concert in Geneva, Switzerland, which would be broadcast on closed-circuit television. Saying he had the backing of United Nations General Secretary Kurt Waldheim, Summers said Elton John had agreed to emcee the concert, and Leonard Bernstein would conduct the Vienna Philharmonic orchestra to perform along with the Beatles. Only the recalcitrant John Lennon was not fully on board with the grand plan,

Summers lamented.[5] Even self-proclaimed "Beatles fan" Muhammad Ali got in on the action, telling an interviewer in 1977 about plans for a lavish Beatles reunion concert with the goal of "feeding and clothing the poor children of the world." "All races love the Beatles. I love the music. I used to train to their music," Ali explained.[6]

The ex-Beatles kept denying rumors they would soon be sharing the stage once again, deflating the hopes of anxious fans everywhere. Some media outlets reported in 1978 that the band was on the verge of reuniting to raise funds for a Greenpeace campaign to save whales and dolphins. Paul McCartney, an animal lover, responded: "I'm happy to do a concert for the whales. I think they shouldn't be hunted to extinction." But he called a Beatles reunion a "nonstarter." "We've all gone in different directions since we split up and there's no way we're just going to walk on stage one day and make fools of ourselves—even for a lot of money," said McCartney.[7] The other three Beatles made comments to the press that echoed Paul's sentiments. "To get the four of us in one room together is very difficult," said Ringo Starr, not because of acrimoniousness, he insisted, but due to busy schedules.[8] George Harrison shrugged off the rumors when asked about them in 1977. He said,

> It's really overwhelming that the Beatles still mean so much to everybody. It's very flattering. We grew up then—a lot of people grew up during that whole Beatle music period. But to me, watching old Beatles film clips, it's like watching the old Laurel and Hardy movies—it's so dated already. So getting together again is a bit like asking me to go back to school again. It's very limiting.[9]

Of all the former Beatles, it was John Lennon—who was often thought to be the holdout preventing Beatles from returning together to the concert stage—that publicly expressed a willingness to consider the possibility of reuniting. Asked by *Los Angeles Times* music critic Robert Hilburn about the likelihood of a reunion album in December 1973, Lennon responded "without hesitation": "Well, it's possible. If you had asked me last year, I would have said, 'No. No way. I'm not going back one step' ... but I just think anything is possible now."[10] Beatles fans struggled to make sense of the many reunion rumors floating around in the 1970s. The confusion stemmed from mixed signals given by the Beatles, dubious claims of concert promoters, and a fervent wish among the band's devoted followers—sparked by the uneven quality of the ex-Beatles solo output—that the band might get together again to recapture the magic.

Those hopes were destroyed with the shocking murder of John Lennon on the night of December 8, 1980, in front of the Dakota Apartments building where he lived.[11] No other event since the Beatles ceased touring in 1966 brought fans out into the public en masse as much as Lennon's tragic and senseless death. Outpourings of grief across the United States, and around the world, occurred on an immense scale, lasting for weeks. Nations flew flags at half-staff. Mourners turned out, in some places by the thousands, at events from coast to coast to bid farewell to Lennon and reflect on his achievements and legacy. From children to the elderly, people participated in candlelight vigils and gathered to sing Lennon's beloved antiwar anthem "Give Peace a Chance." Radio stations played Beatles and Lennon music in round-the-clock tributes. There was a run on Beatles and Lennon albums at record stores nationwide. "We sold out of the John Lennon albums first thing," reported Laura Bylen, who worked at the Record Warehouse in Chicago.[12] Copies of John Lennon and Yoko Ono's latest LP, *Double Fantasy*, which was released the previous month to sluggish sales, flew off shelves particularly fast. In New York City, fans gathered to weep and leave gifts near the entrance of the Dakota.[13] The 55-year-old father of a Beatles fan showed up to pay his last respects because his daughter could not make it. "My daughter admired him very much … She always carried around John Lennon for President buttons and a John Lennon comb, and she was always hoping to meet him outside the Dakota apartments."[14] A flood of tribute magazines, many one-offs, arrived at newsstands and supermarket checkout lanes. Images of Lennon appeared on the December 22 covers of *Time* and *Newsweek*. "Of all the Beatles, Lennon was the one who showed the greatest depth and complexity. His was the growth I expected the most from, and now that has been cut short," wrote music and film critic Jay Cocks, in the special *Time* commemorative issue.[15]

The murder of John Lennon assumed a significance that went beyond the violent extinguishing of one man's life. In the popular imagination, the incident was emblematic of the death of the 1960s, and the hope, idealism, and promise that era seemed to carry. "His death," one distraught fan remarked, "cuts the last thread to the faith we had that love could save us."[16] "When John died, it seemed to me like all the years from 1964 to 1980 died too. I grew up on all his songs," said Judy Flynn, 27 at the time of Lennon's death, who had been a first-generation Beatles fan from Middletown Township, New Jersey. Flynn, like a hundred thousand or so others, attended a farewell ceremony to Lennon in Central Park, New York. "I just had to come today, it was my way of saying goodbye."[17] John Strub, a student at Columbia University, originally from Iowa City, Iowa, was at the Dakota at the time of the shooting. He heard the gunshots and ran over to the scene, reaching the apartment building when Yoko was screaming, and John was lying on the ground. Strub echoed others who thought John Lennon embodied values championed by idealists of the 1960s. "People were comparing him to John Kennedy and Martin Luther King. After all, he presided over a revolution of a kind. He was a symbol of peace and love," said Strub.[18] At a candlelight vigil that drew around 1,200 participants

Cincinnati, Rita Gatton, a 27-year-old Beatles fan, brought a candle with her that she had last lit at an antiwar demonstration in front of the White House in Washington, DC, seven years earlier.[19] Dawn Steen, a 27-year-old fan, was one of 2,500 people who gathered at a tribute to Lennon at Lee Park in Dallas, Texas. "I came by to say goodbye to my youth. Their music was a search that still isn't over for a lot of us and now maybe it's too late," said Steen.[20] Tragically, at least two fans, sixteen-year-old Colleen Costello of Brooksville Florida, and Michael Craig, age thirty, from Salt Lake City, immediately committed suicide upon hearing the news, leaving notes indicating that Lennon's murder was the reason.[21] President Jimmy Carter issued a statement at the White House expressing his sadness, and the shock of "many millions of Americans" at Lennon's death. "John Lennon," said President Carter, "helped create the music and the mood of our time. His spirit, the spirit of the Beatles—brash and earnest, ironic and idealistic all at once ... It is especially poignant that John Lennon has died by violence, though he had long campaigned for peace."[22]

Of course, it was not lost on people in the aftermath of Lennon's murder that his killer, Mark David Chapman, twenty-five at the time of the shooting, was a self-described "Beatles fan." A born-again Christian zealot from Hawaii, Chapman had spent years listening to, and idolizing, the Beatles. "He was very much a Beatles fan, and he played their music constantly," recalled David Moore, who had been the killer's roommate for six months in Chicago in the mid-1970s.[23] The deranged young man had targeted Lennon for saying the Beatles were "more popular than Jesus," and for singing about a world without God and religion in his popular peace anthem, "Imagine." The assassin carried out the murder methodically and deliberately. In response to Lennon's killing, the experts—in this case, psychiatrists, psychologists, social workers, counsellors, academics with expertise on human behavior, and the killer's attorney—psychoanalyzed Lennon's murderer in the press, searching for ways to explain the assassins violent behavior. The reasons behind Chapman's actions, they insisted, were manifold: he endured a troubled childhood. His parents had gotten a divorce that traumatized him. He identified too closely with Lennon. He was overly fixated on Jesus Christ. His wife broke up with him. He had been contemplating suicide and decided to kill Lennon—whom he regarded as his alter ego—instead. He was a religious fanatic. He felt empty and powerless, and this was his horrifying way of trying to empower himself. He was a cautionary tale about fans taking fandom too far. He clung to the "extraordinary belief" that he was Holden Caulfield, the sensitive young protagonist in J. D. Salinger's 1951 coming-of-age novel, *Catcher in the Rye*.[24] There were other reasons, and the analyses kept coming in the press at a steady clip. Stuart Berger, a professor of legal psychiatry at Harvard University, offered this assessment at the time: "There can be such a psychotic loss of ego boundaries with the victim so that the murderer almost perceives himself as one with the victim and ultimately is the victim."[25] David Abrahamsen, a prominent New York City, blamed Lennon's death on Chapman's jealousy: "If Chapman identified so much with Lennon, he could have had a grudge against Lennon because he didn't get as far as Lennon."[26] A police detective on duty on the night of Lennon's slaying put it most succinctly: "We got a psycho."[27]

After Lennon's death, the Beatles' music underwent a rapid process of canonization, with the group achieving—in the eyes of music critics and scholars alike—the lofty status of greatest rock band of all time. Unlike many of their contemporaries in rock music, the Beatles disbanded at the height of their output, resulting in their legacy being forever enshrined in the minds of enthusiasts. Fans in the 1980s and 1990s witnessed waves of nostalgic yearning for an imagined world that the Beatles were thought to represent. The band's 1970 break-up, coupled with the murder of John Lennon, were frequently spoken of as ends of an era. And yet, new generations of fans came of age, nurtured by their elders who kept Beatles' music playing. Fan clubs were revived, and Beatles conventions took place across the United States in this era of nostalgia, celebrating the accomplishments and legacies of the Fab Four. The release of the *Beatles Anthology* in November 1995, a multimedia celebration of the band consisting of a sprawling eight-episode documentary, a three-volume set of double albums, and a glossy book filled with photographs and detailed histories of the band merely reinforced the Beatles' towering stature in the minds of fans as the greatest rock band of all time. Fans explored the history of the band through documentaries and books, and some of them made the pilgrimage overseas to Liverpool, to see the dwellings where the Beatles grew up, and the sights of Penny Lane, and the gates of Strawberry Field, the old overgrown, gated Salvation Army property located in the suburb of Woolton. Journeying Merseyside to Liverpool and touring the city proved a meaningful odyssey for Beatles fans of all ages seeking a deeper connection with the band.[28]

But the pain of losing another Beatle brought more anguish to fans. Toward the end of his life, George Harrison made it clear he did not miss the chaotic days of Beatlemania. "I've never been that good at being a promoter of myself, doing TV interviews or whatever," he admitted in 1987.[29] He found the legions of screaming Beatles fans oppressive and off-putting. He admitted he sometimes experienced moments of joy and excitement during those eventful years in the mid-1960s, but on balance, he often found Beatlemania suffocating and oppressive, and he had a hard time concealing his disdain for it. "We had a great laugh, really, when we were good friends, though we were like caged animals most of the time."[30]

Following the senseless killing of Lennon, Harrison retreated into his own private world of family and gardening, occasionally venturing out to make music, either as a solo artist or with the super group the Traveling Wilburys, consisting of fellow musicians Bob Dylan, Jeff Lynne, Tom Petty, and Roy Orbison. Harrison feared that he would meet the same fate as Lennon. To prevent this, he had his Victorian neo-Gothic mansion known as Friar Park, located on sixty-two acres in Henley-on-Thames, heavily guarded by an elaborate security system and guards staffing a booth. That did not stop deranged 34-year-old Michael Abram from breaking into Harrison's estate in the middle of the night brandishing a knife with a six-inch blade. Abram forcefully entered Harrison's home and a violent clash ensued, with Harrison and his wife Olivia fighting off the attacker. By the time two constables showed up, Harrison had been stabbed around 40 times. He miraculously survived the attack, but it left him in a severely weakened state, and he had already been diagnosed with cancer in 1997. On November 29, 2001, Harrison died at age 58 of metastatic non-small cell lung cancer, with his family at his bedside. At the time, he was staying in a home owned by Paul McCartney in Beverly Hills, California.[31]

Once again, as they did in 1980, fans mourned the loss of another Beatle. More candlelight vigils were held, people gathered in cities and towns to say goodbye, and there were radio and television tributes about the so-called Quiet Beatle. A decade later, Martin Scorsese's three-and-a-half-hour 2011 documentary, *George Harrison: Living in the Material World*, won praise from critics and Beatles devotees alike, capturing memorable fragments of a dramatic and complex life. Two years later, in 2013, a "George Harrison Commemorative Mural" and a detailed plaque were erected by the Illinois State Historical Society along Interstate 57 near Benton, Illinois, the place where, half a century earlier, twenty-year-old George Harrison journeyed with his brother Peter to see his sister Louise and her family. The day of the marker's dedication, September 21, 2013, Louise Harrison was the guest of honor at a large ceremony, and musician Taylor Kearney played Beatles and George Harrison songs. Residents of Benton who remembered Harrison's arrival in town all those years earlier fondly reminisced about their encounters with him. Scores of fans came from all over America to remember their musical hero, including Jim and Diane Denzer, of Decatur, Illinois. Jim explained their reason for making the drive to Benton that day: "We wouldn't have missed this ... We are huge Beatles fans and I love George. Their music changed my life."[32]

That sentiment was widely held among veterans of Beatlemania who were still alive. Into their sixties and seventies by the early 2020s, many of these fans retained vivid memories of the sights and sounds and exhilaration—the screaming crowds, spinning turntables, cries of joy, bonds of friendship—involved with being a first-generation Beatles fan in 1964, 1965, and 1966. They followed the careers of the two remaining Beatles, Paul McCartney and Ringo Starr, both magnificent musicians, still in top form, full of energy and youthful enthusiasm, as they entered their eighties. In his post-Covid "Got Back" Tour during the spring of 2022, McCartney showed no signs of slowing down.

To long-time Beatlemaniacs, a fair number of them grandparents by now, the Beatles were more than a mere rock band. They were saviors. Looking back across the decades to her youth, Lisa Yanak of Hatfield, Pennsylvania, could have been speaking for legions of first-generation Beatles fans when she explained the significance of the Beatles in her personal life: "Sometimes I think that they actually saved my life ... Yes, they had a massive influence on music, our culture in general, and on many generations for years to come, but do they know that they probably saved my life by giving me hope and a reason to live?"[33]

Notes

Introduction

1. The literature on the Beatles is much too long to list here. Books by some of the key chroniclers of the band include: Mark Lewisohn's superlative *The Beatles: All These Years: Volume One—Tune In* (New York: Little, Brown and Company, 2013); Philip Norman's *Shout!: The Beatles in Their Generation* (New York: Fireside/MJF Books, 1981); Bob Spitz's *The Beatles: The Biography* (New York: Little, Brown and Company, 2005); Hunter Davies's pioneering *The Beatles: The Authorised Biography* (New York: McGraw Hill, 1968); and Kenneth Womack's *Solid State: The Story of "Abbey Road" and the End of the Beatles* (Ithaca: Cornell University Press, 2019).

2. Jon Wiener, *Come Together: John Lennon in His Time* (Champaign: University of Illinois Press, 1984); Ian MacDonald, *Revolution in the Head: The Beatles' Records and the Sixties* (London: 4th Estate Books, 1994); Steven D. Stark, *Meet the Beatles: A Cultural History of the Band That Shook Youth, Gender, and the World* (New York: Dey Street Books, 2005); Jonathan Gould, *Can't Buy Me Love: The Beatles, Britain, and America* (New York: Harmony Books, 2007); John F. Lyons, *Joy and Fear: The Beatles, Chicago and the 1960s* (New York: Permuted Press, 2021); Christine Feldman-Barrett, *A Women's History of the Beatles* (New York: Bloomsbury Publishing, 2021); and Kenneth L. Campbell, *The Beatles and the 1960s Reception, Revolution, and Social Change* (New York: Bloomsbury Publishing, 2021).

3. Fan-oriented accounts include Garry Berman's *We're Going to See the Beatles!: An Oral History of Beatlemania as Told by the Fans Who Were There* (Santa Monica, CA: Santa Monica Press, 2008); Candy Leonard's *Beatleness: How the Beatles and Their Fans Remade the World* (New York: Arcade Publishing, 2014); Kit O'Toole and Kenneth Womack, eds., *Fandom and the Beatles: The Act You've Known for All These Years* (New York: Oxford University Press, 2021). Sociologist and first-generation Beatles fan Candy Leonard has written the most significant contribution on the topic with her book *Beatleness: How the Beatles and Their Fans Remade the World* (2014). To date, *Beatleness* is the gold standard of Beatles fan accounts, relying almost exclusively on fan oral histories that were gathered, edited, and arranged by the author into an absorbing and insightful narrative. Her account of the era accomplishes what it sets out to do by surveying Beatles fandom in an era of tumult and rapid changes, and it lets the fans speak for themselves about their varied experiences, with coverage extending beyond Beatlemania's golden age. One of the

few scholarly works that partially focuses on Beatlemania itself is historian André Millard's *Beatlemania: Technology, Business, and Teen Culture in Cold War America* (Baltimore: Johns Hopkins University Press, 2012). The title of Millard's book is something of a misnomer, however, as only one of its twelve chapters examines Beatlemania in broad brush strokes, with one other chapter focusing on Beatlemania-era fans. Much of Millard's history is about the Beatles themselves, with portions of his account detailing their early career and rise to fame, and some engaging commentary on the business side of their story. There is also a lot of space dedicated to transatlantic Anglo-American cultural exchanges. One of the book's chapters explores the era's technological innovations that helped to bring their music across the Atlantic to millions of people in the United States, and another details innovations in studio recording. Despite containing some useful insights about Beatlemania, Millard's *Beatlemania* should not be considered a definitive history of the subject, contrary to what the title partially suggests.

4   Kathy Small, "If You Can't Join 'Em, Beatle 'Em," *Elmira Star-Gazette,* February 16, 1964, 22.
5   Miller Davis and Ian Glass, "4 Beatles = 1 Frenzy," *Miami News,* February 14, 1964, 1.
6   William Tucker, "Beatlemania Havoc Laid to Publicity," *Miami News,* February 14, 1964, 1.
7   Becky Pierce, "They All Shrieked and I Tingled," *Miami News,* February 14, 1964, 3.
8   Jonathan Kasparek, "A Day in the Life: The Beatles Descend on Milwaukee," *Wisconsin Magazine of History*, vol. 84, no. 2 (Winter, 2000–1), 22.
9   Steven R. Hoffbeck, "Memories: The Beatles in Minnesota," *Minnesota History*, vol. 60, no. 5 (Spring, 2007), 197.

Chapter 1

1   Alan Patureau, "The Ridiculous British Beatles," *Newsday,* February 10, 1964, 62.
2   *The Complete Ed Sullivan Shows Starring the Beatles*, 1964. DVD. Toronto: Universal Music Canada, 2010.
3   Amanda Vaill, "We Saw Them Standing There," in Penelope Rowlands, ed., *The Beatles Are Here! 50 Years after the Band Arrived in America, Writers, Musicians, & Other Fans Remember* (Chapel Hill, NC: Algonquin Books of Chapel Hill, 2014), 11–13.
4   Carolyn Tanner recollections, in Phillip Ramati, "Readers Share Their Memories of The Beatles," *The Macon Telegraph*, February 9, 2014, 6A.
5   For example: Gay Stilley, "The Beat of the Beatles Tuned to Teen Tempo," *The Jackson Sun*, February 7, 1964, 5.

   This version of Stilley's column, printed the day The Beatles touched down at New York's John F. Kennedy airport, featured a picture of Gay and her father Francis clowning around in Beatles wigs, holding a toy Ringo Starr doll.

NOTES

6 "The Beatles: Boston Votes Bushy Britons One-Way Ticket to Cuba," *The Boston Globe,* February 10, 1964, 1.

7 Percy Shain, "Barnyard Braying Better'n Beatles," *The Boston Globe,* February 10, 1964, 3.

8 "Please Take Beatles Back, John Bull," *The Greenwood Commonwealth,* February 10, 1964, 2.

9 "TV Brings Americans Shaggy Dogs' Tale," *The Journal Herald,* February 10, 1964, 1.

10 Alan Patureau, "The Ridiculous British Beatles," *Newsday* (Suffolk Edition), February 10, 1964, 62.

11 Cynthia Lowry, "Critic Doesn't Think She'll Ever Become a Beatle-Nut," *Lancaster New Era,* February 10, 1964, 11.

12 Ben Gross, "Run, Men, Run! Beatles Churn Channel Hysteria," *New York Daily News,* February 10, 1964, 21.

13 Cynthia Lowry, "Beatles: Study of the Human Animal," *Lancaster New Era,* February 10, 1964, 11.

14 "George, Paul, Ringo, and John," *Newsweek,* February 24, 1964, 38.

15 "The Beatles: Boston Votes Bushy Britons One-Way Ticket to Cuba," *The Boston Globe,* February 10, 1964, 1.

16 " 'Stamp Out Beatles' Is Their Aim," *The Bismarck Tribune,* February 11, 1964, 1.

17 Berman, *We're Going to See the Beatles!*, 73.

18 Rick Bentley, "Valley Has Golden Beatles Memories," *The Fresno Bee,* February 9, 2014, F2.

19 Michelle Isacoff Rothstein, "Reader Memories," *The Philadelphia Inquirer,* February 9, 2014, H11.

20 Elizabeth Abbe, "What It Was Like 50 Years Ago When the Beatles Came to the U.S.," from the Connecticut Historical Society Museum and Library website, February 9, 2014. https://chs.org/2014/02/what-it-was-like-50-years-ago-when-the-beatles-came-to-the-us/ (accessed August 9, 2021).

21 Gregory Clay, "The 1964 Beatles," *The Winona Daily News,* February 9, 1964, C1.

22 Alan Patureau, "The Ridiculous British Beatles," *Newsday,* February 10, 1964, 62.

23 Mrs. J. V. T., "Beatles Better Than Beaching, She Says," *Orlando Sentinel,* April 2, 1964, 34.

24 "Beatles Wigs, Garb May Net $20 Million," *The Indianapolis Star,* March 1, 1964, 64.

25 "We Wanta Hold Your Purse," *Spokane Chronicle,* February 21, 1964, 4.

26 "Beatles Wreck 1 Man's Nerves," *The Baltimore Sun,* February 23, 2.

27 Accounts of The Beatles' February 1964 US visit include: Bill Eppridge, *The Beatles: Six Days That Changed the World, February 1964* (New York: Rizzoli International Publications, 2014); Chuck Gunderson, *Some Fun Tonight!: The*

Backstage Story of How the Beatles Rocked America: The Historic Tours 1964–1966 (Volumes 1 & 2) (Guilford, CT: Backbeat Books, 2016); Bernie Ilson, *Sundays with Sullivan: How the Ed Sullivan Show Brought Elvis, the Beatles, and Culture to America* (Lanham, MD: Taylor Trade Publishing, 2008); Larry Kane, *Ticket to Ride: Inside the Beatles' 1964 Tour That Changed the World* (Guilford, CT: Backbeat Books, 2014); Gerald Nachman, *Right Here on Our Stage Tonight!: Ed Sullivan's America* (Berkeley: University of California Press, 2009); Jason Richards, *The Beatles in America* (Canton, MA: Wheelhouse Publishers, 2021).

28 "10,000 Fans Mob Beatles on Return," *The Boston Globe,* February 23, 1964, 24.

29 George Harrison's trip to Benton, Illinois, in September 1963 is recounted in the following sources: Alan Pell Crawford, "The Charming Story of George Harrison's Vacation in Small-Town America," *Smithsonian Magazine,* May 2020. https://www.smithsonianmag.com/arts-culture/charming-story-george-harrison-vacationed-small-town-america-180974593/ (accessed August 21, 2021); Louise Harrison, *My Kid Brother's Band, a.k.a. The Beatles* (Morley, MO: Acclaim Press, 2014); Jim Kirkpatrick, *Before He Was Fab: George Harrison's First American Visit* (Vienna, IL: Cache River Press, 2000).

30 Becky Malkovich, "Benton Recalls Beatles' Harrison," *The Southern Illinoisan,* September 15, 2013. https://thesouthern.com/news/local/benton-recalls-beatles-harrison/article_41f02c0e-1dbe-11e3-be93-001a4bcf887a.html (accessed August 21, 2021).

31 Louise Harrison offers a thorough overview of Peter and George's itinerary during their two weeks in Illinois in September 1963 in her memoir, *My Kid Brother's Band*, 32–41.

32 The first instance of a disc jockey in North America playing a Beatles song likely occurred on Canadian radio personality Ray Sonin's *Calling All Britons* show on station CFRB in Toronto, Ontario. Sonin lowered the needle on "Love Me Do" in December 1962, which predated the sudden explosion of Beatles music on American airwaves by over a year. See Bruce Spizer, *The Beatles Are Coming!: The Birth of Beatlemania in America* (New Orleans: 498 Productions, 2003), 27.

33 Kirkpatrick, *Before He Was Fab,* 21–2.

34 Books that emphasize the pivotal events of the so-called "long 1964" (which began with the assassination of President John F. Kennedy in Dallas on November 22, 1963, and concluded roughly in the summer of 1965) include: Fred Logevall, *Choosing War: The Lost Chance for Peace and the Escalation of War in Vietnam* (Berkeley: University of California Press, 2001); Jon Margolis, *The Last Innocent Year: America in 1964—The Beginning of the "Sixties"* (New York: William Morrow, 1999); Doug McAdam, *Freedom Summer* (New York: Oxford University Press, 1995); Robert S. McElvaine, *The Times They Were a-Changin': 1964, the Year the Sixties Arrived and the Battle Lines of Today Were Drawn* (New York: Arcade Publishing, 2021); Rick Perlstein, *Before the Storm: Barry Goldwater and the Unmaking of the American Consensus* (New York: Hill and Wang, 2001); Bruce Watson, *Freedom Summer: The Savage Season of 1964 That Made*

Mississippi Burn and Made America a Democracy (New York: Penguin, 2011); Nancy Beck Young, *Two Suns of the Southwest: Lyndon Johnson, Barry Goldwater, and the 1964 Battle between Liberalism and Conservatism* (Lawrence: University Press of Kansas, 2019). The documentary film *1964*, directed by Stephen Ives, which aired in January 2015 as an episode of the popular American Experience series on PBS, covered much of the same ground as the aforementioned titles, and was partially based on Jon Margolis's book.

35 The best single history of these volatile early years of rock and roll can be found in Glenn C. Altschuler, *All Shook Up: How Rock 'n Roll Changed America* (New York: Oxford University Press 2003).

36 "Rock 'n' Roll: Decline and Fall?," *Time*, December 14, 1959, 66.

37 Histories of the new renaissance of English rock music and the British Invasion include: Barry Miles, *The British Invasion: The Music, the Times, the Era* (New York: Sterling Publishing, 2009); James E. Perone, *Mods, Rockers, and the Music of the British Invasion* (Greenwood, CT: Prager Publishers, 2009); Simon Philo, *British Invasion The Crosscurrents of Musical Influence* (Lanham, MD: Rowman & Littlefield, 2017); Alan J. Whiticker, *British Pop Invasion* (London: New Holland Publishers, 2013).

38 "Beatlemania: It's Happening Everywhere … Even in Sedate Cheltenham," *Daily Mirror*, November 2, 1963, 3.

39 The growing popularity of rock and roll music among British youths is covered in the following books: Dick Bradley, *Understanding Rock 'N' Roll: Popular Music in Britain, 1955–1964* (Maidenhead: Open University Press, 1992); Martin Creasy, *Beatlemania!: The Real Story of the Beatles UK Tours* (London: Omnibus Press, 2011); Pete Frame, *The Restless Generation: How Rock Music Changed the Face of 1950s Britain* (London: Omnibus Press, 2007); Anna Ariadne Knight, *Screening the Hollywood Rebels in 1950s Britain* (Manchester: Manchester University Press, 2021); Tom Lodge, *The Ship That Rocked the World: How Radio Caroline Defied the Establishment, Launched the British Invasion, and Made the Planet Safe for Rock and Roll* (Savage, MD: Bartleby Press, 2010); Philo, *British Invasion*.

40 Timothy Green, "Here Come Those Beatles," *Life*, January 31, 1964, 30.

41 Rita Mueller, "Records: Cockney Lad Sings Spirituals," *Quad City Times-Democrat*, May 25, 1958, 2C.

42 "British Songwriters Declare Independence," *Globe-Gazette*, March 10, 1961, 13.

43 Geoffrey Miller, "Americans Filling British Music Halls," *The Norman Transcript*, December 6, 1957, 8.

44 Spizer, *The Beatles Are Coming!*, 10–23.

45 "Beatles to Get $150,000 For Kansas City Program," *New York Times*, August 24, 1964, 22.

46 Enest Mehl, "Sporting Comment," *Kansas City Star*, September 8, 1964, 13.

47 Karen McNally, *When Frankie Went to Hollywood: Frank Sinatra and American Male Identity* (Urbana: University of Illinois Press, 2008), 15.

48 "25,000 Fans Storm Sinatra's Theater," *Pittsburgh Sun-Telegraph,* October 12, 1944, 24. Hannah Ewens, *Fangirls: Scenes from Modern Music Culture* (Austin: University of Texas Press, 2020), 32.

49 Author Thomas Hine, in his book *The Rise and Fall of the American Teenager* (New York: Avon, 1999), insisted that the first instance of the word "teenager" appearing in print in the United States could be traced back to an issue of *Popular Science* magazine from 1941 (8–9). However, at the time Hine wrote the book, in the 1990s, online newspaper database searches were not available, and researchers were stuck with limited resources, such as the *Reader's Guide to Periodical Literature.* A search of Newspapers.com, a massive collection of more than 21,000 newspapers (as of the date of this search, September 3, 2021) reveals sporadic use of "teenager" in the press by the mid-1920s, with a dramatic increase by decade's end and into the Great Depression.

50 Rob Walker, *Buying In: The Secret Dialogue between What We Buy and Who We Are* (New York: Random House, 2008), 108–10. See also Grace Palladino, *Teenagers: An American History* (New York: Basic Books, 1996); Jon Savage, *Teenage: The Prehistory of Youth Culture: 1875–1945* (New York: Penguin, 2008).

51 Bill Osgerby, "'A Caste, a Culture, a Market': Youth, Marketing, and Lifestyle in Postwar America," in Ronald Strickland, ed., *Growing Up Postmodern: Neoliberalism and the War on the* Young (Lanham, MD: Rowman & Littlefield Publishers, 2002), 18.

52 "Columnist Defends Typical Teenagers," *Metropolitan Pasadena Star-News,* December 21, 1947, 50.

53 "Swooner Crooner" (1944), *Looney Tunes: Golden Collection Volume 3* (New York: Warner Brothers Home Video, 2005), DVD.

54 *The Bachelor and the Bobby-Soxer,* directed by Irving Reis (New York: Turner Home Entertainment, 2004), DVD. The film's screenplay was written by television producer and novelist Sidney Sheldon (1917–2007), who created such television programs as *The Patty Duke Show, I Dream of Jeannie,* and *Hart to Hart.*

55 Annual Movie Chart, Movie Index, 1947, from https://www.the-numbers.com/market/1947/top-grossing-movies (accessed September 4, 2021).

56 Virginia Sheward, "Most Beer Taps Turn Dry for LI Youngsters," *Newsday* (Suffolk ed.), February 4, 1952, 3.

57 Raymond Moley, "Shocking Traffic in Dope Revealed," *Nashville Banner,* January 17, 1952, 4.

58 Ernest Lenn, "Schoolgirl Tells Drug, Liquor Purchases at S.F. 'Thrill Spot'," *San Francisco Examiner,* December 16, 1954, 1.

59 "Sinatra's Bobby-Soxers in Line at 4:30 A.M.; 53 Held by Police," *St. Louis Post-Dispatch,* March 24, 1946, 1.

60 "Object to 'Good, Clean Kids' Being Called Bobby-Soxers," *Hanford Morning Journal,* April 20, 1946, 7.

61 "13-Year-Old Bobby-Soxer Held For Setting Churches Afire," *Rocky Mount Telegram,* April 21, 1952, 1.

NOTES

62 "Bobby-Soxer Roots for Joe Stalin," *Windsor Star,* August 28, 1950, 9.
63 "Bobby-Soxers Send Crooner to Hospital," *News-Herald*, January 24, 1950, 3.
64 "Thrill-Seeking Bobby-Soxers Follow New Fad: Haunt Atlanta Jail to Look at Men," *Dayton Daily News,* February 3, 1950, F-1.
65 Jack Beahan, "Short Change," *Evening Times*, March 4, 1953, 10.
66 Phyllis Brattelle, "She Furnished Antidote for Rock 'n' Roll Noise," *Morning Call*, December 27, 1955, 6.
67 Gertrude Samuels, "Why They Rock 'n' Roll—And Should They?" *New York Times Magazine*, January 12,1958, 19.
68 Altschuler, *All Shook Up*, 6.
69 Phyllis Brattelle, "Rock 'n' Roll Fad: How Harmful Is It?" *Nashville Tennessean,* June 17, 1956, 3B.
70 Phyllis Brattelle, "Cold-Eyed, Hot-Voiced Elvis Is King of Teens," *St. Petersburg Times,* June 24, 1956, 8-E.
71 Molly (no last name), "In Defense of R&R," *Newsday* (Suffolk ed.), July 27, 1956, 25.
72 Phyllis Brattelle, "Rock 'n' Roll Fad: How Harmful Is It?" *Nashville Tennessean,* June 17, 1956, 3B.
73 Bobby Moore, "We're Hep to Music, Not Words, Say Nashville Fans," *Nashville Tennessean,* June 17, 1956, 3B.
74 Linda Deutsch, "Bradley Beach Teen-Ager Proud of Elvis and His Fans," *Asbury Park Evening Press,* March 21, 1958, 17.
75 Dee Hubbard, "Grandmothers Organize Elvis Presley Fan Club," *El Paso Times,* February 16, 1958, 5-C.
76 Ralph Reppert, "Elvis Presley Fan Club Meets Once a Month to Talk about Their Hero," *Baltimore Sun,* May 5, 1957, 18.
77 Eugene Gilbert, "Are Elvis Presley's Fans 'Do Nothings?,'" *Cincinnati Enquirer,* March 15, 1958, 17.
78 Ibid.
79 Ibid.
80 Ibid.
81 Marilyn Van Eaton, "Teens Think Rock 'n' Roll Fades," *Lawton Constitution,* March 10, 1957, 4.
82 Eugene Gilbert, "Rock 'n' Roll Still Growing," *Richmond Times-Dispatch,* March 9, 1958, L-13.
83 "Payola Fails to Dim Fans' Ardor," *Miami Herald,* November 23, 1959, 19-A.
84 Eugene Gilbert, "Rock 'n' Roll Still Growing," *Richmond Times-Dispatch,* March 9, 1958, L-13.
85 "Rock 'n' Roll Said on Way Out in Wake of 'Payola,'" *Tampa Tribune,* November 29, 1959, 10-A.

86 John Crosby, "Being a Teenage Idol Is Like Hard Work," *Oakland Tribune,* June 12, 1960, B-15.
87 Dick Venizelos, "Rock 'n' Roll Here Forever," *Binghamton Press and Sun-Bulletin,* April 26, 1959, C-1.
88 Martin Abramson, "Ricky Nelson Made it on His Own as a Singer with 6,000 Fan Clubs," *Pittsburgh Press,* July 15, 1959, 17.
89 Tom A. Cullen, "World Star Hayley Mills Is a Very Lonely Little Girl," *Philadelphia Daily News,* August 29, 1961, 44.
90 Lloyd Shearer, "Hayley Mills: She's the Greatest Child Find since Shirley Temple," *Dayton Daily News,* November 5, 1961, 115.
91 Rene-Georges Inagaki, "New Japanese Radio Firm Scores Startling Success," *Lansing State Journal,* January 19, 1958, 11.
92 RCA Victor tape cartridge recorder advertisement, *Shreveport Journal,* September 25, 1962, 11.
93 Columbia Record Club advertisement, *Life,* vol. 49, no. 24, December 26, 1960, 11.
94 "Chicago Flips Wig; Beatles and Otherwise," *Billboard,* February 15, 1964, 1, 8.
95 Milton R. Bass, "The Lively Arts," *Berkshire Eagle,* March 4, 1964, 4.
96 Lyons, *Joy and Fear*, 56.
97 Jerry Hames, "Adieu Beatle Clan … but Wait! They May Return," *Windsor Star,* February 20, 1964, 32.
98 The Beatle Fan Club of Massachusetts advertisement, *Boston Globe,* February 17, 1964, 22.
99 Mark Holingworth, "Beatles Bomb Baseball," *Long Beach Press-Telegram,* March 4, 1964, D-1.
100 Patrick Kelly, "In Our Town," *Tampa Tribune,* April 30, 1964, 2-B.
101 Don Clasen, "Beatles Fans Organize," *Rock Island Argus,* August 3, 1964, 3.
102 "Dance Aid Funds," *The Record*, September 5, 1964, 7.
103 "Benefit Beatle Hop Set," *Pittsburgh Press,* May 28, 1964, 10.
104 " 'Keep Jackson Beautiful' is Youth's New Slogan," *Clarion-Ledger*, October 17, 1965, D-16.
105 "These Girls Like That Beatle Beat," *Belvidere Daily Republican,* June 2, 1964, 3.
106 "Beatle Fans Leave Their Phonograph," *News-Journal,* December 19, 1964, 7. "Beatle Fans Hold Empty Stocking Sale," *Wisconsin State Journal,* December 7, 1964, 3.
107 Marji's High-Line, "Sisters Get Out Own Beatle Bulletin," *Hartford Courant,* February 27, 1965, 14.
108 John Terry, "Seven Organize Salem Fan Club," *Capital Journal,* June 10, 1964, 24. John Ericksen, "On the Brighter Side," *Statesman Journal,* June 8, 1964, 1.
109 "Beatle Fan Club and How It Grew," *Nevada State Journal,* April 21, 1964, 11.

NOTES

110 Jim Reid, "Efforts to Squelch Bealtes Backfires," *Daily Oklahoman,* April 17, 1964, 38.

Chapter 2

1 Jim McLaughlin, "Two Ohio Girls Sought in Land of Beatles," *Indianapolis News,* September 23, 1964, 2. *Cincinnati Enquirer,* September 30, 1964, 3.
2 For example, see: "Runaway Girls Found in English City," *Chicago Tribune,* September 19, 1964, 3.
3 "Beatle Fans' Runaway Well-Planned," *Akron Beacon Journal,* October 2, 1964, 16.
4 "Believe Missing Girls Adrift in Beatle Land," *Evening Independent*, October 5, 1964, 8. "Runaways to England Still Missing," *Akron Beacon Journal,* October 5, 1964, 11.
5 "Rolling Stones Homeward Bound," *Windsor Star,* October 8, 1964, 10.
6 "Scotland Yard Ends 2 U.S. Girls' Junket," *Los Angeles Times,* October 9, 1964, 2.
7 Most accounts claim that Martha Schendel and Janice Hawkins had roughly $1,100 at the time of their capture, although an Associated Press story in the Windsor Star (October 8, 1964, 10) insisted they had $1,400 when the police found them.
8 "Scotland Yard Ends 2 U.S. Girls' Junket," *Los Angeles Times,* October 9, 1964, 2.
9 Janice Mitchell, *My Ticket to Ride: How I Ran Away to England to Meet the Beatles and Got Rock and Roll Banned in Cleveland (A True Story from 1964)* (Cleveland: Gray & Company Publishers, 2021), 281–2.
10 "Two Beatles Buffs Biffed by Blunt Juvenile Judge," *Cincinnati Enquirer,* November 3, 1964, 22.
11 Ibid., 278.
12 Connie Gee, "Her Problem: Runaway Children," *Miami News,* May 10, 1964, 20.
13 Louise Sheldon, "Runaway Children Police Headaches," *Citizen-News*, November 28, 1964, 62.
14 Anne Leonard, "Reports Runaway Children Mental Illness Candidates." *Asbury Park Press*, October 13, 1963, 24.
15 "6 Beatles Fans Fly, 2 to England," *Akron Beacon Journal,* September 20, 1964, 54.
16 "Third Youngster Seen Beatle Runaway," *Baltimore Evening Sun,* May 29, 1964, B-19.
17 "2 Virginia Girls Back Home; Plan to Visit Beatles Fails," *Baltimore Sun,* June 1, 1964, 36.

NOTES

18. "It's Back to School for Beatle-Crazed Runaways," *Progress-Index*, June 1, 1964, 1.
19. "4 Missing Beatle Fan Girls Seen," *San Francisco Examiner*, October 19, 1964, 55.
20. "San Rafael Girls May Seek Beatles," *Daily Independent Journal*, October 17, 1964, 1. See also: "Runaway Beatle Fans May Be in Sacramento Region," *Daily Independent Journal*, October 19, 1964, 4.
21. "Tip from Bus Station Leads to Discovery of Runaways," *Daily Independent Journal*, October 19, 1964, 1.
22. "Local Beatles Fan, 13, Drifts Off to Britain," *Boston Globe*, October 23, 1964, 33.
23. Ibid.
24. "Missing Newton Girl, 13, Discovered in London," *Boston Globe*, October 31, 1964, 2.
25. Gloria Negri, "Girl Finds Beatles Hard Way," *Boston Globe*, November 6, 1964, 4.
26. Craig Rosen, "The True Story of the 'Beatles' Runaway," *Yahoo News*, February 19, 2014. https://www.yahoo.com/entertainment/blogs/music-news/true-story-beatles-runaway-223417792.html (accessed October 4, 2021).
27. The Beatles quotes are found in "Runaway Beatle 'Bug' Sees Idols, Has Fun," *Sacramento Bee*, November 2, 1964, 6.
28. Craig Rosen, "The True Story of the 'Beatles' Runaway," *Yahoo News*, February 19, 2014. https://www.yahoo.com/entertainment/blogs/music-news/true-story-beatles-runaway-223417792.html (accessed October 4, 2021).
29. Gloria Negri, "Beatle Fan Back in Dullsville," *Boston Globe*, November 6, 1964, 1.
30. "'Pied Piper Beatles' Lure Girls From Home," *Boston Globe*, May 30, 1964, 9.
31. "Runaway Beatle Fans May Be in Sacramento Region," *Daily Independent Journal*, October 19, 1964, 4.
32. "Two Beatles Buffs Biffed by Blunt Juvenile Judge," *Cincinnati Enquirer*, November 3, 1964, 22.
33. Ron Bergman, "Pandemonium at S.F. Cow Palace," *Concord Transcript*, August 20, 1964, 2.
34. Thomas Fitzpatrick, "Beatles Are a Screaming Smash Here," *Chicago Tribune*, September 6, 1964, 1.
35. Ralph Cosham, "Beatles Go on U.S. Video, Cause Flopover in Audience," *Atlanta Constitution*, February 10, 1964, 13.
36. "Dissecting the Beatles: George, Paul, John, and Ringo! Why Are They Different?," *The Original Beatles Book* (Los Angeles: Petersen Publishing Company). This special one-off issue does not contain page numbers. If the

NOTES

cover is counted as page 1, which many fan magazines from the mid-1960s did, then these quotes appear on pages 15, 17, 19, and 20.

37 Feldman-Barrett, *A Women's History of the Beatles*, 49.
38 Ibid.
39 Berman, *We're Going to See the Beatles!*, 57.
40 "Paper Mates," *Dig*, September 1964, 40.
41 Penelope Rowlands, ed., *The Beatles Are Here! 50 Years after the Band Arrived in America, Writers, Musicians, & Other Fans Remember* (Chapel Hill, NC: Algonquin Books of Chapel Hill, 2014), 185.
42 "63 Ways to Meet the Beatles," *Best of the Beatles* (New York: Macfadden-Bartell Corporation, 1964), 76–7.
43 Sandra Roland, "Teen-Agers Strive for Independence," *Nashville Tennessean*, June 12, 1965, 14.
44 Raymond Olmsted, "Parent Says Beatles Good, Clean Fun," *Des Moines Register*, August 1, 1965, 31.
45 Virginia Riley, "Tampans: You, Too, Can Look Like a Beatle," *Tampa Times*, February 13, 1964, 1.
46 "Beatle Mania Infests S.C. Capital," *Greenville News*, February 11, 1964, 1.
47 Ted Fourkas, "Old Rag Mops for Beatle Brows," *Oakland Tribune*, February 13, 1964, 1, 4.
48 Craig Brown, *150 Glimpses of the Beatles* (New York: Farrar, Straus and Giroux, 2020), 172.
49 "Give Yourself a Beatle Bob," *All About the Beatles*, no. 1 (New York: YOPU Press, 1964), 38.
50 "The Hair Do That Changed the Face of the Nation," *Beatle Mania*, vol. 1, no. 1 (New York: SMP Publishing, 1964), 8–9.
51 Patricia Gallo-Stenman, *Diary of a Beatlemaniac: A Fab Insider's Look at the Beatles Era: A Fab Insider's Look at the Beatles Era* (Malvern, PA: Cynren Press, 2018), 34.
52 Ibid., 35.
53 Stephen Kahn, "How You Can Become a Beatle!," *The Beatles* (New York: Beatle Publishing Corporation, 1964), 28–9.
54 "The Beatle Cut: It's a Mad Fad, Dad!," *The Beatles Personality Annual*, vol. 1, no. 1, 52–3.
55 Gallo-Stenman, *Diary of a Beatlemaniac*, 38.
56 Berman, *We're Going to See the Beatles*, 121.
57 "Young Fans Drop the Veneer of Civilization for Beatles," *Cincinnati Enquirer*, August 28, 1964, 1.
58 Regina Sinnes and Carolyn Plutt, "Here's How Two Napa Teen-Agers Viewed England's Beatles," *Napa Valley Register*, August 20, 1964, 13.
59 Berman, *We're Going to See the Beatles*, 133.

NOTES

60 Bill Roberts, "Winner of Beatles Contest Is Agog Over 'Those Dolls,'" *Indianapolis News,* August 21, 1964, 3.
61 Lyons, *Joy and Fear,* 57.
62 Feldman-Barrett, *A Women's History of the Beatles,* 142–3.
63 Marti Whitman—who later became Marti Edwards—tells the story about meeting Derek Taylor and the Beatles in her self-published book *16 in '64: The Beatles & the Baby Boomers,* 2nd ed. (Kindle, 2015).
64 John C. Thomas, "This Little Miss Actually Kissed One of the Beatles," *Boston Globe,* September 13, 1964, 66. A caption under a photo of Debbie Chase meeting Ringo Starr that goes along with the story refers to her as "Debbie Carter."
65 Nancy Freund, "Teen Finds Beatles Charming," *Wausau Daily Herald,* August 27, 1965, 11,
66 Lyons, *Joy and Fear,* 112.
67 Richard J. Connolly, "Teens Flip Wigs for Beatles," *Boston Globe,* September 13, 1964, 1.
68 Jack Helsel, "Beatles Came, Conquered, Sang—but Weren't Heard," *Philadelphia Daily News,* September 3, 1964, 5.
69 Richard Houghton, *The Beatles: I Was There: More Than 400 First-Hand Accounts from People Who Knew, Met and Saw Them* (Falmouth: Red Planet Books, 2016), 278.
70 Kasparek, "A Day in the Life," 22.
71 Maureen Wheelhouse, "Finds Beatles Relaxed, Witty, Pleasant, Playful," *Clarion-Ledger,* August 26, 1965, 3.
72 For example, see: "Ringo Loses Medal as Fans Vent Love," *Fort Worth Star-Telegram,* August 29, 1964, 9.
73 Houghton, *The Beatles: I Was There,* 291–2.
74 Howard Carl Rubin, "Teens Music No Harm to Anyone," *Tennessean,* June 12, 1965, 14. See also: Howard Carl Rubin, "Teens Don't Use Phone to Excess," *Tennessean,* December 25, 1965, 13.
75 Joe Queenan, "Tools of Satan, Liverpool Division," in Rowlands, ed., *The Beatles Are Here!,* 1–7.
76 Jim Treloar, "Trouble, With a Capital 'B,'" *Detroit Free Press,* February 13, 1964, 45.
77 Patrick Kelly, "In Our Town," *Tampa Tribune,* April 30, 1964, 14.
78 Deborah Paige, "Beatle-Mania Hits at Fan Club Fete," *Salt Lake Tribune,* July 23, 1965, 12.
79 Gloria Steinem, "Beatle With a Future," *Cosmopolitan,* December 1964, 60.
80 Ibid.
81 Gay Talsese, "Beatles and Fans Meet Social Set," *New York Times,* September 21, 1964, 44.
82 James Yuenger, "Beatle Bagger," *Chicago Tribune,* October 10, 1964, 8.
83 Eleanor Nangle, "Whew! Beatle Hair Style Could Sweep the Nation," *Chicago Tribune,* February 14, 1964, B14.

NOTES

84 Helen McLaughlin, "To Suit Your Fancy," *Vermont Times,* February 20, 1964, C1.
85 Victor D. Brooks, *Boomers: The Cold-War Generation Grows Up* (Chicago: Ivan R. Dee, 2009), 9.
86 Marian Matthews, "Take Good Care of Children's Topknots," *Des Moines Register,* January 10, 1953, 5.
87 Amy Vanderbilt, "American Haircut, Clothes Soon Put Immigrant Look to Rout," *Pittsburgh Press,* March 21, 1957, 20.
88 Earl Wilson, "Moore and Wilson: Krew Kut Kids," *Charlotte News*, March 5, 1955, 16.
89 Bob Thomas, "Hollywood: Long Hair: Yes or No?," *The Ithaca Journal,* November 26, 1965, 8.
90 Bob Thomas, "Movie Stars Frown on Long-Haired Boys," *The Sacramento Bee,* November 26, 1965, 34.
91 Bob Thomas, "Hollywood: Long Hair: Yes or No?," *The Ithaca Journal,* November 26, 1965, 8.
92 Bob Thomas, "Frown on Long Hair for Boys," *Kansas City Star,* November 26, 1965, 4.
93 "Find 80% of Public Against Beatle-Type Hair on Boys," *Des Moines Register,* October 6, 1965, 1.
94 Eugene Gilbert, "Beatlemania Will Fade Soon, Teens Say," *Town Talk*, April 4, 1964, 4.
95 Lynne Watson, "They Like The Beatles … Even Wear Haircuts," *Democrat and Chronicle,* February 23, 1964, 84.
96 Rose DeWolfe, "Beatles Bug Barbers, Bushy-Browed Buffs Start Youth Buzzing," *Philadelphia Inquirer,* February 13, 1964, 17.
97 "Beatle Hair-Dos Banned," *Minneapolis Star,* February 14, 1964, 19.
98 "Beatle Hair Ban Lawful, Office Rules," *Reno Gazette-Journal,* September 25, 1965, 10.
99 "Tulsa School Bans Beatle Hair Styling," *Amarillo Globe Times,* January 13, 1965, 7.
100 Joseph M. Harvey, "Georgie Porgie's Turn to Cry," *Boston Globe,* December 7, 1965, 1, 32.
101 Max Rafferty, "Educators See Beatle Hair as More Than a Question of 'Rights,'" *Cincinnati Enquirer,* February 2, 1965, 6.
102 "Cause of Acne: Beatle Hairdos Are Blamed," *Asbury Park Press,* September 8, 1965, 3.
103 "Beatle Skin: Mops Called Face Irritant," *Fort Worth Star-Telegram,* October 4, 1965, 9.
104 H. L. Herschensohn, "Hair on Face Can Cause Acne," *The Times,* February 24, 1966, 15.
105 "Beatle Bangs Banned," *The Times,* February 12, 1964, 10.

106 Mary Lu Dickey, "Yeah, They're Great," *News Journal*, February 18, 1964, 27.

107 Michael H. Rhea, "Beatle Cuts Fad," *Baltimore Sun*, February 10, 1964, 16.

Chapter 3

1 "Hang the Lanterns in the Tower: The British Are Coming!," *Minneapolis Star*, February 7, 1964, 1A.

2 Hugh Stevens, "Quick, Henry, the SWAT," *Daily Tar Heel*, February 15, 1964, 2.

3 Frank Holeman, "D.C. is Alarmed as Another British Invasion Nears, *New York Daily News*, February 11, 1964, 52.

4 Richard B. Stolley, "The Beatles of Foggy Bottom," *Life Magazine*, April 3, 1964, 38.

5 Pat Lloyd, "Around the Town," *Pensacola News Journal*, February 16, 1964, 8C.

6 Some estimates of the cost of the EMI-Capitol publicity blitz climb as high as $100,000, but most accounts place it more around $40,000. These figures are found in Michael R. Frontani, *The Beatles: Image and the Media* (Jackson: University Press of Mississippi, 2007), 23–4. See also: Philo, *British Invasion*, 35–7. Walter Everett, *The Beatles as Musicians: The Quarry Men through Rubber Soul* (New York: Oxford University Press, 2001), 205–6. Bill Harry, *The British Invasion: How the Beatles and Other UK Bands Conquered America* (New Malden, Surrey: Chrome Dreams Publications, 2004), 24–8.

7 News item, *Billboard Magazine*, January 4, 1964, 10.

8 Bill Whitworth, "Laugh Pal, but These 'Rockers' Have Rolled Up to 76 Million!" *Boston Globe*, November 29, 1964, 77.

9 *Who Will Beat the Beatles?* (New York: Magnum Productions, 1964); *The Beatles Meet the Dave Clark 5* (New York: Kahn Communications Corporation, 1964); *Dave Clark 5 vs. the Beatles* (New York: Tempest Publications, vol. 1, no. 1, September 1964).

10 "The Dave Clark 5 vs. the Beatles," in *Dave Clark 5 vs. the Beatles*, 5.

11 "Follow the Leader," *Time*, September 3, 1965, 84.

12 Steven X. Rea, "Their Sound Was Glad All Over," *Philadelphia Inquirer*, March 8, 1984, 7-D.

13 Lynn Birch, "Presenting the Dave Clark Five: In Concert," *Macon Telegraph and News*, December 20, 1964, 16.

14 Donna Seman, "Letter to the Editor," *Orlando Sentinel*, June 21, 1964, 17B.

15 Terry Pattishall, "Letter to the Editor," *Orlando Sentinel*, June 26, 1964, 3B.

16 "Dave Clark Five to Bring 15 Special Police with Them," *Passaic Herald-News*, May 18, 1964, 22.

17 Phil Chen, "They're Wild, Gorgeous, Cute, Great, Say Girls," *Passaic Herald-News*, June 3, 1964, 8.

NOTES

18 Nick Jones, "Platter Potpourri: British Music Invasion Still Gaining Momentum," *Indianapolis News,* August 13, 1964, 11.

19 Leonard, *Beatleness,* 71. It turns out, according to Paul McCartney, that behind the scenes, the Beatles were quietly apprehensive about the startling success of the Dave Clark Five. He confirmed the band's fears in an interview that originally appeared in a French magazine in January of 1985, and was later translated and published in the October / November 1985 issue of *Write Thing* fanzine. Paul told the interviewer:

> In the beginning, in Liverpool, we were anxious because of a group called Gerry and the Pacemakers. Later on, in London, we used to feel threatened by the Dave Clark Five. In fact, as far as I was concerned anyway, I didn't trust anyone. I remember one day somebody came into our office saying, "Dave Clark is number one in the chart." There was dead silence. It was serious stuff. Today it makes you laugh to think that the Beatles were scared of Gerry or Dave Clark. But we were.

See "French Interview With Paul," on the Meet the Beatles For Real blog, January 28, 2015. http://www.meetthebeatlesforreal.com/search?q=%22Dave+Clark+Five%22 (accessed July 25, 2022).

20 Quoted in Anthony DeCurtis, James Henke, and Holly George-Warren, eds., *The Rolling Stone Illustrated History of Rock and Roll: The Definitive History of the Most Important Artists and Their Music* (San Francisco: Random House / Straight Arrow Press, 1992), 205.

21 John McMillian, *Beatles vs. Stones* (New York: Simon & Schuster, 2013), 122. Philip Norman, *Sympathy for the Devil: The Rolling Stones Story* (New York: Simon & Schuster, 1984), 104.

22 Bill Whitworth, "After Beatles Came the Deluge," *Los Angeles Times,* Calendar Section, December 5, 1964, 26.

23 Miles, *The British Invasion,* 129.

24 George McKinnon, "Wayne Newton: The 'Happy Music' Man," *Boston Globe,* November 30, 1966, 52.

25 Bernard M. Corbett and Peter Fornatale, *50 Licks Myths and Stories from Half a Century of the Rolling Stones* (London: Bloomsbury Publishing), 25.

26 Dorothy Kilgallen, "New British Invaders Outdo Beatles," *Washington Post,* May 26, 1964, D5.

27 "Rolling Stones Top Beatles in Popularity," *Times and Democrat,* September 9, 1964, 1.

28 "Stones Displace Beatles," *Elmira Star Gazette,* September 9, 1964, 27.

29 "Cleveland Beatle-Chasers Now Like Rolling Stones," *Lancaster Eagle-Gazette,* November 2, 1964.

30 "Rolling Stones Replace Beatles as No. 1 Group," *San Angelo Standard-Times,* September 9, 1964, 13A.

31 "Freakier Rivals of the Beatles, 'Rolling Stones,' Coming Tuesday," *Rutland Daily Herald,* June 1, 1964, 3.

32 Mary Campbell, "A 'Rolling Stone' Speaks," *Cincinnati Enquirer*, April 23, 1966, Special "Teen-Ager" Section, 2.

33 Bill Byers, "Meet the Rolling Stones: Forget the Moss, They Gather 'Lolly,'" *Philadelphia Daily News*, June 10, 1964, 41.

34 "They're Buggin' the Beatles," *Rutland Daily Herald*, June 1, 1964, 3.

35 Kay Reimler, "A Fan Is Cute and Wears in Clothes," *Charlotte News*, October 9, 1965, 8.

36 Charles Champlin, "Rolling Stones Ready to Go into Orbit," *Los Angeles Times*, December 10, 1965, 39.

37 B. J. S., "Letter to the Editor," *Orlando Sentinel*, June 21, 1964, 17-B.

38 Frederick James, "Beatles Talk: John and George," *The Beatles Monthly Book*, no. 19, February 1965, 9.

39 John Lennon later famously skewered Mick Jagger, not once, but multiple times, in an interview with Jan Wenner of *Rolling Stone* magazine, conducted on December 5, 1970. At one point, an irate Lennon said of the Rolling Stones' lead singer:

> I think Mick got jealous. I was always very respectful about Mick and the Stones, but he said a lot of sort of tarty things about the Beatles, which I am hurt by, because you know, I can knock the Beatles, but don't let Mick Jagger knock them. I would like to just list what we did and what the Stones did two months after on every fuckin' album. Every fuckin' thing we did, Mick does exactly the same—he imitates us. And I would like one of you fuckin' underground people to point it out, you know Satanic Majesties is Pepper, "We Love You," it's the most fuckin' bullshit, that's "All You Need Is Love."

See: Jan S. Wenner, "John Lennon: *The Rolling Stone* Interview, Part One," Rolling Stone. https://www.rollingstone.com/music/music-news/john-lennon-the-rolling-stone-interview-part-one-160194/ (accessed July 28, 2022). Over the decades, the war of words between members of the two bands steadily escalated, reaching a fever pitch in the 2010s and 2020s, with Paul McCartney and Mick Jagger being the main culprits. For examples, see: Bonnie Stiernberg, "A Brief History of the Beatles and the Rolling Stones Insulting Each Other," *InsideHook*, October 14, 2021. https://www.insidehook.com/article/music/beatles-stones-rivalry (accessed July 28, 2022).

40 Joyce Maynard, "My Secret Life with the Rolling Stones," *New York Times*, June 22, 1975, 107.

41 Examples: "Rolling Stones Fans Run Wild," *Palm Beach Post*, October 31, 1965, 41; "Rolling Stones Fans Riot at Berlin Show," *Passaic Herald-News*, September 16, 1965, 11; Welton Jones, "Shreveport Teenagers Shriek for the Stones," *Shreveport Times*, November 21, 1965, 12; "Rolling Stones' Fans Faint and / or Fight," *Long Beach Press-Telegram*, June 16, 1965, D-3; "Girls Like Maniacs When Rolling Stones Perform in R.I.," *Holyoke Transcript-Telegram*, November 5, 1964, 7.

42 Bob Talbert, "On the Scene," *The State and the Columbia Record*, November 14, 1965, 8-E.
43 McMillian, *Beatles vs. Stones*, 3.
44 Don Morrison, "Don Morrison's 2 Cents' Worth," *Minneapolis Star*, August 11, 1964, 78.
45 Dwight MacDonald, *Dwight Macdonald on Movies* (Englewood Cliffs, NJ: Prentice-Hall, 1969), 400–1.
46 Walter Winchell, "Chaplin's Memoirs Sales Slow," *Indianapolis Star*, September 19, 1965, 38.
47 Giles M. Fowler, "Merry Chase in Fantasyland Has Beatles Howling 'Help!,'" *Kansas City Star*, August 22, 1965, 93.
48 Bob Neaverson, *The Beatles Movies* (London: Cassell, 1997), 44.
49 Mae Tinee, "Beatle Film Chaotic, but is Good Fun: *A Hard Day's Night*," *Chicago Tribune*, September 3, 1964, C10.
50 Christine McConnell, "Beatles Sing, Fans Scream," *Independent Star-News*, August 16, 1964, 63.
51 Ibid.
52 Ibid.
53 David Mannweiler, "Theater Man Breathes Prayer as 'They' Arrive," *Indianapolis News*, August 26, 1964, 1.
54 Stanley Eichelbaum, "How About That New Beatle Movie!" *San Francisco Examiner*, August 12, 1964, 50.
55 *A Hard Day's Night*, directed by Richard Lester (New York: Criterion Collection, 2014), Blu-ray.
56 *Help!*, directed by Richard Lester (New York: Universal Music, 2013), Blu-ray.
57 Dede Lawless, "N.E. Fans Flip Wigs Over First Beatles Movie," *Boston Globe*, August 13, 1964, 1.
58 Gallo-Stenman, *Diary of a Beatlemaniac*, 109.
59 Ibid., 109–10.
60 Jean Walrath, "New-Type Hollywood Heroines—And Why Beatle Fans Scream," *Democrat and Chronicle*, August 22, 1965, 3E.
61 Berman, *We're Going to See the Beatles*, 104.
62 Bobby Hart and Glenn Ballantyne, *Psychedelic Bubble Gum: Boyce & Hart, The Monkees, and Turning Mayhem into Miracles* (New York: SelectBooks, 2015), Chapter 18, Kindle Edition.
63 John Larson, "Monkees Rocketed to Fame by Way of Madness Contest," *San Bernardino Daily Sun*, October 1, 1966, C8.
64 The most thorough discussion of Beatles' promotion films is found in Stephanie Fremaux, *The Beatles on Screen: From Pop Stars to Musicians* (London: Bloomsbury Publishing), 78–98.
65 In addition to producing over 200 *Popeye the Sailor* cartoons between 1960 and 1962 for King Features, Al Brodax (1926–2016) produced such cartoon

programmes as *Krazy Kat, Beatle Bailey, Snuffy Smith and Barney Google,* and *Blondie* during the 1960s. His most famous productions were *The Beatles* on ABC and *Yellow Submarine* (1968), an animated film about the Beatles uniting with Captain Fred in his yellow submarine on a journey to Pepperland to liberate it from the Blue Meanies, a bizarre species of music-hating beings. Like the Saturday morning cartoon of the Fab Four, *Yellow Submarine*—which was more heavily infused with psychedelia than its TV counterpart—did not feature the actual voices of the Beatles, but it included multiple songs by the band. Decades later, Brodax wrote a book titled *Up Periscope Yellow: The Making of the Beatles' Yellow Submarine* (Lanham, MD: Limelight eds., 2004), in which he chronicled the challenges involved with making the film. He died in 2016 at age eighty.

66 Mel Helmer, "My New York," *Fort Pierce News Tribune,* June 21, 1965, 12.
67 "Beatles in Cartoon Win Highest Rating," *Hackensack Record,* November 5, 1965, 10.
68 Harvey Pack, "TV Keynotes: Beatles in Cartoons," *Allentown Morning Call,* November 5, 1965, 42.
69 John Blaney, *Beatles for Sale: How Everything They Touched Turned to Gold* (London: Jawbone Press, 2008), 196. According to the *Sydney Morning Herald*, Nicky Byrne was also "a racing driver who also has interests in the fashion trade." See: "Making a Mint of Money Out of the Beatles," *Sydney Morning Herald,* May 6, 1964, 2.
70 Ibid., 197.
71 Norman, *Shout!*, 217.
72 "Beatlewear—£35,000,000 Business," *Liverpool Echo and Evening Express,* June 8, 1964, 6.
73 Robert McDonald, "Charge Beatle Broker Spent It All," *New York Daily News,* December 9, 1964, 5.
74 Blaney, *Beatles For Sale,* 205.
75 Ibid., 206.
76 Leroy Pope, "$50,000,000 U.S. Jackpot From the Beatles," *St. Louis Post-Dispatch,* February 25, 1964, 34.
77 Ibid.
78 Martin Arnold, "Moneywise," *New York Times,* February 17, 1964, 1.
79 Woolworth's advertisement, *Kansas City Star,* September 15, 1964, 9.
80 Woolworth's advertisement, *Greeley Daily Tribune,* August 20, 1964, 23.
81 Gertrude Trawick, "Local Stores Riding Crest of Beatlemania," *Macon News,* March 25, 1964, 13.
82 Harriet Van Horne, "Relax, Mom, Beatlitis Has Run Its Course in the U.S.," *El Paso Herald-Post,* November 27, 1964, 10. Lloyd Stewart, "Beatle Fad Helps Girl Slim Down," *Fort Worth Star-Telegram,* July 16, 1964, Section 2, 3.
83 Ron Gibson, "Beatles? Yay!! All of the Walls!," *Lincoln Journal and Star,* March 29, 1964, B-1.

NOTES

84 "Action Line: Beatle Game," *Detroit Free Press,* January 24, 1981, 10.
85 Advertisement for Caldor Stores, *Port Chester Daily Item,* December 16, 1964, 27.
86 Hunter Davies, *Confessions of a Collector* (London: Quercus Books, 2009), 34.
87 Karyn Snead, "Memorabilia Fuels the Mania," *South Florida Sun Sentinel,* February 7, 1984, E-1.
88 "New Yule Disc Opening Doors for Becky, 10," *Columbus Ledger,* December 10, 1964, 44.
89 Tom Gray, "Columbus Girl Records Beatle Christmas Disc," *Columbus Ledger,* December 13, 1964, 43.
90 George Harrison, "Epstein Takes Court Action Against the Beatleggers," *Liverpool Echo and Evening Express,* February 16, 1964, 5. Coincidentally, the *Liverpool Echo and Evening Express* had a columnist named George Harrison writing for the newspaper, who was no relation to George Harrison of the Beatles, and was the author of this piece, as well as numerous other articles about the Beatles. He accompanied the Beatles on their tours, and his name was occasionally the source of some confusion and excitement in the 1960s.
91 Geoffrey Ellis, *I Should Have Known Better: A Life in Pop Management: The Beatles, Brian Epstein and Elton John* (London: Thorogood Publishing, 2005), 111.
92 Will Jones, "Clever Sale Goes Well," *Minneapolis Star Tribune,* August 9, 1965, 37.
93 Davies, *Confessions of a Collector,* 34.

Chapter 4

1 James Baldwin, "This Nettle, Danger…," in *James Baldwin: Collected Essays* (New York: The Library of America, 1998), 690.
2 For more on the pivotal new generation of Black actors in cinema and on television, see: Ossie Davis and Ruby Dee, *With Ossie and Ruby: In This Life Together* (New York: William Morrow, 1998); Ruth Feldstein, *How It Feels to Be Free: Black Women Entertainers and the Civil Rights Movement* (New York: Oxford University Press, 2013): Aram Goudsouzian, *Sidney Poitier: Man, Actor, Icon* (Chapel Hill: University of North Carolina Press, 2011); Mark Whitaker, *Cosby: His Life and Times* (New York: Simon & Schuster, 2014).
3 Accounts of these influential African American artists include: Ian Carr, *Miles Davis: The Definitive Biography* (New York: HarperCollins, 1998); Robert Gordon, *Can't Be Satisfied: The Life and Times of Muddy Waters* (New York: Back Bay Books, 2003); James Gavin, *Stormy Weather: The Life of Lena Horne* (New York: Atria Books, 2009); R. J. Smith, *Chuck Berry: An American Life* (New York: Hachette Books, 2022); Peter Guralnick, *Dream Boogie: The Triumph of Sam Cooke* (New York: Back Bay Books, 2006); Ray Charles and

David Ritz, *Brother Ray: Ray Charles' Own Story* (Boston: Da Capo Press, 2004; and David Ritz, *Respect: The Life of Aretha Franklin* (New York: Back Bay Books, 2015).

4   For more on Motown, see: Peter Benjaminson, *The Story of Motown* (Los Angeles: Rare Bird Books, 2018); Stuart Cosgrove, *Detroit 67: The Year That Changed Soul* (Edinburgh: Polygon, 2016); Lamont Dozier, *How Sweet It Is: A Songwriter's Reflections on Music, Motown and the Mystery of the Muse* (New York: BMG Books, 2019); Nelson George, *Where Did Our Love Go?: The Rise and Fall of the Motown Sound* (Champaign: University of Illinois Press, 2007); Brian Holland, Edward Holland and Dave Thompson, *Come and Get These Memories: The Story of Holland-Dozier-Holland* (London: Omnibus Press, 2019); Gerald Posner, *Motown: Music, Money, Sex, and Power* (New York: Random House, 2009); Mark Ribowsky, *The Supremes: A Saga of Motown Dreams, Success, and Betrayal* (Boston: Da Capo Press, 2009); Adam White, *Motown: The Sound of Young America* (London: Thames and Hudson, 2019).

5   Larry Kane, *When They Were Boys: The True Story of the Beatles' Rise to the Top* (Philadelphia: Running Press Book Publishers), 79–80.

6   Quoted in Lyons, *Joy and Fear*, 54.

7   Ibid.

8   Ibid.

9   Peter Benjaminson, *Mary Wells: The Tumultuous Life of Motown's First Superstar* (Chicago: Chicago Review Press), 74.

10 Ibid.

11 Creasy, *Beatlemania!*. https://www.scribd.com/read/347302720/Beatlemania-The-Real-Story-of-the-Beatles-UK-Tours-1963-1965#a_search-menu_293231 (accessed September 17, 2022).

12 Mary Wells, *Love Songs to the Beatles* (New York: 20th Century Fox, 1965). Vinyl LP.

13 Benjaminson, *Mary Wells*, 74.

14 The best account of the relationship between Motown and the Beatles is to be found in Jack Hamilton's *Just Around Midnight: Rock and Roll and the Racial Imagination* (Cambridge, MA: Harvard University Press, 2016), 121–68.

15 Aretha Franklin, *Aretha: From These Roots* (New York: Villard Books, 1999), 139.

16 The history of the Beatles on Vee-Jay Records is chronicled in Bruce Spizer's *The Beatles Records on Vee-Jay: Songs, Pictures & Stories of the Fabulous Beatles Records on Vee-Jay* (New Orleans: Four Ninety-Eight Productions, 1998).

17 Lyons, *Joy and Fear*, 31–3. According to Lyons, the Vee-Jay 7" single of "From Me to You" sold a measly 13,000 copies and failed to chart on Billboard.

NOTES

18 Quoted in Kenneth Womack, *The Beatles Encyclopedia: Everything Fab Four, Volume 2: K-Z* (Santa Barbara: ABC-CLIO/Greenwood Press, 2014), 964.

19 Spizer, *The Beatles Are Coming!*, 227–31.

20 Kitty Oliver, "The Beatles Gave Me My First Taste of Freedom," *Pride*, November 25, 2016. https://www.pridemagazine.com/dr-kitty-oliver-the-beatles-gave-me-my-first-taste-of-freedom/ (accessed January 24, 2022).

21 *The Beatles: Eight Days a Week*, DVD, directed by Ron Howard (New York: Universal Music, 2016).

22 Joyce Chen, "Oprah Winfrey jets into Washington D.C. with BFF Gayle, boyfriend Stedman for Kennedy Center Honors," *New York Daily News*, December 5, 2010. https://www.nydailynews.com/entertainment/gossip/oprah-winfrey-jets-washington-bff-gayle-boyfriend-stedman-kennedy-center-honors-article-1.472374 (accessed March 7, 2022).

23 What few studies have been undertaken on Beatles fans are mostly devoid of discussions about race. A few accounts, however, have discussed the relationship between Beatles fans and African Americans. In sociologist Leonard's *Beatleness*, an early trailblazing work on Beatles fandom, the author writes:

> Most young Beatle fans did not feel personally connected to [Martin Luther King Jr.] but saw his assassination as part of the encroaching chaos—another act of violence that bubbled up where chaos and violence frothed just below the surface. Beatle fans, like many other white Americans, had very little contact with "Negroes," and so their impressions were formed, for the most part, by the images they saw on television: stereotypes on sit-coms and dramas, singers on variety shows, athletes on playing fields, and depending on one's perspective, as oppressed citizens or rioters; maybe both. (177)

Although Leonard was an academic, she also prided herself on being a "first-generation Beatles fan," and she wrote her book to appeal to a broad popular readership. Other academics have not been as inclusive when it comes to the issue of race. In the anthology *Fandom and the Beatles*, edited by Kenneth Womack and Kit O'Toole, chapters by Beatles scholars cover a wide range of issues, including gender, the media, religion, heritage tourism, and fandom across generations. But the weighty issue of race is conspicuously absent from the book. One of the few scholarly works to incorporate a great deal of commentary on the Beatles and race—including the experiences of racialized minority fans—is historian John F. Lyons's outstanding book *Joy and Fear*. Moreover, Christine Feldman-Barrett's *A Women's History of the Beatles* does an excellent job of exploring the intersections of race and gender among Beatles fans.

24 "Beatles Tell Memphis Newsmen They Like Negro Vocal Groups," *Jet*, September 8, 1966, 60.

25 Maureen Mahon, "Black Like This: Race, Generation, and Rock in the Post-Civil Rights Era," *American Ethnologist*, May 2000, vol. 27, no. 2, 289.

26 Kitty Oliver, "The Beatles Gave Me My First Taste of Freedom," *Pride*, November 25, 2016. https://www.pridemagazine.com/dr-kitty-oliver-the-beatles-gave-me-my-first-taste-of-freedom/ (accessed January 24, 2022).

27 Joyce Chen, "Oprah Winfrey jets into Washington D.C. with BFF Gayle, boyfriend Stedman for Kennedy Center Honors," *New York Daily News*, December 5, 2010. https://www.nydailynews.com/entertainment/gossip/oprah-winfrey-jets-washington-bff-gayle-boyfriend-stedman-kennedy-center-honors-article-1.472374 (accessed April 3, 2022).

28 *The Beatles: Eight Days a Week*, DVD, directed by Ron Howard (New York: Universal Music, 2016).

29 Lyons, *Joy and Fear*, 90–1.

30 Lenore Bennett Jr., "Stokely Carmichael: Architect of Black Power," *Ebony*, vol. 21, no. 11, September 1966, 30.

31 Stokely Carmichael, "Speech given at Garfield High School, Seattle, Washington April 19, 1967." https://www.aavw.org/special_features/speeches_speech_carmichael01.html (accessed April 4, 2022).

32 Doris Raynes Johnson, "Beatles Just the Thing for Kids 8 to 88," *Chicago Defender*, March 28, 1964, 9.

33 Theophilus and Associates, "I Still Say … Ban the Beatles," *Chicago Defender*, June 20, 1964, 16.

34 Cynthia Jackson, "Teen-Town Chatter," *Chicago Defender*, June 13, 1964, 13.

35 Amiri Baraka, *Black Music* (New York: William Morrow and Company, 1968), 201–2.

36 Eldridge Cleaver, *Soul on Ice* (San Francisco: Ramparts Press, 1968), 194–204.

37 Julius Lester, *Look Out Whitey, Black Power's Gon' Get Your Mama* (New York: Dial Press, 1968), 91–2.

38 Ibid., 90–1.

39 Ibid., 91.

40 For more on the Schwerner, Chaney and Goodman murders, see: Seth Cagin and Philip Dray, *We Are Not Afraid: The Story of Goodman, Schwerner, and Chaney, and the Civil Rights Campaign for Mississippi* (New York: Nation Books, 2006). See also: William Bradford Huie, *Three for Mississippi* (Jackson: University Press of Mississippi, 2017; reprint of 1965 ed.).

41 *Mississippi Cold Case*, DVD, directed by David Ridgen (New York: Films Media Group, 2009).

42 Emily Wagster Pettus, "Posthumous Medals 'Distort History': Family," *Montreal Gazette*, November 24, 2014, A14.

43 For key works on the Mississippi Freedom Summer Project, see: Jon N. Hale, *The Freedom Schools: Student Activists in the Mississippi Civil Rights Movement* (New York: Columbia University Press, 2018); McAdam, *Freedom Summer*; Laura Visser-Maessen, *Robert Parris Moses: A Life in Civil Rights and Leadership at the Grassroots* (Chapel Hill: University of North Carolina Press, 2016); Bruce Watson, *Freedom Summer: The Savage Season That Made Mississippi Burn and Made America a Democracy* (New York: Viking, 2010).

NOTES

44 For example, decades later, Paul McCartney explained to an interviewer:

> I was sitting around with my acoustic guitar, and I'd heard about the Civil Rights troubles that were happening in the '60s in Alabama, Mississippi, Little Rock in particular. I just thought it would be really good if I could write something that if it ever reached any of the people going through those problems, it might give them a little bit of hope. So, I wrote "Blackbird."

See: Joe Taysom, "How the Beatles Wrote 'Blackbird' to Fight Back at Racism," *Far Out,* January 7, 2021. https://faroutmagazine.co.uk/the-beatles-paul-mccartney-blackbird-anti-racism-message/ (accessed April 5, 2022).

45 Robert D. Jacobus, *To Live and Play in Dixie: Pro Football's Entry into the Jim Crow South* (Amherst, NY: Prometheus Books, 2021), 164.

46 Jason Richards, *The Beatles in America 1964* (Canton, MA: Wheelhouse Publishers, 2021), 198.

47 Leslie Hart, "What the Beatles Were Really Like: Reporter Recalls His 'Ticket to Ride,'" Consider This Blog, *Al Jazeera America,* February 7, 2014. http://america.aljazeera.com/watch/shows/consider-this/Consider-This-blog/2014/2/7/larry-kane-recallshistimeontourwiththebeatles.html (accessed April 5, 2022).

48 Kenneth L. Campbell, *The Beatles and the 1960s: Reception, Revolution, and Social Change* (London: Bloomsbury Publishing, 2021), Chapter 4, Kindle.

49 Mark Lewisohn, *The Complete Beatles Chronicle* (New York: Harmony Books, 1992), 171.

50 John C. Winn, *Way Beyond Compare the Beatles' Recorded Legacy, Volume 1* (New York: Three Rivers Press, 2008), 249.

51 Jason Berry, Jonathan Foose, and Tad Jones, *Up from the Cradle of Jazz: New Orleans Music since World War II* (Lafayette: University of Louisiana at Lafayette Press, 2009), 149.

52 Michael Hurtt, "It Was 40 Years Ago Today Frogman Henry and the Beatles Came to Play," *OffBeat Magazine,* September 1, 2004. https://www.offbeat.com/articles/it-was-40-years-ago-today-frogman-henry-and-the-beatles-came-to-play/ (accessed April 7, 2022).

53 "Ex-Manager Must Repay 'Frogman' Henry $1,000," *Pittsburgh Courier,* April 18, 1964, 12.

54 Michael Hurtt, "It Was 40 Years Ago Today Frogman Henry and the Beatles Came to Play," *OffBeat Magazine,* September 1, 2004. https://www.offbeat.com/articles/it-was-40-years-ago-today-frogman-henry-and-the-beatles-came-to-play/ (accessed April 7, 2022).

55 Ibid.

56 "Teens Scream Fond Farewell to Wealthy Beatles," *Central New Jersey Home News*, September 21, 1964, 13.

NOTES

57. For the finest account of Ella Baker's remarkable life, see Barbara Ransby's outstanding book *Ella Baker and the Black Freedom Movement: A Radical Democratic Vision* (Chapel Hill: University of North Carolina Press, 2003).

58. Unpublished fundraising manual, n.d. (circa 1964). Student Nonviolent Coordinating Committee (SNCC) Papers, 1959–1972. ProQuest (0531154).

59. Constancia Romilly letter to Joan Baez, July 9, 1965. Student Nonviolent Coordinating Committee (SNCC) Papers, 1959–1972. ProQuest (0450986).

60. Constancia Romilly letter to Manuel "Manny" Greenhill, July 21, 1965. Student Nonviolent Coordinating Committee (SNCC) Papers, 1959–1972. ProQuest (0450986).

61. Betty Garman Robinson letter to Elizabeth Sutherland, James Forman, and Constancia Romilly, August 1, 1965. Student Nonviolent Coordinating Committee (SNCC) Papers, 1959–1972. ProQuest (0450986).

62. Unknown SNCC organizer (unsigned) to Jay Lockard, Boston Friends of SNCC, October 2, 1964. Student Nonviolent Coordinating Committee (SNCC) Papers, 1959–1972. ProQuest (0340052).

63. Roberta Jones to Lucia Hatch, August 18, 1965. Student Nonviolent Coordinating Committee (SNCC) Papers, 1959–1972. ProQuest (0270350).

64. Betty Garman Robinson letter to Bobbi Jones, August 17, 1965. Student Nonviolent Coordinating Committee (SNCC) Papers, 1959–1972. ProQuest (0270350).

65. Kenneth Womack, *Maximum Volume: The Life of Beatles Producer George Martin, The Early Years, 1926–1966* (Chicago: Chicago Review Press, 2017), 285.

66. For a poignant account of Peter Simon's life, see Bill Eville, "Peter Simon, 71, Chronicled Island with His Camera," *Vineyard Gazette,* November 21, 2018. https://vineyardgazette.com/news/2018/11/21/peter-simon-71-chronicled-island-his-camera (accessed April 11, 2022).

67. Peter Simon, "Beatles Concert at Shea Stadium: Three African American Girls in a cCowd of Fans Outside the Stadium, August 15, 1965," Photograph, Special Collections and University Archives, University of Massachusetts Amherst Libraries, Amherst, MA. https://credo.library.umass.edu/view/full/muph009-d6508-sl001-i014 (accessed April 11, 2022).

68. Lenore Bennett Jr., "Confrontation on the Campus," *Ebony,* May 1968, 32.

69. Nelson George, *The Death of Rhythm and Blues* (New York: Pantheon, 1988), 92–3.

70. Quoted in Jude Rogers, " 'I Was Shattered'—Paul Weller, Booker T and More on the Day the Beatles Split." *The Guardian,* April 9, 2020. https://www.theguardian.com/music/2020/apr/09/shattered-paul-weller-booker-beatles-split-50-years-ago-fans (accessed April 11, 2022).

Chapter 5

1. Anthony Burton, "It's All a Big Giggle to the Beatles," *New York Daily News,* February 11, 1964, 52.
2. "A Line O' Type Or Two: Beatles," *Chicago Tribune,* November 20, 1964, 16.
3. The Beatle Editor, "Mom Miffed By Son's Beatle Bob," *Philadelphia Daily News,* August 26, 1964, 5.
4. "School Suspends Student Here with 'Beatle Haircut,' " *Daily Times Advocate,* September 14, 1964, 1.
5. Vivian K. Ruby, "We Have Put up with That Noise," Letters to the Editor, *Hartford Courant,* February 19, 1964, 14.
6. James Devane, "You Said It!" *Cincinnati Enquirer,* February 17, 1964, 40.
7. Lucy E. Hagen, "Can't 'See' Beatles," Letters to the Editor, *Alton Evening Telegraph,* March 2, 1964, 4.
8. William Long, "It Isn't Music," Letters to the Editor, *Asheville Citizen-Times,* March 5, 1964, 4.
9. J.R., "I Have Had It up to Here with the Beatles," *Greenwood Commonwealth,* February 18, 1964, 10.
10. "Unbelievable Beatles," editorial in the *Minneapolis Star,* February 12, 1964, 14.
11. "A Beatle Hater? What an Insect!" *Charlotte Observer,* February 14, 1964, 4.
12. "Rival Beatle Factions Battle," *Eureka Humboldt Standard,* September 5, 1964, 11.
13. " 'Stamp Out Beatles' Is Their Aim," *Bismarck Tribune,* February 11, 1964, 1.
14. Don and Robert Engelhardt, "Letters to the Editor," *Evening Independent,* February 18, 1964, 4.
15. "Beatles Fans Let Their Hair Down," *Chicago Tribune TV Week,* March 28, 1964, 4.
16. John Place, "Anti-Beatles Stir Antis with Fans Mopping Up," *Pittsburgh Press,* February 23, 1964, 2. See also: Kaspar Monahan, "Arnold Girl Interviews Beatle Relative," *Pittsburgh Press,* April 6, 1964, 26.
17. Bob MacKenzie, "TV Mailbox," *Oakland Tribune,* May 11, 1964, 14.
18. John Place, "Anti-Beatles Stir Antis with Fans Mopping Up," *Pittsburgh Press,* February 23, 1964, 2.
19. A history of the film can be found in Steven Rosen, "Judge's Response to Beatles Lives on in Internet Age," *Cincinnatti Enquirer,* August 25, 2014. https://www.cincinnati.com/story/news/history/2014/08/25/judges-response-beatles-lives-internet-age/14560519/ (accessed April 24, 2022). For the YouTube video of Judge Schwartz's rant, see: AcmestreamingDOTcom, "The Beatles Are a threat to Our children, Especially girls. A Warning From Cincinnati August 1964," YouTube Video, 3:57, September 29, 2013. https://www.youtube.com/watch?v=R0nY33UgHmo (accessed April 24, 2022).
20. "Judge Scores Beatles at Landmark Meet," *Wilmington News-Journal,* August 29, 1964, 1.

21. Andrew J. Taylor, "The Expert in American Life," *National Affairs*, Fall 2021. https://www.nationalaffairs.com/publications/detail/the-expert-in-american-life (accessed April 25, 2022).
22. "Firmer Hand by Parents Vogue Today," *Herald-News,* March 3, 1960, 17.
23. Llewellyn Miller, "Old Enough to Date," *Pittsburgh Sun-Telegraph, American Weekly Magazine,* October 2, 1955, 2.
24. J. Edgar Hoover, "Crisis in Juvenile Delinquency Tide," *Kansas City Star,* January 2, 1959, 8.
25. Bernard Saibel, "Beatle-Mania Frightens Guidance Expert," *Washington Post,* August 26, 1964, C4.
26. Charles H. Hapgood, "Beatles Do Not Create Emotion," *Boston Globe,* September 6, 1964, 39.
27. Inez Robb, "Let's Not Worry about the Beatles but about the Fans," *Gazette,* February 17, 1964, 17.
28. "Beatles Beat Echoes Prewar Nazi Chants," *Washington Post,* August 21, 1964, A5.
29. David Dempsey, "Why the Girls Scream, Weep, Flip," *New York Times,* February 23, 1964, 71.
30. Amy Larkin, "Ask Amy: All-Out Beatle Craze May Be Quite Normal for Teen Girl," *Atlanta Constitution,* July 8, 1964, 18.
31. Ibid.
32. Phyllis Lee Levin, "The Sound of Music?," *New York Times,* March 14, 1965, SM72.
33. Joyce Brothers, "Teen Revolt Aids Beatles," *Fort Worth Star-Telegram,* February 16, 1964, 19.
34. Lloyd Shearer, "The Beatles: How Long Will They Last?," *Boston Globe,* August 2, 1964, C4.
35. Harry Nelson, "Beatle-Mania: New Name for an Old Craze," *Los Angeles Times,* August 23, 1964, F1.
36. Margaret Josten, "Nothing New, This Beatle-Mania, UC Expert Says," *Cincinnati Enquirer,* Kentucky ed., August 28, 1964, 29.
37. William F. Buckley, "Why Do We Deserve the Beatles?" *Boston Globe,* September 13, 1964, 95.
38. Ibid.
39. Ibid.
40. Ibid.
41. Alfred Aronowitz, "The Return of the Beatles," *Saturday Evening Post,* August 8, 1964, 28.
42. "We Sneer and Jeer at Religion," *Life Lines,* vol. 6, no. 137, November 13, 1964, 2.
43. William V. Lord, "Beatles Communist," *Fort Myers News-Press,* July 25, 1965, 11.
44. Stan Fisher, "Birchers Blast Beatles," *Montreal Star,* August 6, 1965, 26.

45 John Clemens, "Beatles Said Red," *Paterson Morning Call,* September 7, 1966, 5.
46 H. L. Hunt, "Youthful Leaders for Freedom," *Chicago Tribune,* September 20, 1965, 20.
47 David Pritikin's column is quoted in Reverend Lyonel Watkins, "Explains Threat Beatles Pose," *Freeport Journal-Standard,* February 24, 1965, 11. The original column appeared on February 17, 1965. But for some reason, that issue of the *Freeport Journal-Standard* is missing from the Newspapers.com database. Pritikin's other "Teen Routine" columns appeared monthly in the newspaper.
48 "Beatles Called Sirens for Reds," *Detroit Free Press,* February 21, 1965, 7. See also: "Anti-Red Rally Slated," *Allentown Morning Call,* November 15, 1964, 6.
49 David A. Noebel, *Communism, Hypnotism and the Beatles: An Analysis of the Communist Use of Music—the Communist Master Music Plan* (Tulsa: Christian Crusade, 1965).
50 Ibid., 15.
51 Ibid., 12.
52 There are countless newspaper articles between 1964 and 1970 that refer to Reverend David Noebel's Christian Crusade–sponsored cross-country tours throughout the decade. Many of them contain his remarks about the Beatles. For example: Paul Coates, " 'Marxist Music Depreciation' Act Still Barnstorming the Country," *Los Angeles Times,* February 19, 1965, A6.
53 "Announcing! Christian Crusade Anti-Communist Rallies" advertisement, *Tipton Daily Tribune,* November 1, 1969, 5. See also: "Crusade to Begin with Talk Here," *Shreveport Times,* November 12, 1968, 8. According to the article, Rev. David Noebel was beginning "an 11-city tour of Louisiana and Texas."
54 "Cleric Links Beatles, Canines, Communism," *Long Beach Independent,* January 18, 1965, 11.
55 "Beatles Called a Red Plot," *Honolulu Star-Bulletin,* July 15, 1965, 15.
56 Judy Gilhousen, "Teeners Protest 'Beatles A Red Plot' Pamphlet," *Akron Beacon Journal,* May 29, 1965, A4.
57 Stephen Allen, "Beatle Fans Help! Writer Digs That Style," *Camden Courier-Post,* February 18, 1966, 15.
58 Jean Basil, "Beatle Fan's Efforts Attracting Letters," *Daily Independent Journal,* February 10, 1965, 31.

Chapter 6

1 The best, most authoritative single book on The Beatles in the pivotal year 1966 is Steve Turner's masterful *Beatles '66: The Revolutionary Year* (New York: Ecco Press, 2016).

2. Among the best accounts of the increasing volatility of the United States and the world in 1966 are: Kevin Boyle, *The Shattering: America in the 1960s* (New York: W.W. Norton, 2021); Dennis L. Breo and Bill Kunkle, *The Crime of the Century: Richard Speck and the Murders That Shocked a Nation* (New York: Skyhorse Publishing, 2016); Ronald Collins and David Skover, *The Trials of Lenny Bruce: The Fall & Rise of an American Icon* (Oak Park, IL: Top Five Books, 2012); Gary M. Lavergne, *A Sniper in the Tower: The Charles Whitman Murders* (Denton: University of North Texas Press, 1997); Mark Atwood Lawrence, *The Vietnam War: A Concise International History* (New York: Oxford University Press, 2010); Jon Savage, *1966: The Year the Decade Exploded* (London: Faber & Faber, 2016); Tom Wells, *The War Within: America's Battle Over Vietnam* (Berkeley: University of California Press, 1994).

3. Essential books about the rise of the Black Power Movement and the state of race relations in the mid-1960s include: Joshua Bloom and Waldo Martin, *Black against Empire: The History and Politics of the Black Panther Party* (Berkeley: University of California Press, 2013); Jeffrey Haas, *The Assassination of Fred Hampton: How the FBI and the Chicago Police Murdered a Black Panther* (Chicago: Chicago Review Press, 2009); Peniel Joseph, *Waiting 'Til the Midnight Hour: A Narrative History of Black Power in America* (New York: Henry Holt, 2006); Peniel E. Joseph, *Stokely: A Life* (New York: Basic Books, 2014); Peter B. Levy, *The Great Uprising Race Riots in Urban America During the 1960s* (New York: Cambridge University Press, 2018); Clay Risen, *The Bill of the Century: The Epic Battle for the Civil Rights Act* (New York: Bloomsbury, 2014).

4. More than any other works of Beatles' literature, Walter Everett's magisterial two-volume set *The Beatles as Musicians* brilliantly chronicles the evolution of the band's music in a manner both scholarly and accessible. The details are abundant, yet the narrative is never anything less than gripping. Interestingly, Everett ends the first volume with *Rubber Soul* (1965) and opens the second volume with *Revolver* (1966), two albums that many Beatles lovers consider companion pieces. Both books are essential reading for anyone seeking a deeper understanding of the band's musical history. See: Everett, *The Beatles as Musicians*; and Walter Everett, *The Beatles as Musicians: Revolver through the Anthology* (New York: Oxford University Press, 1999).

5. Maureen Cleave, "How Does a Beatle Live? John Lennon Lives Like This," *Evening Standard*, March 4, 1966, 10; Maureen Cleave, "Ringo Starr: So Who's Afraid of Dogs and Babies!" *Evening Standard*, March 11, 1966, 10; Maureen Cleave, "George Harrison: Avocado with Everything," *Evening Standard*, March 18, 1966, 8; Maureen Cleave, "Paul All Alone: Running Hard to Catch up with the Music," *Evening Standard*, March 25, 1966, 8.

6. Paul Brannigan, "Danny Says: How Danny Fields Changed Music Forever," *Louder,* April 21, 2016. https://www.loudersound.com/features/danny-says-how-danny-fields-changed-music-forever (accessed August 19, 2022).

7. The shortened versions of Maureen Cleave's profiles of Paul McCartney and John Lennon ran in *Datebook,* vol. 5, no. 8, September 1966, 8–11.

NOTES

8 Maureen Cleave, "Paul All Alone: Running Hard to Catch Up with the Music," *Evening Standard*, March 25, 1966, 8.

9 Unlike Maureen Cleave's original profile of John Lennon, which buried Lennon's quote deep in the story, Datebook highlighted the quote repeatedly in the magazine, displaying it in a large font on the first page of the excerpted Lennon profile. See: "John: I Don't Know Which Will Go First—Rock 'n' Roll or Christianity," *Datebook*, vol. 5, no. 8, September 1966, 8–11. See also: Peter Brown and Steven S. Gaines, *The Love You Make: An Insider's Story of the Beatles* (New York: New American Library, 2002), 193.

10 Mark Sullivan, " 'More Popular Than Jesus': The Beatles and the Religious Far Right," *Popular Music*, vol. 6, no. 3, Beatles Issue (October 1987), 313–14.

11 Wayne Greenhaw, "Beatles Decline Comment on Ban; Other Stations Rallying to Fight," *Alabama Journal*, August 4, 1966, 31.

12 Ibid.

13 "Local Radio Station Joins 'Ban Beatles' Campaign; Others Study It," *Danville Register*, August 4, 1966, 10.

14 Paul Rowan, "Ban Doesn't Hurt Beatles in Angelo," *San Angelo Standard-Times*, August 11, 1966, 17.

15 Pat Ammann, "Radio Station's 'Beatle Ban' Spreads," *Birmingham Post-Herald*, August 4, 1966, 30.

16 "Radio Stations Ban Beatles," *Brazosport Facts*, August 16, 1966, 7.

17 "Three More Radio Stations Ban Beatles," *Tampa Tribune*, August 6, 1966, 20-C.

18 "Beatles Dropped for Anti-Religious Remarks," *Tampa Times*, August 4, 1966, 1.

19 "Local Radio Station Joins 'Ban Beatles' Campaign; Others Study It," *Danville Register*, August 4, 1966, 10.

20 "Beatles Dropped for Anti-Religious Remarks," *Tampa Times*, August 4, 1966, 1.

21 Ibid.

22 "Local Radio Station Bans Beatle Records," *Shamokin News-Dispatch*, August 10, 1966, 1.

23 Ibid.

24 "Local Radio Station Joins 'Ban Beatles' Campaign; Others Study It," *Danville Register*, August 4, 1966, 10.

25 Tom Slayton, "Rutland Radio Station Lifts Beatle Ban," *Rutland Daily Herald*, August 8, 1966, 9.

26 "Radio Stations Lift Bans on Beatles Discs," *Muncie Star Press*, August 17, 1966, 15.

27 " 'Ban the Beatles' Protest Fails to Call Off Tour," *Tampa Tribune*, August 6, 1966, 20-C.

28 "Beatles Dropped for Anti-Religious Remarks," *Tampa Times*, August 4, 1966, 1.

29 "Local Radio Station Joins 'Ban Beatles' Campaign; Others Study It," *Danville Register,* August 4, 1966, 10.
30 Ibid.
31 "El Paso Radio Stations Won't Ban the Beatles," *El Paso Herald-Post*, August 5, 1966, 1.
32 Beverly Gewertz, "500 Teenagers Add Fuel to Beatle Bonfire Here," *Alexandria Town Talk,* August 8, 1966, C-1.
33 Ibid.
34 "Beatle Records Burned," *Tampa Tribune,* August 7, 1966, 20-A.
35 "Beatle Bonfire," *Cincinnati Post,* August 12, 1966, 6. " 'Beatle Bonfire' Held By Alabama Teenagers," *El Paso Post-Herald,* August 12, 1966, 5.
36 "Beatle-Burning Is 'A Smash' for Thousands," *Longview News-Journal,* August 14, 1966, 17.
37 "Klan Gets in on Move to Ban Beatles," *Durham Sun,* August 10, 1966, 10C. "Beatles Are 'Last,' Says Klan's Scoggin," *Columbia State,* August 11, 1966, 6-C.
38 "Beatle Protest Brings Scalping," *Greenwood Commonwealth,* August 8, 1966, 2.
39 "Boy Has Hair Cut to Protest Beatles," *Poughkeepsie Journal,* August 8, 1966, 2.
40 "Beatle Record Burning Set By Baptist Youth," *Orlando Sentinel,* August 13, 1966, 29.
41 Norman Vincent Peale, "Jesus vs. the Beatles? It's Really No Contest," *Chicago Tribune,* October 29, 1966, C11.
42 Turner, *Beatles '66*, 283.
43 Ray Coleman, *The Man Who Made the Beatles: An Intimate Biography of Brian Epstein* (New York: McGraw-Hill, 1989), 282. Turner, *Beatles '66*, 275.
44 "Beatles Leave for U.S. with Bibles by Seats," *Wilmington News Journal,* August 11, 1966, 1. Music critic Richard Goldstein, in the pages of the Village Voice, attributed the quote to New York-born Beatles fan Barbara Ruben, who lived in England at the time. It is possible a few different people expressed that sentiment. See: Richard Goldstein, "Report from Swinging London: 'Revolver' Revolution," *Village Voice,* August 25, 1966. https://www.villagevoice.com/2020/03/27/pop-eye-on-revolver/ (accessed August 25, 2022).
45 Milton Benjamin, "Beatles Get Brushoff by Boston Teens," *Newport Daily News,* August 12, 1966, 21.
46 Gloria Negri, "Beatlemania: The Throb's Still There," *Boston Globe,* August 12, 1966, 14.
47 Turner, *Beatles '66,* 223–54.
48 "Beatle Lennon Sorry about Jesus Remark," *Fort Worth Star-Telegram,* August 12, 1966, 8.
49 "Lennon of Beatles Sorry for Making Remark on Jesus," *New York Times,* August 12, 1966, 38.

50 Ibid.

51 Kevin Courrier, *Artificial Paradise: The Dark Side of the Beatles' Utopian Dream* (Westport, CT: Praeger Publishers, 2009), 139. See also: Lee Thomas-Mason, "The Disastrous Moment John Lennon Compared the Beatles to Jesus," *Far Out Magazine*, December 26, 2021. https://faroutmagazine.co.uk/when-john-lennon-compared-the-beatles-jesus/ (accessed August 22, 2022).

52 For example, in journalist Beverly Gewertz's account of the August 6 Beatles Bonfire in Alexandria, audience members declared themselves to be ex-Beatles fans. See Beverly Gewertz, "500 Teenagers Add Fuel to Beatle Bonfire Here," *Alexandria Town Talk*, August 8, 1966, C-1.

53 "Burning Beatles," *Syracuse Post-Standard*, August 11, 1966, 1.

54 Kathy Pepper, "John Lennon's Jesus Opinion Gets Reaction," *Pensacola Journal*, August 12, 1966, 8C.

55 Beverly Gewertz, "500 Teenagers Add Fuel to Beatle Bonfire Here," *Alexandria Town Talk*, August 8, 1966, C-1.

56 "Memphis Wants to Cancel Beatles' Shows," *Daily Oklahoman*, August 10, 1966, 17.

57 "Two American Girls in Support of Beatles," *Port Angeles Evening News*, August 7, 1966, 11.

58 Berman, *We're Going to See the Beatles!*, 250.

59 The radio statistics for 1966 come from the United States Department of Commerce, Bureau of the Census, *Bicentennial Edition: Historical Statistics of the United States, Colonial Times to 1970* (Washington, DC: US Government Printing Office, 1975), "Radio and Television Stations, Sets Produced, and Households with Sets: 1921 to 1970" (Series 4 93–105), 796.

60 For example, see: "Radio Stations Lift Bans on Beatles Discs," *Muncie Star-Press*, August 11, 1966, 15; "Some Beatle Bans Lifted," *Wilmington Morning News*, August 17, 1966, 13.

61 "Beatles Manager Here to Quell Storm Over Remark on Jesus," *New York Times*, August 6, 1966, 13.

62 "Pastor to Ban Beatle-Goers," *Akron Beacon Journal*, August 13, 1966, 11.

63 "More Critics Join the Beatles 'Ban Wagon,'" *Chicago Tribune*, August 6, 1966, 55.

64 Kathy Ahlfeld and Merideth Robb, "Singer's Remark Has Area Teens Jumping," *Dayton Daily News*, August 5, 1966, 19.

65 The increasingly controversial positions held by the Beatles by 1966—on a host of issues—are covered effectively in the following books: Campbell, *The Beatles and the 1960s*; Gould, *Can't Buy Me Love*; Stark, *Meet the Beatles*; Turner, *Beatles '66*.

66 W. Fraser Sandercombe, *The Beatles: The Press Reports, 1961–1970* (Burlington, ON, Canada: Collector's Guide Publishing), 181.

67 Karen Call, "Open Letter to Beatle Fans," *KRLA Beat*, December 4, 1965, 11.

68 Ibid.

69 Ibid.

70 The Beatles, *Revolver,* Parlophone, 1966, LP. For the definitive book on *Revolver*, see Robert Rodriguez's *Revolver: How the Beatles Re-Imagined Rock 'n' Roll* (Milwaukee: Hal Leonard Corporation, 2008).

71 Klaus Voormann, *Birth of an Icon: Revolver 50: The Making of the Legendary Cover Artwork for the Beatles Album Revolver*, English edn. (Bielefeld, Germany: Delius Klasing Verlag).

72 Berman, *We're Going to See the Beatles,* 219.

73 Ibid., 220. In her oral history in Berman's book, Wendi Tisland hastened to add: "And now that I'm older I know they had to do that, and that's where their best music came from, in their later days."

74 Linda Schultz, ed., *Tales of the Awesome Foursome: Beatles Fans Share Their Personal Stories, Poems and Memories of the Fab Four* (West Conshohocken, PA: Infinity Publishing, 2004), 50.

75 Leonard's *Beatleness*, 122.

76 "Tops in Pops," *Los Angeles Times,* August 31, 1966, 73.

77 Matthew Schneider, *The Long and Winding Road from Blake to the Beatles* (New York: Palgrave Macmillan, 2008), 121.

78 Jerry Zolten, "The Beatles as Recording Artists," in Kenneth Womack, ed., *The Cambridge Companion to the Beatles* (New York: Cambridge University Press, 2009), 44.

79 Houghton, *The Beatles: I Was There,* 345.

80 Ibid., 347.

81 Ibid., 354.

82 Patti Pjerrou and Arcelia Senz, "Two San Bernardino Teens Report on Beatle Concert," *San Bernardino County Sun,* September 3, 1966, 5.

83 Ibid.

84 Beatles Interview: Carnegie Hall February 12, 1964. See: Beatles Interviews Database. http://www.beatlesinterviews.org/db1964.0212.beatles.html (accessed August 26, 2022).

85 George Harrison (journalist), "The Beatles Made It: An Electrifying Show," *Liverpool Echo,* February 12, 1964, 15.

86 Henrietta Leith, "Beatles' Carnegie Hall Performance Awesome," *Marion Star,* February 13, 1964, 16.

87 Vernon Barchard, "Beatles Are Crowning Blow to Hectic Week in Jacksonville," *Tampa Tribune,* September 13, 1964, 12.

88 Beatles Press Conference: Seattle, Washington, August 21, 1964. See: Beatles Interviews Database. http://www.beatlesinterviews.org/db1964.0821.beatles.html (accessed August 25, 2022).

89 William Leonard, "Beatles' Class Comes Thru," *Chicago Tribune,* September 6, 1964, 2. Everett, *The Beatles as Musicians*, 250.

90 Larry Kane, Interview with The Beatles, Chicago, August 20, 1965. See: Beatles Interviews Database. http://www.beatlesinterviews.org/db1965.0820.beatles.html (accessed August 26, 2022).

91 Murray Schumach, "Shrieks of 55,000 Accompany Beatles," *New York Times,* August 16, 1965, 29.
92 Spitz, *The Beatles*, 578.
93 Thomas MacFarlane, *The Beatles' Abbey Road Medley: Extended Forms in Popular Music* (Lanham, MD: Scarecrow Press, 2007), 16.
94 Lyons, *Joy and Fear,* 225–6.
95 Gloria Negri, "Beatlemania: The Throb's Still There," *Boston Globe,* August 12, 1966, 14.
96 "US Notes," *The Beatles Monthly Book,* no. 39, October 1966, 12.
97 Nancy W. Ellis, "Anatomy of a Beatle Fan," *Boston Globe,* September 11, 1966, A-3.
98 Ibid.
99 Ibid.
100 Frederick James (a.k.a., Tony Barrow), "Why Haven't the Beatles Fixed Another Concert Tour?" *The Beatles Monthly Book,* no. 45, April 1967, 6.
101 Ibid.
102 "Beatle Fan Clubs Unite," *Akron Beacon-Journal,* April 7, 1968, E19.
103 Tom A. Cullen, "And It's Bye-Bye Beatles!" *Santa Cruz Sentinel,* December 4, 1966, 30.
104 "Beatlemania Ending; Echo Lingers On," *Los Angeles Times,* November 19, 1966, 21.
105 "Beatles Near Splitsville; Americans Invade England," *Lafayette Daily Advertiser,* November 28, 1966, 14.
106 "The End to Beatlemania," *Tampa Bay Times*, January 1, 1967, "Leisure and Arts Section," 11.
107 Joan Deppa, "Are Beatles Really Breaking Up?" *Lansing State Journal,* November 27, 1966, E-9.
108 Gallo-Stenman, *Diary of a Beatlemaniac,* 143–4.
109 Ibid., 160.

Chapter 7

1 Tony Barrow, *John, Paul, George, Ringo & Me: The Real Beatles Story* (London: André Deutsch, 2005), 261.
2 Books and articles that cover the music and the making of *Sgt. Pepper's Lonely Hearts Club Band,* as well as the critical responses to it and its legacies, include Jonathan W. Bernard, "The Beatles: Sgt. Pepper's Lonely Hearts Club Band." *Music Theory Spectrum,* 25, no. 2 (2003): 375–82; Kathryn B. Cox and Kenneth Womack, *The Beatles, Sgt. Pepper, and the Summer of Love* (Lanham, MD: Lexington Books, 2017); Everett, *The Beatles as Musicians*; Graham Fuller, "It Was Fifty Years Ago Today: Beatlemania Lives On in an Intimate Memoir and a Countercultural

Study," *Cinéaste*, 39, no. 2 (2014): 4–7; Olivier Julien, ed., *Sgt. Pepper and the Beatles: It Was Forty Years Ago Today* (New York: Routledge, 2008); Gabriel Lubell, "Spatial Counterpoint and the Impossible Experience of *Sgt. Pepper's Lonely Hearts Club Band*," in Katie Kapurch and Kenneth Womack, eds., *New Critical Perspectives on the Beatles: Things We Said Today* (London: Palgrave Macmillan, 2016), 95–118; Barry Miles, *The Beatles: A Diary: An Intimate Day by Day History* (London: Omnibus Press, 1998); Allan F. Moore, *The Beatles: Sgt. Pepper's Lonely Hearts Club Band* (Cambridge: Cambridge University Press, 1997).

3 "Beatle Album Cover 2-Fold Experiment," *Los Angeles Times*, May 19, 1967, Part IV, 16.

4 Ibid.

5 Barry Miles, *Paul McCartney: Many Years from Now* (New York: Henry Holt, 1997), 303.

6 Theodore Roszak, *The Making of a Counter Culture: Reflections on the Technocratic Society and Its Youthful Opposition* (Garden City, NY: Doubleday., 1969).

7 Ibid., 162.

8 Ibid., 72.

9 Ibid., 44.

10 Andrew Grant Jackson, *1965: The Most Revolutionary Year in Music* (New York: Thomas Dunne Books, 2015), 1.

11 Savage, *1966*.

12 D. A. Pennebaker's documentary *Monterey Pop* (1968) remains the best single source on the historic Monterey Pop Festival of 1967. See: *Monterey Pop*, directed by D. A. Pennebaker (New York: Criterion Collection, 2017), Blu-ray.

13 Leonard, *Beatleness*, 153.

14 Ann Landers, "Clean-Cut Fellow's Fed Up with Hippies," *Charlotte Observer*, September 18, 1967, 11.

15 "S.F. Hippies Plead for 'Summer of Love' Aid," *Sacramento Bee*, May 14, 1967, A17.

16 Deanne and David Heller, " 'Hippie' Tourists are Shivering These Days during S.F.'s 'Summer of Love,' " *Naugatuck Daily News*, September 26, 1967, 4.

17 Claude Burgett, "The New Breed—That 'Hippie Tribe,' " *Oneota Star*, May 9, 1967, 2.

18 "Summer of Love in Hippieland Falls Apart as Violence Grows," *Cincinnati Post and Times-Star*, August 16, 1967, 19.

19 Berman, *We're Going to See the Beatles*, 134, 227.

20 Sandy Johnson, "Yea Monkees," *Teen Scoop*, June 1968, 7.

21 Dan Bond, "Anti-Beatle II," *Teen Screen*, June 1968, 64.

22 Barb Haig, "Serendipity," *Daily Herald*, December 13, 1967, 15.

23 David Michaelis, "The Back of the Album," in Rowlands, *The Beatles Are Here: 50 Years After the Band Arrived in America, Writers, Musicians and Other Fans Remember* (Chapel Hill, NC: Algonquin Books, 2014), 213–14.
24 Sandercombe, *The Beatles: The Press Reports*, 191.
25 "The Beatles Reveal: Our Plans for the Future," *16 Magazine,* September 1966, 33.
26 "Beatles Plan to Move Forward," *Odessa American,* June 17, 1967, 21.
27 Ibid.
28 Marian Ross, "Public Recovering from Beatlemania?" *Los Angeles Times*, August 27, 1968, Part IV, 14.
29 Michaelis, "The Back of the Album," 214.
30 Norman Moss, "Beatles Show No Sign of Fading Away," *Pensacola News Journal,* February 7, 1968, 5C.
31 Ibid.
32 Patti (last name unknown), "Beatle-In," *Fresno Bee*, July 13, 1967, 40.
33 Dave Schwensen, *The Beatles in Cleveland: Memories, Facts & Photos about the Notorious 1964 & 1966 Concerts* (Vermilion, OH: North Shore Publishing, 2007), 162.
34 Leonard, *Beatleness*, 148.
35 For the authoritative work on the subject, see Malcolm McLaughlin, *The Long, Hot Summer of 1967: Urban Rebellion in America* (New York: Palgrave Macmillan, 2014).
36 Barry Weisberg, "Selective Service: An American Institution" (n.d., circa 1967), Students for a Democratic Society Papers, Microfilm, Reel 19, Correspondence, 1965–1970. ProQuest (0190004).
37 Students for a Democratic Society (New York region), *News,* November 1967, 2, Students for a Democratic Society Papers, Microfilm, Reel 24, Folder 50, "Cortland State College - New York City Regional Office, 1965-1969." ProQuest (0240531).
38 Paul Wasserman, "The Beatles: Grooving in the Midst of Atrocity?" *Granpa,* vol. 1, no. 2, December 22, 1967, 8.
39 Marty Jezer, *Abbie Hoffman: American Rebel* (New Brunswick, NJ: Rutgers University Press, 1993), 73.
40 Ian Inglis, ed., *The Beatles, Popular Music and Society: A Thousand Voices* (London: Palgrave Macmillan UK, 2016), 17. There is evidence that Abbie Hoffman, though he listened to the Beatles in the 1960s, developed ambivalent views about the band. In an interview for a 1987 Granada Television special in the UK about *Sgt. Pepper's Lonely Hearts Club Band*, an interviewer asked Hoffman: "Is love all you need?" The lifelong agitator, now a half century old, considered with the question with a smile and a laugh. "No," he replied. "It's nice to have. It's nice, as is peace. But it is not, and this is basically the flaw in Beatle politics: Justice is all you need." See: John Kimsey, "The Beatles for Sale and for Keeps," in Kenneth Womack, ed., *The Cambridge Companion to the Beatles* (Cambridge, UK: Cambridge University Press, 2009), 239.

41 Roszak, *The Making of a Counter Culture*, 30.
42 Lyons, *Joy and Fear,* 275
43 Dave Lippman, "The Beatles as Counterrevolutionaries," *Helix*, vol. 5, no. 8, December 5, 1968, 6.
44 Ralph J. Gleason, "The Beatles' Revolution," *Liberation News Service*, no. 102, September 2, 1968. D-17—D-18. In fairness, not all radicals attacked John Lennon and the Beatles for "Revolution 1," or regarded the song as counterrevolutionary. "I did note the transformation of the Beatles when their song 'Revolution' came out," recalled Angela Davis decades later in the documentary *The U.S. vs. John Lennon* (2006), which treated the song as a plea for revolutionary nonviolence that complemented the work being done by anti-Vietnam War activists across the United States. See: *The U.S. vs. John Lennon*, directed by David Leaf and John Scheinfeld (New York: Alliance Films, 2007), DVD.
45 John McMillian, *Beatles vs. Stones* (New York: Simon & Schuster, 2013), 182.
46 Susan Lydon, "Would You Want Your Sister to Marry a Beatle?" *Ramparts Magazine*, vol. 7, no. 8, November 30, 1969, 66–8.
47 Wiener, *Come Together*, 66.
48 Ibid., 78.
49 *The Beatles: Rock Band,* directed by Josh Randall (New York: MTV Games, 2009).
50 E.M., "Lest We Forget," *Teen World,* March 1969, 54.
51 Elaine Svientek, "Old Beatles," *Teen Screen*, July 1968, 64.
52 "Granny's Gossip," *Hit Parader,* July 1968, 46.
53 Troy Irvine, "Swing Around the Valley," *Arizona Republic,* March 16, 1968, 75.
54 Troy Irvine, "Swing Around the Valley," *Arizona Republic,* February 17, 1968, 58.
55 Tom Campbell, "Beatles May Go Back on Word," *San Francisco Chronicle,* November 16, 1968, 12.
56 "Beatle & English News," *16 Magazine,* February 1969, 64.
57 Leroy F. Arons, "John Lennon Inside the Fishbowl, Working for Peace," *San Francisco Chronicle,* June 15, 1969, *Date Book* section, 2.
58 "Public Beatle-ing Past, Ringo Says," *Tampa Bay Times*, March 28, 1969, 2.
59 Alan Smith, "George Harrison—Songwriting and Recording," *Hit Parader,* April 1969, 56.
60 Robb Baker, "John & Yoko Rocking It," *Chicago Tribune,* September 16, 1969, Section 2, 1. At the time, many newspapers reported that Yoko Ono's avant-garde performance at the Toronto Rock and Roll Revival—which involved a great deal of non-melodic shrieking and noisemaking—was booed by the audience. In his review of the concert, Robb Baker challenged this version of the event: "Her thing is weird. But the audience listened politely [reports that there was a good deal of booing are simply not true], and some [this writer included] obviously dug it a lot."

NOTES

61 Andre Ouimet, "Rocks Roll in Pot Smoke," *Windsor Star,* September 15, 1969, 40.

62 For a detailed account of John Lennon, Yoko Ono and the Plastic Ono Band, see John Kruth's *Hold on World: The Lasting Impact of John Lennon and Yoko Ono's Plastic Ono Band, Fifty Years On* (Lanham, MD: Backbeat Books, 2021).

63 Maris Ross, "Can You Dig Beatles Making Like Animated Cartoon Characters?" *Cincinnati Enquirer,* July 13, 1968, 19.

64 Marjory Adams, "Beatles' Shiny 'Yellow Submarine' Mad Vehicle," *Boston Globe,* November 20, 1968, 38.

65 Courrier, *Artificial Paradise,* 200–2.

66 Bruno Edera, *Full Length Animated Feature Films* (London: Focal Press, 1977), 87.

67 Vincent Bugliosi, with Curt Gentry, *Helter Skelter: The True Story of the Manson Murders* (New York: W.W. Norton, 2001; originally published in 1974), 323–6.

68 Jonathan C. Friedman, *The Routledge History of Social Protest in Popular Music* (New York: Routledge / Taylor & Francis, 2013), 144. See also: Greg Marquis, *John Lennon, Yoko Ono and the Year Canada Was Cool* (Toronto: Lorimer, 2020), 19–22, 28–32.

69 Liberation News Service, "Interview with John Fogerty of Creedence Clearwater Revival," no. 243, March 28, 1970, 30.

70 Richard J. Tofel, "Misinformation and the Saga of 'Paul Is Dead,' " *Columbia Journalism Review,* December 20, 2021. https://www.cjr.org/analysis/misinformation-paul-mccartney-dead.php (accessed September 11, 2022).

71 The best single volume on the history of conspiracy theories and culture in the United States is Robert Goldberg's *Enemies Within: The Culture of Conspiracy in Modern America* (New Haven: Yale University Press, 2001).

72 "Beatle Spokesman Calls Rumor of McCartney's Death Rubbish," *New York Times,* October 22, 1969, 8.

73 Such gatherings are mentioned in Jackie Ross, "Rumor Paul McCartney Dead Keeps Beatles Fans Buzzing," *Hartford Courant,* October 21, 1969, 36.

74 Edward L. Kenney, "Death Rumor Haunts Beatle," *Ithaca Journal,* July 5, 1989, 23.

75 Mary Campbell, "McCartney Elegies Proliferate: Dead or Alive, Paul is Potent Influence," *Arizona Star,* October 31, 1969, Section B, 9; "It's 'So Long Paul' and Hello Werbley Finster," *Oakland Tribune,* November 5, 1969, 26.

76 Victor Keegan, "Reverse Charge Dialogues with a Beatle By Proxy," *Manchester Guardian,* October 23, 1969, 1.

77 B.J. Phillips, "McCartney Death Rumors," *Washington Post,* October 22, 1969, B1.

78 Ritchie Yorke, "McCartney Fans Conduct Morbid Investigation," *Journal News,* October 25, 1969, 11.

79 Sandercombe, *The Beatles: The Press Reports,* 280.

80 Ibid.

81 Albert Goldman, "The Beatles Decide to Let It Be—Apart," *Life,* April 24, 1970, 38.

82 So far, the authoritative work on the Beatles' break-up is Ken McNab's *And in the End the Last Days of the Beatles* (New York: St. Martin's Giffin, 2022). Other key works on this pivotal period include: David Bennahum, *The Beatles – After the Break-Up: In Their Own Words* (London: Omnibus Press, 1991); Keith Badman, *The Beatles Diary Vol. 2: After the Break-Up 1970-2001* (London: Omnibus Press, 2001); Peter Doggett, *You Never Give Me Your Money: The Beatles After the Breakup* (New York: HarperCollins, 2010); Tom Doyle, *Man on the Run: Paul McCartney in the 1970s* (New York: Random House, 2014); Geoffrey Giuliano, *Lennon in America: 1971-1980, Based in Part on the Lost Lennon Diaries* (New York: Cooper Square Press, 2001); Elliot J. Huntley, *Mystical One: George Harrison: After the Break-up of the Beatles* (Toronto: Guernica Editions, 2004); and Kenneth Womack's outstanding *Solid State: The Story of Abbey Road and the End of the Beatles* (Ithaca: Cornell University Press, 2019).

83 Berman, *We're Going to See the Beatles,* 248.

84 Hy Gardner, "Glad You Asked That!" *Dayton Daily News,* June 4, 1970, 26.

85 Linda Schultz, ed., *Tales of the Awesome Foursome: Beatles Fans Share Their Personal Stories, Poems and Memories of the Fab Four* (West Conshohocken, PA: Infinity Publishers, 2004), 51.

86 Ibid., 68.

87 Mike Crowley, "Teen Fans Give Views About Paul Leaving Beatles," *Courier-Post,* April 11, 1970, 15.

88 "Beatles Break-Up Has All England in a Fog," *Honolulu Advertiser,* November 9, 1966, 16.

89 "Manager Refuses to Deny Rumor of a Beatles Break-Up," *Herald-Sun,* November 9, 1966, 28.

90 "Rumored Beatles Break-Up Denied," *Morning News,* November 16, 1966, 37.

91 "Beatles Break-Up Coming?" *Lansing State Journal,* November 8, 1966, E3.

92 "Beatles May Break Up as Top Singing Group," *Zanesville Times Recorder,* November 10, 1966, 10-C.

93 "Paper Says Beatle Paul Got 'Help' from Friends in Quitting," *Miami News,* April 13, 1970, 4-B.

94 Alvin Shuster, "McCartney Breaks Off with Beatles," *New York Times,* April 11, 1970, 20.

95 Christian Appy, American Reckoning: The Vietnam War and Our National Identity (New York: Penguin Books, 2016), 183.

96 Philip Elwood, " 'Let It Be'—Fluff For Beatle Buffs," *San Francisco Examiner,* May 16, 1970, 5. Not all critics pounced on the film like Elwood. Charles Champlin, film critic for the *Los Angeles Times,* said of the Let It Be: "It

makes for the warmest and most engaging hour and a half of film I've seen in weeks, maybe longer." See: Charles Champlin, " 'Let It Be'—A Documentary By the Beatles," *Los Angeles Times,* May 20, 1970, Part IV, 1.

97 Vernon Scott, "Beatles Split Recorded in Latest Film," *Terre Haute Tribune,* May 27, 1970, 11.

98 Director Peter Jackson's acclaimed 2021 documentary, *Get Back,* used extensive of footage discarded by Michael Lindsay-Hogg over a half century earlier. With a running time of nearly eight hours, *Get Back* purported to present a fuller, more complex portrait of the making of the *Get Back / Let It Be* album, including happier moments in the studio that were omitted from the much shorter *Let It Be* documentary. The famous "Rooftop Concert" atop Apple Corps headquarters at 3 Savile Row in London, was also featured in its 42-minute entirety in *Get Back,* as opposed to the 21 minutes of it included in *Let It Be.*

99 Robert Hilburn, " 'Yesterday' For Today's Beatles Buffs," *Los Angeles Times,* September 6, 1977, Part IV, 1.

100 "Beatles File Suit for $60 Million," *Atlanta Constitution,* September 28, 1979, 1-B.

101 The Clash, "London Calling," 1979, track 1 on *London Calling,* Epic Records, 1979, vinyl LP.

Epilogue

1 Michael Frontani, "The Solo Years," in Womack, ed., *Cambridge Companion to the Beatles*, 161.

2 Robert Hilburn, "Beatles Reunion: I Wanna Pull Your Leg," *Los Angeles Times,* August 7, 1977, Calendar Section, 78.

3 Cliff Radel, "Reunite the Beatles—for Only a Dollar," *Cincinnati Enquirer,* September 26, 1976, F-16.

4 Wayne Harda, "Quite Certain of a Beatles Reunion," *Honolulu Advertiser,* September 24, 1979, C-7.

5 Thomas Sabulis, "Will the Beatles?" *Boston Globe,* October 28, 1979, E1, E8,

6 Stan Mieses, "Can Muhammad Ali Ally the Beatles?" *Poughkeepsie Journal,* January 30, 1977, 11B.

7 "Whales Won't Spur Beatles Reunion," *Evening Press,* March 23, 1978, 2.

8 Lisa Robinson, "Rock Talk: Beatles Reunion?" *Argus-Courier,* February 12, 1977, 23.

9 Bruce Meyer, "A Beatles Reunion? Hmmm … Well … Maybe …" *Detroit Free Press,* January 16, 1977, 7F.

10 Robert Hilburn, "Beatles Again? Anything Is Possible, Says Lennon," *Los Angeles Times*, December 30, 1973, Calendar Section, 1.

11 There exists a number of titles about the tragic murder of John Lennon, most notably: Alison Behnke, *Death of a Dreamer: The Assassination of John Lennon* (Minneapolis: Lerner Publishing Group, 2012); Fenton Bresler, *Who Killed John Lennon?* (New York: St. Martin's Press, 1990); Jack Jones, *Let Me Take You Down: Inside the Mind of Mark David Chapman, the Man Who Killed John Lennon* (New York: Villard Books, 1992); Lesley-Ann Jones, *Who Killed John Lennon?: The Life, Loves And Deaths of the Greatest Rock Star* (New York: Pegasus Books, 2020); Keith Elliot Greenberg, *December 8, 1980 the Day John Lennon Died* (Milwaukee: Backbeat Books, 2010); James Patterson, Casey Sherman and Dave Wedge, *The Last Days of John Lennon* (New York: Grand Central Publishing, 2022); and Kenneth Womack, *John Lennon 1980: The Last Days in the Life* (London: Omnibus Press, 2020).

12 Sam Smith, "Record-Shop Rush 'Worse Than for Elvis,'" *Chicago Tribune*, December 10, 1980, 18. See also: "Lennon Fans Mob Stores; Latest Album Sold Out," *Pittsburgh Press*, December 10, 1980, 19.

13 Robert D. McFadden, "Half-Staff Flags Among Tributes to John Lennon," *New York Times*, December 13, 1980, 31.

14 "Crowds of Lennon Fans Gather Quickly at the Dakota and Hospital," *New York Times*, December 9, 1980, B7.

15 John A. Meyers, "Letter From the Publisher," *Time*, December 22, 1980, 1.

16 Lee Weisbecker, "Suspect Stalked Lennon for 3 Days," *Charlotte Observer*, December 10, 1980, 1.

17 Walter Patrick, "Love Dominated Tribute," *Asbury Park Press*, December 17, 1980, B17.

18 Diana Arman, "Iowa Citian Tells of Chaos after Shooting," *Iowa City Press-Citizen*, December 9, 1980, 1.

19 "'I Never Thought He'd Die': 1,200 Gather at Candlelight Vigil in Cincinnati to Honor Ex-Beatle," *Dayton Daily News*, December 10, 1980, 13.

20 Patty Ryan, "Lennon Fans Pay Tribute in Song," *Tampa Tribune*, December 11, 1980, 11.

21 "Two John Lennon Fans Take Own Lives Tuesday," *Albany Democrat-Herald*, December 11, 1980, 25. Tragically, Costello's father had recently committed suicide a short time before she did, leaving the teenage girl despondent over two major losses in her life.

22 "'Music, Mood of Our Time,'" *Spokesman Review*, December 10, 1980, 14.

23 "The Accused: A 'Wild Kid' Whose Girl 'Unglued' Him," *San Francisco Examiner*, December 10, 1980, 3.

24 Carl Hiassen, "Lennon's Slayer: God Told Me to Plead Guilty," *Miami Herald*, June 23, 1981, 5A.

25 Edward Edelson, "Chapman May Have Lost Identity," *New York Daily News*, December 11, 1980, 7.

26 Ibid.

27 Michael Daly: "From Out of Obscurity: Assassins Get the Attention they Crave," *New York Daily News*, December 11, 1980, 6.

28 For more on these pilgrimages to Liverpool, see Michael Brocken, "Beatles Heritage Tourism in Liverpool: Standing at the Crossroads?" in Kit O'Toole and Kenneth Womack, eds., *Fandom and the Beatles: The Act You've Known for All These Years* (New York: Oxford University Press, 2021), 255–73.
29 Geoff Boucher, "'Quiet Beatle' Sought Spirituality, Privacy," *Los Angeles Times,* December 1, 2001, A22.
30 Ibid.
31 Elliot J. Huntley, *Mystical One: George Harrison: After the Break-up of the Beatles* (Toronto: Guernica edns.), 288–95.
32 Becky Malkovich, "George Harrison Remains Forever Fab," *Southern Illinoisian,* September 22, 2013, 5.
33 Schultz, ed., *Tales of the Awesome Foursome,* 17.

Index

16 magazine 14, 41, 120
1960s: *see* Sixties

Abbe, Elizabeth 13
Abbey Road Studios: *see* EMI Studios
Abram, Michael 173
African Americans 2, 18
    in 1960s' popular culture 80
    attitudes toward the Beatles 79, 85–86, 90
    Beatles' debt to Black musicians 80–81
    Black musicians covering Beatles' songs 82–83
    Black Power 87–89, 119–129, 145
    Civil Rights Movement 2, 15–16, 79–80, 90–96, 119, 130
    and Vee-Jay Records 83–84
    violence in the South against 90–92
Aladdin Industries 59
albums
    Abbey Road 155, 161
    Beatles (White Album) 153, 155, 157, 159
    Help! 120
    Magical Mystery Tour 155, 161
    Revolver 120, 128, 130, 131–132, 140, 148, 162, 202 n. 4
    Rubber Soul 120, 131, 132, 202 n. 4
    Sgt. Pepper's Lonely Hearts Club Band 144, 145, 146, 148–149, 150–151, 152, 153, 155, 156, 161
Ali, Muhammad (Cassius Clay) 14, 30, 169
Allen, Linda G. 56
Amron, Alan 168
Animals, the 1, 61, 73
Anka, Paul 25

anticommunism 101–102, 116, 117, 118, 129, 201
Anti-Vietnam War Movement, the 2, 113, 151–152, 157
    John Lennon and 159–163, 170–171
Aoki, Rocky 168
Apple Corps, Ltd. 161, 164, 165, 213 n. 98
Apple Records 157, 162
Associated Press 12
Avalon, Frankie 25–26
Awad, Mary Ann 128

Babbs, Reverend Thurman H. 129
Baby Boom generation, 2
Baez, Joan 95
Baker, Ella 94
Baldwin, James 80
Baraka, Amiri
    on the Beatles 87–89
Beach Boys 146
Beatlemania (musical) 165–166
Beatlephobes 3, 4, 12–13, 103
    Beatle bans 120–130
    criticisms of fans 106–108
    dislike of screaming 107
    first Anti-Beatles Club in Bismarck, North Dakota 12, 104
    inability to sustain clubs, 105–106
    media coverage of 106
    right-wing Beatlephobes 113–118
Beatles, the
    adults' views on 13–14, 23, 35–39, 108–111
    and African American musicians 80–83
    albums of 29, 31, 33, 38, 41, 48, 50, 51, 60, 68, 75, 84, 98, 125,

126, 128, 132, 148, 149, 155, 170, 202 n. 4
Aretha Franklin on 83
break-up of 3, 140, 155, 163–164, 167
Civil Rights Movement and 90–96
critics of 11–12, 14
debut on the *Ed Sullivan Show* (February 9, 1964) 4, 9–14, 29, 39, 51, 53, 55, 60, 61, 72, 75, 79, 80, 103, 107, 110, 116, 130, 134, 135, 141, 143–144
fashion style of 12, 71, 135, 148
Gator Bowl Stadium Concert (1964) 92–93
and Clarence "Frogman" Henry 93
literature on 2–4
Marvin Gaye on 81
Deacon John Moore on 93–94
Motown and 80–82, 88, 131
opposition to racism 80–81
public image of 78, 140
rapport with African American musicians 79–83
radical leftist critiques of 153–155
reunion rumors, 163, 167, 168, 169
rivalry with the Dave Clark Five, 62–63, 189 n. 19
rivalry with the Rolling Stones, 63–68
Smokey Robinson on 81
solo careers of 78, 162, 165, 167–169, 172–173
and Mary Wells 81–82
Otis Williams on 81
Mary Wilson on, 81
and touring 7, 81, 85, 132–133, 136, 139, 143, 149–150, 151, 157, 169
and Vee-Jay Records 83–84
The Beatles (ABC animated series, 1965–1967) 72–73, 118, 158, 192 n. 65
Beatles fans 3–7, 10
African American fans 84–87, 93–94, 98–99
Beatles National Fan Club 29
and Beatles reunion rumors 140
and the Civil Rights Movement, 195 n. 23

clashes with Beatlephobes 3, 32, 53, 104–106, 113, 129
compared to bobby-soxers 20–23, 29, 32, 111
compared to early Elvis Presley fans, 23–25
culture of, 40–43
end of Beatlemania 140–141, 142–144, 150
enduring love for the Beatles 169, 172–174
and fan clubs 2, 3, 17, 29–31, 32, 33, 41, 42–43, 46–47, 48, 50, 51–52, 61, 66, 70, 85, 102
and fan magazines 3, 14, 26, 27, 28, 31, 41, 43–44, 59, 61, 62, 74, 76, 86, 125, 128, 141, 167, 170
and "favorite Beatle" 41, 45–46
and *A Hard Day's Night* (1964 film) 68–71, 77
and *Help!* (1965 film) 68–69, 70–71, 141
gender 10–11, 20–21, 32, 39, 40–41, 43–44, 45, 52–53, 54–55, 89, 103, 112, 117, 146
male fans, 50–57
meeting the Beatles 46–49
parents of 10–13, 23, 30, 31, 33, 35–39, 53, 55, 78, 108–111, 129, 149, 171
pen pals 41
post-Beatlemania 148–151
reactions to the Beatles' break-up 162–164
as runaways, 33–39
screaming of 4, 5, 6–7, 9, 10, 12–13, 15, 19, 20, 23, 26, 39, 46, 61, 63, 69, 71, 86, 93, 103, 110, 133, 135, 136–139, 149, 150, 151, 156, 165, 166, 172, 173
shrines to the Beatles 42–43, 50, 76–77, 114
Beatles hairstyles 4
acne and 56–57
controversy 13, 87, 88, 101, 102–104, 114, 123
media coverage of 12, 60, 61, 64, 77, 87, 89, 112, 169

INDEX

on females 36, 42, 43–44, 45–46, 53, 112
on males 2, 33, 42, 51–57, 125, 158
masculinity 54–55
school board bans 55–57
versus traditional hairstyles, 53–55
Beatles merchandise
  alarm clocks 77
  bed sheets and pillow cases 67
  bobbleheads 14, 67
  dolls 14, 59, 75, 76, 77
  Beatleggers 75
  Beatles Flip Your Wig Game, 59, 77
  Beatles Magnetic Hair Game 77
  Beatles wigs 14, 30, 43, 55, 59, 76, 77, 122, 125, 149, 176 n. 5
  Brian Epstein and 73–74, 77
  bubble bath 59, 67, 118
  as collector's items 78
  jewelry 45, 75
  lunch boxes 59, 67
  necklaces 77
  notebooks 77
  profitability of 14, 74–75, 77–78
  promotional films 71–72
  shampoo 77
  trading cards 31, 67, 75, 77
Beatles Monthly Book 139–140
beatniks 53, 57, 62
Beck, Becky Lee 77
Benson, George 83
Benton, Illinois 14–19
Bernstein, Sid 96, 168
Berry, Chuck 16, 17, 26, 72, 80, 81, 82, 88, 97, 157
Bartram, Lorraine 127
Best, Shirley 36–37
Bilk, Acker 18
Billy J. Kramer and the Dakotas, 17
Biondi, Dick 84
Black, Cilla 37
bobby-soxers 20–23, 29, 32, 111
Boggiano, Barbara 129
Boorman, John 61
Braceland, Francis 23
Bracken, James C. 83–84
Brattelle, Phyllis 22
Breazele, David 125
British Invasion

bands 1, 59, 61
and the Beatles 59, 60
first wave 64–65, 80
literature on 179 n. 37
origins of name 60
Brodax, Al 75, 158, 192 n. 65
Brothers, Dr. Joyce 53, 112
Brown, Craig 43
Brownlee, Rodger 50
Byrne, Nicky 74–75, 192 n. 69

Call, Karen 131
Campbell, Kenneth L. 3, 92
Canada
  1969 Plastic Ono Band Performance in 157
  Bed-ins For Peace in 159
  and Beatles tours 32, 40, 46, 63, 126, 135, 151
  Capitol Records in 83
  pen pals in 41
Capitol Records 29, 42, 51, 60–61, 83–84, 188 n. 6
Carmichael, Stokely, 87, 88, 119
Carroll, Diahann 80
Carter, Jimmy 171
Carter, Vivian 83–84
Carvalho, John J. 125–126
Casbah Coffee Club 18
Cash, Johnny 25
Catcher in the Rye 171
Cavern Club, 18, 41, 135, 139
CBS network 9, 19, 28, 65, 72
  and Studio 50 9
Chad & Jeremy, 61
Champlin, Charles 66
Chaney, James 90–92
Chapman, Mark David 171–172
Charles, Ray 80
Charles, Tommy 122–126, 129
Chase, Debbie 48
Chess, Leonard 84
Chess, Phil 84
Chess Records 84
Chicago Transit Authority 157
Christ, Jesus 118, 120–121, 122, 124–128, 129, 131, 137, 138, 161, 171
  Christianity 114, 121, 124, 127, 130

Christians 104, 114, 116–118, 126, 129–130, 171
cities
　Atlanta 22, 95, 11, 165
　Austin 119
　Boston 11, 23, 30, 37, 38, 40, 46, 48, 49, 56, 60, 70–71, 127, 134, 138, 148, 158, 165
　Berkeley 151, 152
　Birmingham 122, 123, 151
　Chicago 17, 19, 24, 29, 40, 48, 53, 69, 84, 86, 87, 98–99, 105, 119, 127, 148, 152, 154, 156, 165, 171
　Cincinnati 46, 49, 103, 107, 108, 112, 171
　Cleveland 33–35, 36, 39, 65, 129, 133, 151
　Dallas 4, 13, 16, 50, 67, 171
　Des Moines 148, 160–161
　Detroit 17, 29–30, 51, 80, 88, 151, 156, 161
　Houston 49, 57
　Kansas City 19–20, 69, 75
　Los Angeles 25, 29, 36, 41, 47, 77, 133, 156, 165, 168, 169
　Madison, 116, 130
　Memphis 85, 86, 122, 128, 129, 133
　Miami 4–15, 14, 25, 35, 92, 150
　Milwaukee 6, 12, 49, 85, 151
　Minneapolis 48, 55, 60, 68, 104, 151, 156
　Montreal 159
　New Orleans 93–94
　New York City 9, 11, 14, 20, 34–35, 51, 52, 60, 74, 94, 97, 101, 120, 126, 135, 138, 152, 154, 166, 168, 170
　Newark 88, 151
　Oklahoma City 31
　Philadelphia 13, 25, 29, 36, 45, 49, 51, 62, 68, 102, 138, 140–141
　Salt Lake City 52, 56, 124, 171
　San Francisco 29, 35, 40, 43, 52, 70, 76, 88, 89, 104, 105, 131, 132, 147–148, 153, 156, 165
　Seattle 87, 109, 135, 153
　Toronto 126, 151, 157
　Tulsa 55, 116
　Washington, D.C. 10, 14, 16, 60, 90, 114, 133, 135, 138, 171
　Wilmington 57, 161
Civil Rights Act of 1964 119
Civil Rights Movement, the 2, 15–16, 90–96, 119, 130
　And Black Power 87–89, 119–129, 145
　and the song "Blackbird" 197 n. 44
　at high tide 79–80
　Beatles and 91–92
　Beatles' opposition to Southern segregation 92
　Mississippi Freedom Summer Project 94
　Murder of James Chaney, Andrew Goodman and Michael "Mickey" Schwerner 90–92
　Student Nonviolent Coordinating Committee (SNCC) 91, 94–95
Clapton, Eric 157
Clark, Dave: see Dave Clark Five, the
Clark, Petula 37, 61
Clarke, David 51
Clash, the 166
Classical music 18
Claussen, Sheryl 5
Cleave, Maureen 120–121, 127–128, 130
Cleaver, Eldridge
　on the Beatles 88–89
Cocks, Jay 170
Cole, Nat King 16
Columbia Record Club 28
Como, Perry 24, 54
Congress of Racial Equality (CORE) 91
conservatives 7, 39, 101–102
　claiming Beatles are communists 116–117, 118
　Buckley, William F. 114
　John Birch Society, 116, 117
　Goldwater, Barry 115
　Noebel, Rev. David 116–118
　objections to the Beatles 113
　religious objections to the Beatles 114, 116
Cosby, Bill 80
Costello, Colleen 171
counterculture 3, 113

INDEX

Beatles as symbols of 114, 152–153
Beatles fans and 149–150
formation of 145–146
hippies 86, 147–148, 152
psychedelic rock 72, 132, 146, 149, 152, 155
Sgt. Pepper's Lonely Hearts Club Band and 145, 146, 148–149, 150–151, 155
Cox, Carol 132
Craig, Michael 171
Creedence Clearwater Revival 160
crew cuts 12, 54
Crowley, Mike 163

Dagnal, Cynthia 86–87
Darin, Bobby 25
Datebook 27, 120–121, 130
Dave Clark Five, the 1
  Carnegie Hall performance of 63
  Catch Us If You Can (1965 film) 62
  Dave Clark 61–63, 131
  decline of 63–64
  fan magazines and 62
  fans of 62–63
  Ed Sullivan Show and 61, 63
  hits in the United States 61
  Mike Smith 62
  rivalry with the Beatles, 62–63, 189 n. 19
  Tottenham Sound and 62
Daytona Beach 14
Davies, Hunter 2, 78
DeCurtis, Anthony 65
Dee, Henry Hezekiah 91
Dee, Ruby 80
Denzer, Diane 173
Denzer, Jim 173
DeShannon, Jackie 93
Deutsch, Linda 23
Diddley, Bo 157
Dig magazine 14
disc jockeys 5, 16, 48, 122, 123, 124, 139, 140, 156, 161
Dixon, Ivan 80
Dobbs, Susan 129
Domino, Fats 18, 26, 81
Doors, the 157
Dow, Jack 78

Duke, Patty 54
Dylan, Bob 144, 146, 173
  John Lennon's love of 67

Earles, Theresa 129
Ed Sullivan Show, the
  Beatles debut on (February 9, 1964) 4, 9–14, 29, 39, 51, 53, 55, 60, 61, 72, 75, 79, 80, 103, 107, 110, 116, 130, 134, 135, 141, 143–144
  Dave Clark Five on 61, 63
  Rolling Stones on 64–65
Ellis, Geoffrey 77
Ellis, Nancy 137–139
EMI Records 60, 83–84, 188 n. 6
EMI Studios 96, 140, 144, 155
Epstein, Brian 143, 150
  Beatles merchandizing and 73–74, 77
  Beatles' 1966 U.S. tour and 126
  Beatles' early success and 19
  and Beatles' opposition to racism 92
  Student Nonviolent Coordinating Committee (SNCC) and 95
  runaway Beatles fans and 34, 38
  death of 155
Etengoff, Dave 163
Evans, Mal 48
Everly Brothers 16, 26, 29
experts 108–113
  on bobby-soxers 20–22
  on rock 'n' roll 22–25

Fabian 25
Faithfull, Marianne, 1
fans: *see* Beatles fans
Feldman-Barrett, Christine 3
feminism, 2, 52, 57, 113, 145
Fencsak, John 51
Ferris, Barbara 62
Finley Charles O. 19–20
Fitzpatrick, Thomas 40
Fogerty, John 160
Four Seasons, the 83
Fowler, Giles M. 69
Frampton, Peter 167–168
Freedman, Barbara 37–38
Freedman, Elizabeth 37–38
Frees, Paul 73

INDEX

Gaffney, Edward 34
Gagliardo, Judge Angelo J. 39
Gallo-Stenman, Patricia (Patti) 45, 71, 140, 141
Gatton, Rita 170–171
Gatzman, Liz 13
Gaye, Marvin 81, 83, 146
George, Nelson 97–98
Gerry and the Pacemakers 1, 17, 61, 189 n. 19
Gilbert, Eugene 24–25, 55
Gleason, Ralph J. 153–154
Goldberg, Whoopi 85–86
Goldman, Albert 162
Goldwater, Barry 115
Goodman, Andrew 90–92
Gould, Jonathan 3
Great Society, the 16
Green, Cindy 30
Greer, Bonnie, 98–99
Gross, Ben 12

Haenel, Judy 43
hair: see Beatles hairstyles
Haley, Bill 17
Hamburg 18, 132, 135, 139, 157
Hansen, Margaret 31
A Hard Day's Night (album) 38
A Hard Day's Night (1964 film)
   budget of 68
   Catch Us if You Can (1965) and 62
   cinéma verité and 68
   critical acclaim of 68–71
   and *Help!* (1965) 69
   fan reactions to 69–71, 77, 141
   release of 68
   screenings of 69–71
Hargis, Rev. Billy James 116
Harrison, George 1, 3, 38, 45, 71, 78, 91, 92
   1963 trip to Benton, Illinois 14–19, 178 n. 29
   on Beatles' stage sound 135–136
   cartoon version of 73
   on Christianity 127
   commemorative mural and plaque for 173
   death of 173
   dislike of Beatles' public image 150
   end of touring and 132, 135–136
   fan support of 106–107
   fans meeting 46–49
   friendship with Mary Wells 81
   hair 102
   likeness on merchandise 77, 131
   opposition to by right-wing extremists, 101
   "Quiet One" nickname 41
   reclusiveness of 172–173
   on Rolling Stones fans 66–67
   on Shea Stadium concert 136
   and the Traveling Wilburys, 172–173
Harrison, George (journalist) 193 n. 90
Harrison Caldwell, Louise 14–15, 18, 21, 48, 173, 178 n. 29
Harrison, Olivia 173
Harrison, Peter 14, 16, 18, 173
Harvard University 161, 171
Hatfield, Nancy 30
Hawkins, Janice 33–37, 39, 183 n. 7
Hebb, Bobby 134
Help! (album) 120
Help! (1965 film) 68–69, 70–71, 141
Hendrix, Jessica 128
Hendrix, Jimi 83, 126, 146, 147
Herman's Hermits 1, 17, 61, 131
Herschensohn, H.L. 56
Hickey, Dee 128
Hilburn, Robert 169
Hoffman, Abbie 152, 209 n. 40
Holly, Buddy 16, 17
Hollywood, 27, 30, 54–55
   Hollywood Bowl 47, 133
Hubbell, Carroll 36–37
Huislander, Nancy 128
Hullabaloo 61, 73
Hunt, H.L. 116

Ibuka, Masaru 28
International Committee to Reunite the Beatles 168
Isacoff Rothstein, Michelle 13

Jack Paar Program 19
Jackson, Andrew Grant 146
Jackson State killings (May 15, 1970) 163
Jagger, Mick 64–66, 131, 154

INDEX

John Lennon on 190 n. 39
jazz 18, 19, 27, 29, 37, 80, 83, 84, 147, 153
John, Elton 168
John F. Kennedy Airport (New York) 9, 29, 53, 60, 79, 103, 176 n. 5
Johnson, Lyndon, 16
Jones, Bobbi 95
Jones, Nick 63
Joplin, Janis 146

Kane, Larry 92, 135
Kearney, Taylor 173
Kennedy, John F. 170
   assassination of 4, 15–16, 51, 178 n. 34
   presidency of 16
Kennedy, John, Jr. 55
Kennedy, Robert 98
Kent State killings (May 4, 1970) 163
King, Martin Luther, Jr. 15, 170
Kinks, the 1, 17, 61, 75
Kirkham, Lewis 56
Krzmarcik, Lynn 48–49
Ku Klux Klan (KKK) 91, 125

Laffin, Maryanne 163
Lasker, Jay 84
Layton, Doug 122–126, 129
Leigh, Janet 54
Lennon, Cynthia 126
Lennon, John 1, 3, 15, 71, 78, 92
   cartoon version of 73
   Maureen Cleave's profile of 120–121, 127, 130
   fan support of 106–107
   fans meeting 46–49
   fashion of, 41, 46
   friendship with Mary Wells 81
   hair 102
   Gloria Steinem and 52
   likeness on merchandise 77, 131
   on the Monkees 149
   "More Popular Than Jesus" controversy 120–130, 131, 132, 137, 138, 161, 171
   murder of 166, 169–172
   opposition to by right-wing extremists, 101
   radicalism of 153–155, 160
   on Rolling Stones fans 66–67
   "Witty One" nickname 41
Leonard, Candy 63, 132, 175 n. 3
Leonard, George 55
Lester, Julius 89–90
Lester, Richard 68
Let It Be (1970 film) 165–166, 213 n. 98
Lewis, Jerry Lee 16, 25, 157
Lewisohn, Mark 2
Lindsay, John 164
Lindsay-Hogg, Michael 164–165, 213 n. 98
Lippman, David 153
Liszt, Franz 19
Little Richard (Richard Wayne Penniman) 16, 25, 81, 157
London, Laurie 17
Louis Dow Company 78
Lowry, Cynthia 12
Lulu 1
Lyons, John F. 3, 29

MacDonald, Dwight 68–69
MacDonald, Ian 3
Mad Magazine 104
Manson, Charles 158–159
Marroletti, Lena 132
Martin, George 19
masculinity 3, 32, 53, 54, 112, 146
Masserman, Jules 23
Matthews, Marian 54
Maynard, Joyce 67
McCartney, Paul 1, 3, 14, 71, 78, 92
   in 2020s 173–174
   cartoon version of 73
   fan support of 106–107
   fans meeting 46–49
   friendship with Mary Wells 81
   hair 102
   "Handsome One" nickname 41
   likeness on merchandise 77, 131
   love of animals, 169
   opposition to by right-wing extremists, 101
   and "Paul is Dead" rumors 160–163
McCormack, John F. 128
McEnery, Dixie Jo 36–37
McLaughlin, Helen 53

McLean, Mickey 163
McMillian, John 68, 154
Miami 4–5, 14, 25, 35, 92, 150
Miami Pop Festival 150
Michaels, David 150
Midnight, Johnny 123
Miller, Mitch 23
Mills, Hayley 27
Mills, John 27
Milton Berle Show, the 65
Milton Bradley 77
Mitford, Jessica 95
Monkees, the 132, 147, 148, 149
   John Lennon on 149
   television show 71, 149
Monterey Pop Festival 146
Moore, Allison 36, 38–29
Moore, Harold 38–39
Moore, Charles Eddie 91
Moore, Garry 54
"More Popular Than Jesus" controversy 120–130, 131, 132, 137, 138, 161, 171
Morrison, Don 68
Moser, Suzanne 36–37
Motown 29
   Amiri Baraka on 88
   Beatles' love of 81
   British Invasion and 86
   Detroit and 17, 80
   influence on *Revolver* 132
   literature on 194 n. 4
   Mary Wells and 81–82

National Association for the Advancement of Colored People (NAACP) 91
Neaverson, Bob 69
Nelson, Ricky 25–26
Nesmith, Michael 71
New Left, 151–152, 153–155
Newsweek 12
Nieliwocki, Daryl 57
Noone, Peter 131
Norman, Philip, 2
nostalgia 1, 166, 167, 172, 173

Oldham, Andrew Loog 64, 65, 66
Oliver, Dr. Kitty 84–85, 86

Olmstead, Raymond 43–44
Ono, Yoko 155, 157, 159, 170, 210 n. 60

Paar, Jack 19
Pantas, Carol 36
Park, Eric 168
Parker, Tom 75
Paul, Fred 52–53
"Paul is Dead" rumors: see Paul McCartney
Paul Revere and the Raiders 132
Payola scandal 16–17
peace movement: see Anti-Vietnam War Movement
Peale, Norman Vincent 126
Percival, Lance 73
Percoski, Betsy 31
Percoski, Joanne 31
Peter and Gordon 61
Pierce, Becky 5
Philippines 127
Plutt, Carolyn 46
Poitier, Sidney 80
Precht, Bob 13
Precht, Elizabeth 13
Presley, Elvis 5, 10, 15, 16–17, 20, 26, 29, 65, 75, 89, 102
   fans of 23–26

Queenan, Joe 51

racism 2, 80, 92, 119
   Beatles' opposition to 92
   counterculture opposition to 145
   Paul McCartney's comments on 121
   and police abuse 120
radio stations: see technology
Rafelson, Bob 71
record stores 7, 20, 22, 29, 41, 60, 61, 131, 144, 165, 170
Redding, Otis 83, 146
Reefer Madness (1936) 56
Reid, Jim 31
Revere, Paul 60
Reynolds, Debbie 54
Richard, Cliff 37
Richards, Keith 66
Roberts, Paddy 18
Robinson, Betty Garman 95

INDEX

Robinson, Smokey 80–83
rock music
   African Americans and 80, 89; *see also* African Americans
   British 1, 5, 19–20, 61
   counterculture and 145, 146
   diversification of 28–29
   early rock and roll 16–17, 22–26, 32, 103
   emergence of Classic Rock 146–147
   in England 18
   radio stations and 123, 129
   right-wing opposition to 117
   teens and 131
Roland, Sandra 42
Rolling Stones, the 1, 17, 25, 39, 61, 86, 88
   Bill Whitworth on, 64
   Ed Sullivan Show and 64–65
   fans of 65–68
   media coverage of 64, 65, 66, 67
   merchandizing and 67
   rivalry with the Beatles, 63–68
   "Street Fighting Man" 154–155
Romilly, Constancia 95
Roszak, Theodore 145–146, 152
Rubin, Howard Carl 51
Rubin, Miles 75

Salinger, J.D. 171
Saturday Night Live 167
Saunders, Lou 43
Schafer, Marcia 15
Schendel, Martha, 33–37, 39, 183 n. 7
Schneider, Bert 71
Schumach, Murray 136
Schwartz, Feather 52
Schwerner, Michael "Mickey" 90–92
Scoggin, Bob 125
Screen Gems Television 71
Scorsese, Martin 173
Searchers, the 17, 61
Seltaeb 74, 76, 77
Seventeen magazine 21, 22, 120
Shacove, Gene 45
Shea Stadium Concert (1965) 49, 96, 136–137, 168
Shindig! 61, 72
Shipper, Mark 167–168

Simon and Garfunkel 146, 147
Simone, Nina 83, 147
Sinatra, Frank 10, 16, 20–22, 24, 25, 26, 29
Sinnes, Regina 46
Sixties, 3, 15, 83, 173, 176
   Beatlemania in 20, 31, 33, 78
   consumerism of 27, 59
   counterculture 145–147
   events of 2, 3, 15, 7, 32, 101–102, 170, 172
   experts 108–109
   gender 41
   generational divide 36
   hair 51–57
   music of 17, 25–26, 83, 97–98
   right-wing opposition to the Beatles 117
   technology in 28
Sly and the Family Stone 146
Smith, Mike 62
Sommer, Elke 54
songs
   "All My Loving" 10
   "All Together Now" 158
   "And I Love Her" 83
   "Ask Me Why" 84
   "Band on the Run" 165
   "Blackbird" 159, 197 n. 44
   "Can't Buy Me Love" 6, 31
   "Cold Turkey" 157
   "A Day in the Life" 83
   "Day Tripper" 83
   "Doctor Robert" 131
   "Eleanor Rigby" 83, 130, 131, 140, 158
   "From Me to You" 19, 84
   "Give Me Love (Give Me Peace On Earth)" 165
   "Give Peace a Chance" 157, 170
   "Good Day Sunshine" 132
   "Got to Get You Into My Life" 131
   "A Hard Day's Night" 83
   "Help!" 72
   "Helter Skelter" 159
   "Here Comes the Sun" 83, 167
   "Here, There and Everywhere" 83
   "Hey Bulldog" 158
   "I Am the Walrus" 72

"I Feel Fine" 72
"I Saw Her Standing There" 49, 102, 136
"I Should've Known Better" 70
"I Want to Hold Your Hand" 6, 31, 102
"I'm Only Sleeping" 132
"If I Fell" 70
"Imagine" 165
"It's All Too Much" 158
"Let It Be" 83
"The Long and Winding Road" 82
"Love Me Do" 102, 141
"Love to You" 131
"Lucy in the Sky With Diamonds" 158
"Michelle" 83
"Nowhere Man" 158
"Only a Northern Song" 158
"Paperback Writer" 72
"Penny Lane" 72, 172
"Piggies" 159
"Photograph" 165
"Please Please Me" 19, 84
"Rain" 72
"Revolution" 153–155
"Revolution 1" 159
"Revolution 9" 159
"Savoy Truffle" 83
"She Loves You" 6, 15, 19, 31, 102
"Something" 83
"Strawberry Fields Forever" 72, 172
"Tell Me Why" 70
"Thank You Girl" 84
"Tomorrow Never Knows" 131, 132
"Twist and Shout" 136
"We Can Work It Out" 72, 83
"When I'm Sixty-Four" 158
"Yellow Submarine" 130, 131–132, 152–153
"Yer Blues" 157
"Yesterday" 83
Songwriters' Guild of Great Britain, the 18
Spector, Phil 29
Spitz, Bob 2
Springfield, Dusty 1, 17
Stanley, George 55–56
Stark, Steven D. 3

Starr, Ringo 1, 71, 78, 92
  in 2020s 173–174
  cartoon version of 73
  on Christianity
  fan support of 106–107
  fans meeting 46–49
  friendship with Mary Wells 81
  "Funny One" nickname 41
  hair 102
  likeness on merchandise 77, 131
  opposition to by right-wing extremists, 101
  on reunion rumors 169
Steen, Dawn 171
Steinem, Gloria 52
Stewart, Alan 5
Stilley, Gay 10–11, 176 n. 5
Stoars, Lona 31
Stramsact 74, 76, 77
Strub, John 170
Strummer, Joe 166
Student Nonviolent Coordinating Committee (SNCC) 91, 94–95
Students for a Democratic Society (SDS) 151–152
Sullivan, Ed 9–10, 13, 65
Summers, Dirk 168
Sweed, Ron 150–151
Supremes, the 80, 81

Talbert, Bob 67
Talese, Gay 52
Tarrish, Laura 42
technology
  phonographs 28, 29, 31, 33, 77, 90, 140, 146, 161, 165, 173
  radio stations 15, 25, 84, 101, 104, 122, 124–125, 129–131
  tapes 28
  television 9, 10, 11, 12, 13, 14, 18, 19, 26, 27, 28, 41, 46, 48, 50, 53, 54, 59, 60, 61, 68, 71, 72, 80, 85, 92, 94, 98, 102, 104, 105, 108, 111, 112, 114, 123, 124, 126, 138, 140, 147, 150, 167, 168
  transistor radios 14, 27–28, 33, 52, 135
  Wall of Sound 29
teen idols 25–26

INDEX

Temple, Shirley 21
Temptations, the 80, 81, 90
Tornados, the 18
tours
   1964 UK tour 81–82
   and Beatlemania 143
   Beatles' decision to stop 132, 133, 136, 139, 150, 151, 169
   importance of 149
   North American tours (1964–1966) 5–6, 39–40, 46, 49, 85, 92–94, 96–97, 107, 114, 119, 126–128, 135–139, 151
   rumors of reunion tour 157
Traynor, Mark 43
Troggs, the 75

Vaill, Amanda 10
Valentino, Rudolph 10, 19
Vanderbilt, Amy 54
Vee, Bobby 25
Vee-Jay Records 19, 83–84
Veterans of Foreign Wars 15
Vietnam War 15, 108, 119, 126, 130, 140, 145, 151, 154, 159, 163, 164, 166
Vincent, Gene 157
Voormann, Klaus 132, 157
Voting Rights Act of 1965 119

Wagner, Penny 12–13
War on Poverty, the 16
WAQY Birmingham 122–123
Wayne Fontana and the Mindbenders 17, 61
Weisberg, Barry 151
Wells, Mary 81–82
Wexler, Jerry 83
Wheelhouse, Maureen 49–50
Whitman, Marti 47–48, 49, 186 n. 63
Whitworth, Bill 61, 64
Who, the 1, 146
Wiener, Jon 3
Williams, Otis 81
Winchell, Walter 69
Winfrey, Oprah 85–86
Womack, Kenneth 3
Workman, Roger 52

Yanak, Lisa 174
Yardbirds, the 1, 17, 61
Yellow Submarine (1968 animated film) 158
Youth International Party (Yippies) 152

Zizzamia, Michael 55
Zombies, the 61